D1363080

RE-VISIONS

New Perspectives on the African

Collections of the Horniman Museum

Contributions in Critical Museology and Material Culture.

RE-VISIONS

New Perspectives on the African
Collections of the Horniman Museum

Edited by

Karel Arnaut

The Horniman Museum and Gardens, London

Museu Antroplógico da Universidade de Coimbra

Contributions in Critical Museology and Material Culture is produced by the Horniman Museum and Gardens, London and the Museu Antropológico da Universidade de Coimbra.

Series Editors
Anthony Shelton, Horniman Museum, London
Paulo Gama Mota, Universidade de Coimbra

Editorial Board
Karel Arnaut, Ghent University
Mary Bouquet, University of Utrecht
Nélia Dias, Instituto Superior Das Ciências do
    Trabalho e da Empresa, Lisbon
Pieter ter Keurs, Rijksmuseum voor
    Volkenkunde, Leiden
Frances Palmer, Royal College of Music,
    London
Nuno Porto, Universidade de Coimbra
Mike Rowlands, University College, London

Production
Daria Neklesa

Contents

Foreword   Jan Vansina   7

Preface   Anthony Shelton   9

Introduction. Re-visioning Collections and Ethnography
at the African Worlds Gallery   Karel Arnaut   13

1   If You See Ijele Masquerade, You Have Seen It All   Emmanuel Arinze   23

2   The Lobi People of the Upper West Region, Ghana in September 1999   Michael Pennie   31

3   When Ghede met Barbie: Syncretism in Haitian Vodou Culture   Phil Cope   47

4   Recontextualizing the Horniman's collection of Benin Bronzes   Joseph Eboreime   61

5   Siren Seductress of the Seven Seas: Mammy Wata in the Global Village   Jill Salmons   73

6   Agents of Order and Disorder: Kongo Minkisi   Hein Vanhee   89

7   'Imina Sangan' or 'Masques à la Mode':
    Contemporary Masquerade in the Dogon Region   Polly Richards   107

8   Candomblé Shrines   Tania Costa Tribe   125

9   Contradictory Images: Bwaba Leaf Masks
    and Fibre Masks with Carved Heads (Burkina Faso)   Michèle Coquet   143

10 Masks and Styles: Yoruba Masquerade in a Regional Perspective   William Rea   159

11 Two Masks from the Yoruba-Speaking Region of Nigeria   John Picton   171

12 Quest for the Cross River Skin-Covered Mask:
    Methodology, Reality and Reflection   Keith Nicklin   189

13 Tradition as Object of Derision and Desire:
    The Bedu Masquerade of North-Eastern Côte d'Ivoire   Karel Arnaut   209

    Notes on contributors   231

African Worlds Gallery, Horniman Museum and Gardens, 2000.

(Photograph: Horniman Museum, Heini Schneebeli).

Foreword

If only the walls could speak, if only this mask could speak… but they don't. Even objects fashioned to proclaim a message remain mute to those who do not know beforehand. To find the intended and unintended messages a viewer must first look and appreciate, look again and ask for meaning. Looking again is what *Re-Visions* is all about. This book selects a number of objects in the museum and invites the visitor to start on a journey of exploration that begins with the unhurried view of a concrete unchanging object, follows up with explanation and finally lets meaning dissolve in a maelstrom of creativity in which certainties give way to dialogue and cherished assumptions about culture, change and identity are all challenged. Even if that visitor stems from the African and African diaspora which should be the 'natural audience' for such objects – indeed more visitors from there visit the museum physically or electronically than ever before – still in the end such a person also meets the same challenges.

Re-visions heralds also a new approach in the study of objects by anthropologists, art historians, or others and new ways for this museum to present the results of such studies. But what then exactly is new here? A generation or so ago nearly all specialists studied objects from two major angles, especially those objects that qualified by some unspoken criterium as art. A study of form established styles and connected them to specific 'tribes' (one tribe, one style), while field studies dealt primarily with use and function, in which function included some reference to meaning as well. Every scholar held that the population of Africa had all been rural, consisted of tribes since time immemorial, and that tribal tradition was immutable. Museum labels identified tribe, style, use and function. That this approach denied history, change, and any genuine creativity was not perceived until the evidence burst that straightjacket. It appeared successively that Africans, not all of them rural, had a complex history, that many objects such as masks could not be separated from the performing arts, that performance was both crucial and creative, that one tribe one style was nonsense because most objects originated in workshops and many travelled to be adopted elsewhere, that the forms, uses and functions of various classes of objects changed over time, sometimes radically, that creativity saw potential in all sorts of new materials including junk discards and fashioned new and striking objects from them, that the affinities between the arts of Africa and those of the diaspora, especially but not only in Brazil and in Haiti, were undeniable, and ultimately that objects are not just signs so that one shape carries only and always one meaning, but that objects are multi-vocal and ambiguous: they carry many meanings at once, different meanings for different people and not always the same meanings over time.

Re-visions as a book is a precipitate of such revisionary research. In it the reader meets with nearly all the various facets of the activities of contemporary ongoing research and experiences how they apply to concrete objects. And there is more. Until recently a chasm existed between museums in rich 'collector countries' and

Africans. Museum bought or received objects from collectors and had no contact with people from the milieu in which such objects had flourished. Indeed the very Africans who made, used, or gave meaning to such objects were themselves also objects of research condemned to be providers of raw material or 'informants', but excluded from the discourse of the researchers about the productions of their creativity. Now, no longer. As one can see in this museum and book the chasm has given way to collaboration and dialogue. African scholars help to interpret, African and diaspora artists are commissioned to create objects and ensembles for the museum, sometimes in the very gallery where the work will be shown, and their voices become equal to others. Thanks to modern electronics the museum itself becomes accessible to its natural constituency: the parts of Africa from where the objects stem. Indeed, *Re-visions* is an exuberant celebration of this new reality. The old static and ethnocentric certainties are gone, creativity bubbles everywhere, and the answer is not a statement but a dialogue. Answers change as the questioner changes and questions change as situations change. Through the portals of *Re-visions* the viewer-reader enters into a complex labyrinth of cultures which has no centre and no dead ends, for every way leads somewhere. Here new images and thoughts, new people, new dialogues, new insights emerge at every twist and turn. Travel in this labyrinth, revel in it, dialogue in it, reflect on it all and you will emerge much richer in thought and wiser in feeling than when you went in.

Professor Jan Vansina
University of Wisconsin-Madison

Preface

The Horniman Museum, and the Horniman family, have an established tradition of sponsoring field research and field collecting which dates back to the first half of the last century. Emslie Horniman, the son of Frederick John Horniman, the Museum's founder, and himself a keen observer of humankind, though never a professional fieldworker, regularly took advice from the Horniman's curators, Herbert Spencer Harrison and Alfred Cort Haddon on what he should collect for them during his frequent trips abroad. He also provided funds to allow Haddon to purchase material required to 'fill the gaps' in the Museum's new evolutionary displays which were being mounted in the early 1900s. Emslie's most outstanding contribution to field studies, however, was his endowment of the Emslie Horniman Anthropological Scholarship Fund, administered by the Royal Anthropological Institute. In his will of 1932, he stated his intention that the Fund should contribute to:

> *The promotion of the scientific study of the growth of civilisation habits, customs religions and*
> *physical characteristics of the non-European races inclusive of prehistoric man in Europe and*
> *including anthropology in its wider sense and departments such as ethnology ethnography and*
> *all that relates to their physical and natural developments.*

Emslie was not motivated by soley scholarly considerations, and urged that the Fund would best benefit those wanting to enter government service or a recognised profession through which they could aid humanity by their future researches. Although Emslie proved a generous patron to the Museum and anthropology generally, the discipline's focus on cultural evolution did not require the concerted single-minded attention to specific cultures, that later subject developments would come to demand. Nevertheless, the legacy of the Scholarship Fund provided an important impetus to the work of the British School of Social Anthropology which, indirectly shaped the future role of the Horniman as a committed field museum.

The Horniman is fortunate in that it has been associated not only with one master of fieldwork in the guise of Alfred Cort Haddon (Advisory Curator from 1901-1915), often named as the father of anthropological field studies, but with a second, in the person of Otto Samson (Curator... from 1947-1965), a distinguished Oriental scholar. Samson, interested in the transmission of cultural traits from one part of the world to another, conducted research in Orissa to help ascertain the cultural and historical relationship between India and China. Although his own theoretical position was shaped by diffusionism, he did not fail to see that fieldwork provided a highly effective means of acquiring well documented objects for public display as well as unique interpretative opportunities which were justification enough for the Museum's research programme. It was under Samson's directorship that the first systematic field collection, made by Colin Turnbull from among the Mbuti, arrived at the Museum in 1956. In 1959 Turnbull was commissioned to make another collection, which resulted in a further 109 objects from the Sua. In 1958 Samson encouraged Ms. Jean Jenkins, the Museum's first Keeper of Musical Instruments to undertake research and collecting in Bulgaria. Seven years later she began her first of three seasons work in Ethiopia (1965-1969), interviewing musicians, recording musical performances and assembling a collection of no less than 408 items. Samson's interest in performance also brought the Museum Beryl de Zoote's superb photographic collection on Balinese life, and her lesser known photographs of Romania. Other field collections were made from Asia, the Americas, and Papua New Guinea, but the main focus of most work, from Samson's period to the present day, has probably been Africa.

Under David Boston's directorship (1966-1993), a succession of field collections were made from the Hadza of Tanzania (James Woodburn, 1966), the San of Botswana (Valerie Vowles 1970-1), the Tuareg of Algeria (Jeremy Keenan, 1971), the Xhosa and neighbouring peoples in southern Africa (Erich Bigalke 1972), and the Samburu of Kenya (Jean Brown and Cordelia Rose, 1972).

A second phase of African fieldwork projects began during the tenure of Keith Nicklin as Keeper of Ethnography from 1982-1994. Unlike the previous period, from the mid 1980s, fieldwork was mainly conducted by the Museum's curatorial staff with Keith taking a leading role. With the exception of Keith and Jill Salmon's 1987 season among the Luo and their neighbours in Kenya, research and field collecting became re-focused on Nigeria. In 1988, as part of the Cameroonian Quadrant Expedition, Keith Nicklin visited south-east Nigeria and the adjacent territory of Cameroon. He returned to south-east Nigeria with Jill Salmons in 1992, when he collected among the Ogoni. Among other things he acquired examples of contemporary Karikpo masks which illustrated the use of modern materials in Ogoni mask making. In 1990, in preparation for an exhibition on the Yoruba, Keith visited south-west Nigeria to collect examples of the objects that the Yoruba encounter and use in their everyday life. Notable among these collections was the full and complete contents of a market stall which was re-assembled in the Museum during the Yoruba exhibition.

The results of the third period of research beginning in 1996, sponsored or co-sponsored by the Museum, includes the projects undertaken by Karel Arnaut, Polly Richards, Michael Pennie, Keith Nicklin, Emmanuel Arinze, Joseph Eboreime, Kathryn Chan, Tania Tribe, and Phil Cope, presented in the current volume. Work in Nigeria was continued by two eminent Nigerian anthropologists, Emmanuel Arinze and Joseph Eboreime. Emmanuel Arinze did research in the Igbo region around Achalla on Ijele masquerades. Not only did he conduct original research, making recordings of the music of Kings and filming the making and performance of Ijele, but, on behalf of the Museum, he commissioned an Ijele to be made as the centre piece for the Horniman's 1999 permanent exhibition, *African Worlds*.

As in the case of Emmanuel, our collaboration with Joseph Eboreime also went back to 1996, when he kindly accepted our invitation to sit on the advisory board for the new gallery and undertake research to re-present, from the point of view of his own people, the Benin material most of which Frederick John Horniman had purchased from W. J. Hider in 1897. If the original acquisition was not contentious at the time, the ensuing history of European and American rights over the legal ownership of Benin artefacts has been a continuous source of friction with Nigeria, which we felt an ethical incumbency to confront. The partial and more equitable resolution we devised involved returning the voice of interpretation, if not the disputed objects, to the Bini people themselves. The response of Joseph and the team he put together with the co-operation of the Nigerian National Commission on Museums and Monuments was, to say the least, gracious and immensely rewarding. For over two years Joseph tirelessly directed research on the iconography and history of the bronzes in our collection, using written, archival, and most important, oral sources from within the Royal Palace itself. Furthermore, by recording royal ceremonies he was able to relate historically situated events to their contemporary ritual re-enactments.

Another corpus of research was instigated to examine Africa beyond its continental shorelines; to explore the process of bricolage or syncretism, through which Africa was reborn in the Antipodes. The estate of the late John Povey generously provided Keith Nicklin the funding to investigate and collect Mami Wata shrines in Togo and The Republic of Benin, and for a second trip, with Jill Salmons and Tania Tribe, to Brazil to provide visual examples of the incorporation of Yoruba deities in candomblé ritual. Phil Cope researched Haitian vodou and collected shrine material to furnish the gallery's third altar, which while also echoing powerful African influences, is perhaps even more remarkable for the fantastic syncretism between local beliefs and the expansive global imagery which it domesticates. Work on Trinidadian Carnival was carried out by the accomplished artist Kathryn Chan, another member of the curatorial advisory team and a committed researcher into the history, iconography, and performance of Midnight Cowboys.

The final research corpus that *African Worlds* gave rise to, were those projects on or related to the cultures of French speaking Africa. Since 1996, the Museum's acquisition policy signalled a re-focusing of attention away from English speaking Africa, which is well represented in other museums in the United Kingdom, to the cultures of Côte d'Ivoire, Mali, Burkina Faso, the Benin Republic, and elsewhere. In this new endeavour we have been fortunate not only to count the support of Karel Arnaut himself who has been associated with research for the Horniman's new gallery from 1996, and, before that provided the British Museum and Brighton Museum with excellent collections from the Bondoukou region of Côte d'Ivoire, but Polly Richards who is currently working on contemporary Dogon masquerades. Michael Pennie is another researcher who has not only carried out a great deal of work on the Lobi of Ghana and Burkina Faso, but has helped develop the first museum in the Lobi country which he furnished through the gift of his own collection.

The Horniman Museum is extremely proud that over the 44 years in which it has worked in Africa, many of its fieldwork projects have been carried out in association with the museums of that continent; the National Museum and Art Gallery, Gaborone; the East London Museum, South Africa; the Nigerian National Commission on Museums and Monuments; the Ghana Museums and Monuments Board; and the Musée Historique d'Ouidah, Republic of Benin. The Horniman, is committed to working towards developing new, equitable and respectful relationships not only with the peoples of Africa, but with the rest of the world. In attempting to contribute to balancing the one-way flow of information from the southern to the northern hemisphere, we have put exhibitions and collections on the world wide web, and, in the case of Benin, have supplied the National Museum with computer facilities to enable school children and researchers to access the exhibition to which the Benin people have themselves contributed so much. This publication brings to the fore some of the research which has contributed to making *African Worlds* such a success, and, like its sister publication, Keith Nicklin's *Ekpu: The Oron Ancestor Figures from South Eastern Nigeria*, will be distributed gratis to universities and museums throughout the African continent in acknowledgement of the very great honour they have done us by supporting not only this project, but almost half a century of fieldwork.

Anthony Alan Shelton
Horniman Museum, London

Introduction: Re-visioning Collections and Ethnography at the African Worlds Gallery

Karel Arnaut

In the promotion booklet for the Horniman Museum and Gardens, the *African Worlds* gallery is said to celebrate 'diversity, history and creativity'. This is also what the essays in this volume do, in different respects. Contributors were asked to focus on particular items that are on display in the *African Worlds* gallery. Some were actively involved in collecting and researching the objects, while others were asked to use their research findings to re-interpret particular objects or collections. The result is a diverse set of essays; thirteen individual attempts to relate research, ethnographic work, and personal experience to important objects and collections in the Horniman Museum.

Most of the contributors met for the first time during the 1999 MEG Conference *Glimpses of Africa*. In the title of this volume the idea of glimpses is recuperated in the term 're-visions'. Revision first of all refers to the fact that people were asked to look back on objects collected, and research, conducted in the past. This (field) working one's way to the past through recent research and experience is necessarily a hazardous undertaking. The term 'revision', so often used in morally and politically thorny historical debates, is meant to bring out the dangers involved in re-reading the past. Indeed, most contributors will be seen struggling with ways to revive history, lost tradition, present transformations, personal experience, and past research in the presence of objects. Some have chosen to glimpse at the objects through the eyes of their impassioned makers and users or to narrate their personal explorations, others opted for a more detached view by adopting the 'typical' researcher's stance.

One essay is unambiguously celebratory. In his essay on the Ijele masquerade, Emmanuel Arinze very much

Karel Arnaut

Figure 1:
Ethnographic
installations. Nwa-DC
figure mounted at
the apex of the Ijele,
Horniman Museum,
1999.
(Photograph: E. Arinze).

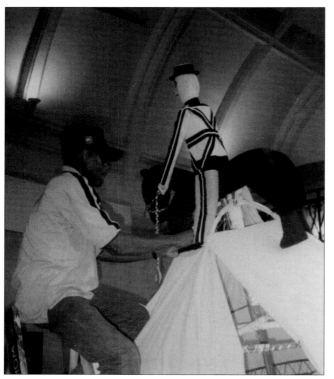

shares the *laudatio* of an Achalla elder whom he quotes saying 'no masquerade is bigger than Ijele'. The author tries to capture the aesthetic and moral appreciation of Ijele by the Igbo of north-east Nigeria. Michael Pennie equally speaks of his sympathy for the Lobi but uses his travel account to tell about his everyday irritations with local conditions and cultural routines. In this volume, he presents a report of his eleventh trip to the Lobi who inhabit a region stretching over Burkina Faso, Ghana, and Côte d'Ivoire. In the case of Phil Cope, enthusiasm gives way to an outspoken commitment to make known the creativity of Haitians under the strains of poverty, the outcome of 150 years of wild capitalism and neo-colonialism. In a neat move Phil Cope locates artistic inventiveness in the way the people of Haiti recuperate materials, recycle religious leftovers from their Amerindean and African pasts as well as the by-products or simply the waste of the contemporary global economy.[1]

Tellingly, the three authors who indulge in enthusiasm and/or discontent, are not academics in the strict sense of the word, but exhibition professionals who in their essays consider first and foremost *people*. The evaluation of these people's artistic exploits is, one could say, instrumental to appreciating their living makers and users.

This is not to say that such esteem for *human* history and creativity is entirely absent from the second group of more scholarly, historical papers. Joseph Eboreime, for example, could be said to somehow celebrate the past in his historical re-interpretation of the collection of Benin bronze plaques on display in the *African Worlds* gallery. He endeavours an iconographic analysis on a double basis. He compares the imagery of the bronze plaque's imagery with contemporary ritual performance such as the Igue festival during which the 'the beauty and power of royalty are paraded in procession and dance'. On the other hand he relies on exegesis by people who are connected to the present court of the Oba at Benin City, now the capital of Edo state in south-central Nigeria.

The Mammy Wata shrine in the *African Worlds* gallery was put together by two artists (man and wife) from Ouidah (Republic of Benin), with Keith Nicklin acting as an 'impresario'. The latter's wife, Jill Salmons, contributes to the present volume a text that combines her own research findings on Mammy Wata in south-east Nigeria in the early seventies and early nineties with data from publications and exhibitions which in themselves index the recent interest, if not the hype, concerning the Mammy Wata cult in West and Central Africa and in the New World. Salmon's paper above all brings us in the right state of mind to start exploring this many-layered phenomenon which seems to indicate a space of creativity, historical imaginations, and ritual practices in which, for one, the aesthetic and the religious merge. Furthermore, Mammy Wata as an exemplary hybrid phenomenon comes to reveal the other side of 'hybridity': the occasion it offers for so many people (including researchers) to recognise in it something of themselves, their own cultures and religions, or, in the case of researchers, the ones they study. Ultimately, it exposes these things as appropriations in their own right by insinuating the question: who borrowed from whom? For instance, the backdrop of the Mammy Wata altar in the *African Worlds* gallery shows a figure in which one can see a (European?) mermaid, a (West African?) female water spirit, and a (Hindu?) snake-charmer. These recognitions are supplemented by researchers claiming that Mammy Wata as a cult was formed in Haiti or Surinam and uses Eskimo imagery. Further to this, Jill Salmons urges us to see every manifestation of Mammy Wata as a local assemblage which deserves the detailed attention of researchers.

Another historical re-interpretation is Hein Vanhee's contribution on Kongo *minkisi* (sing. *nkisi*), the well-known 'power figures' from the western region of the Democratic Republic of Congo (DRC). His research in mission archives in Europe and in Mayombe brought to light new texts on *minkisi,* produced by local people in the Kiyombe language. The texts are related to two previously unknown historic collections built by Belgian Catholic missionaries. In his discussion of this material, Hein Vanhee touches upon the question of what the presence of the so-called Lower Congo 'nail fetishes' in the *African Worlds* gallery actually tells us about the transformation of Kongo culture at the beginning of the twentieth century.

Polly Richards also revisits the Horniman collection of masks from the Dogon people of south-eastern Mali and north-western Burkina Faso. The Dogon masks currently on display in the *African Worlds* gallery, she describes as 'curiously homogeneous', illustrating the canon laid down in Marcel Griaule's classic inventory (1938). In contrast, she tells of the Dogon's contemporary mask production and performance. The masks Polly Richards commissioned for the Horniman demonstrate the drastic changes in style and subject matter over the last 70 years. Moreover her essay amply illustrates recent changes in performance practice. Likewise, Tania Tribe combines extensive ethnographic sensitivity with historical awareness. Her account of Brazilian Candomblé shrines explores the African, notably the Yoruba, origin of the *orixás* or 'saints' and the changing organisation of the 'large body of beliefs and ritual practices' in the urban environment of present-day Rio de Janeiro. The Candomblé shrine on display in the *African Worlds* gallery bears witness to this urban 'reformulation' of the cults. It was built by Pai Roger de Omulu, 'one of a new breed of *pais-de-santo* [male religious leaders] who strive to re-inscribe the sacred within the social space of a modern metropolis'.

A third group of essays are less historical but rather look at (regional) diversity and cultural creativity. In a meticulously documented paper Michèle Coquet presents some of her findings based on extensive fieldwork among the Bwa people of Burkina Faso and Mali. The numerous Bwa communities spread over a large area, share the Doo cult which involves the performance of the well-known zoomorphic masks worn with fibre costumes, and the less familiar leaf masks. This differential popularity in itself appears to be of some relevance. Michèle Coquet's description of the different aesthetics of both masquerade genres, throws some light on the still under-explored issue of degrees of objectification in 'material cultures'.[2] In themselves the leaf 'masks' are rather amorphous and their expressiveness resides almost entirely in the way they are performed. Contrarily, the wooden masks are expressive *per se* and lend themselves more easily to de-contextualisation and re-contextualisation – they travel well. The Bwa borrowed the latter mask genre from the Winiama and the Nuna. In their turn, tourists, government officials, and collectors have found them with the Bwa and recontextualised these transportable 'items of Bwa culture' in their interiors and collections. Lury (1997: 78) described this process in general terms in connection with 'traveller-objects'. These are objects 'whose immanent bounded-ness is secured in relation to an original dwelling by practices of symbolic binding that may occur, paradoxically, in their transit (or, more commonly, the transit of their images)'. Paradoxically indeed, the Bwa still consider their wooden masks as foreign although they have inscribed them with a rich vernacular vocabulary of graphic signs stemming from scars, divination, and their visual environment.

Figure 2: The travelling curator as bush creature. Keith Nicklin in a 'Beast' outfit. The costume is made of dyed raffia fibre, and is of the type representing the 'Beast' in so-called 'Beauty and the Beast' masquerades among the Igbo and neighbouring peoples. The costume was intended for use in Keith's 'Urban Gorilla' masquerade group. Here it has been adapted for use in the innovatory role of perambulatory Christmas tree. (Photograph: Keith Nicklin).

William Rea equally explores regional diversity and creative reformulation in connection with the Epa, Gelede, and Egigun masquerades. Like Michèle Coquet, he combines a regional survey and in-depth analysis to account for a history of multiple exchange and local idiosyncracy. For their surveys, both authors breach established boundaries delineating conventional zones of material culture. Michèle Coquet situates the Bwa within a larger culture area composed of myriad groups – sometimes unduly categorised as *either* Mande *or* Voltaic – who have been exchanging mythological themes, mask types, decorative patterns, etc. over centuries. William Rea deplores the reduction of the masking practices of the Yoruba (south-western part of Nigeria) to 'ethnic performances'. As a result a number of unwarranted associations have been fixed between the centralised Yoruba and Egungun, the south-western Yoruba and Gelede, and the north-eastern Yoruba and the Epa masquerade. Surely, this ethnic typecasting of masquerades does not match with the living diversity that prevails. More generally, William Rea criticises the often invented one-to-one relationship between a specific cultural area, a cult institution, and a mask practice.

Like Michèle Coquet and also John Picton, William Rea argues that categorisation should first of all be based on local (regional) conceptualisations and the aesthetic schemes of the different masquerades, understood 'both within their own performances' (cult institutions and practices) and 'as against each other' (the local Epa as against the local Egigun, for instance). John Picton, in his detailed study of the Epa masquerade in comparison with Egungun and Gelede, illustrates Henry Louis Gates' statement, quoted by William Rea, that 'style draws upon and plays with a chain of signifiers and not on some supposedly transcendent signified'. In Opin, a group of villages that are part of the Ekiti kingdoms of south-western Nigeria, John Picton found that the Orisa, so well known among the other Yoruba were replaced by Imanle and Ebora, respectively 'empowered' artefacts, and natural objects. Here also, Epa-type masks exist under the name of Aguru. In his deconstruction of masquerades, John Picton goes as far as to argue that there is no easy one-to-one relationship between mask performance and mask sculpture: sculpture and performance do not merely illustrate each other; they have to be discretely located within their respective 'chains of signifiers'.

The papers by Keith Nicklin and Karel Arnaut are more difficult to classify in terms of celebrating the expressive lives of people, or attempts at historical reconstruction and comparison. Keith Nicklin tells the story of thirty years of research into the skin-covered masks of the Cross River peoples who inhabit the border region between south-eastern Nigeria and north-western Cameroon. Karel Arnaut looks at the Bedu masquerade of the Bondoukou region in north-eastern Côte d'Ivoire. He explores the traditional guises in which the Bedu mask is presented in contemporary discourse and (political) performance. Although quite different in outlook, both essays offer the occasion to address two matters with which most of the papers in this collection seem to be concerned.

Through his travelogue, Keith Nicklin addresses the key-issue of what he calls 'appropriate ethnographic collecting' as an alternative for 'cultural appropriation'. In his 'self narrative' he explains his many ways of directly interacting with the local 'art world' and ritual associations up to the point of founding his own masquerade group, the 'Urban Gorilla', with personnel of the Oron National Museum. In 1984 Keith Nicklin, then already Keeper of Ethnology at the Horniman Museum, commissioned a skin-covered mask from the master-carver Thomas Ogwogwo whose work he had documented and whom he had supported for a long time. This project may be seen as a precedent to the many projects that were set up in connection with the *African Worlds* gallery in the late 1990s, under the instigation of Anthony Shelton.

For sure, ethnographic museums have a long history of field collecting. From the early stages of the colonial era we remember the scramble for material culture specimens in Africa, run by ethnographic museums of the imperial metropoles and carried out by collectors-ethnographers like Emile Torday, Leo Frobenius, and Arnold Ridyard (see also Schildkrout & Keim 1998). Later, the expeditions of Marcel Griaule for the Musée de l'Homme (Paris) in the 1930s and 1940s, attempted to develop more 'scientific' ways of collecting. Ethnographic objects were considered as 'witnesses' ('témoin') of a given culture ('civilisation'). As Leiris (1931: 8) explained in a manual for potential collectors, neither the aesthetic excellence nor the stylistic purity of objects was of any importance; in fact any object which in some way or other illustrated a technique, a material or mental action was to be considered of possible relevance.[3] From this state of affairs in which Africans were seen as unwitting producers of culture and ethnographers as conscious consumers, it is indeed a large step to the projects of artistic patronage conducted by Keith Nicklin and later by others for the Horniman Museum. In most of the essays in this collection, one can see the field collector acting more as 'cultural broker' than as go-between or runner. 'Runner' implies that the producer is at best half-informed about the destination of his produce after a quickly concluded deal. In contrast, brokerage could imply that the consumers and producers are somehow on an equal footing both economically and 'conceptually'.[4] Many essays attest to this double implication of cultural brokerage: commissioning is a long process of negotiating collaboration, and setting conditions of quality and content that are acceptable for both parties (see Michael Pennie in this volume). All this involved financial compensation. Some of these aspects of cultural brokerage are evoked by Tania Tribe when she writes about Pai Roger and his agreement with the Horniman Museum:

'Although he agreed to supply a *peji* [Candomblé shrine] in return for a substantial sum of money, he was careful to point out that he would only do so on condition that the *assentos* [sacred materials] supplied would not contain the sacred matter that consecrates the emblems of the *orixás*, activating their *axé* [life force].'

The flip-side of travelling curators moving into the artists' working places is the artists doing their work at the museum. Emmanuel Arinze describes how the Ijele mask was first mounted and performed in Achalla, and many months later entirely rebuilt in the *African Worlds* gallery. The same happened in the case of the Candomblé shrine, the Mammy Wata shrine and the Haitian vodou shrine. But in the latter case not even all the materials were brought back from Haiti; some materials were acquired *in situ*. Whatever the practical reasons for doing so, it must be clear that the boundaries between contemporary art installations on the one hand and ethnographic artistic projects like the shrines on the other hand are becoming interestingly thin.[5] Michel Leiris (1931: 8), in his attempt to explain to the potential collector what kind of banal cultural objects ethnographers were interested in, wrote: 'A tin of food, for instance, characterises our societies better than the most expensive piece of jewellry or the rarest stamp.' We may now encounter such banal objects in ethnographic museums, only to find that they have been incorporated in a 'Haitian' or 'Brazilian' shrine installation, conceived by an artist who thereby extends 'the process of re-sacralisation into the urban environment' (Tania Tribe), mediated by a cultural broker of the kind that looms large in Keith Nicklin's auto-ethnography.

From Nicklin's 'appropriate ethnographic collecting' to 'appropriate ethnography', seems only a small step. One of the most critical points which most contributors in this volume seem to recognise is that in research and collecting the artists and performers as well as the audience members are not mere sources of data or producers/consumers of art objects but intellectual partners who can make substantial theoretical contributions (after Bauman and Briggs 1990: 61). John Picton, further exploring his 'What's in a mask?' question, asks to take into consideration 'local conceptual orders' and Hein Vanhee in his discussion of Kongo *minkisi*, proposes to make proper use of 'indigenous theory'. William Rea, while trying to further dismantle the one tribe-one style paradigm, points towards 'an underlying ontology' which probably surpasses or intersects the Yoruba ethnic or linguistic boundaries.

However, postulating an equal intellectual exchange in the reconstruction of vernacular theory-building poses the problem of projection and, above all, intellectual appropriation. This Valentin Mudimbe has demonstrated persuasively in his *The invention of Africa* (1988) where he argued rather gloomily that African knowledge (he calls it 'gnosis') remains incarcerated in Western epistemological territory. One possible way out of this intricacy is to dislocating ethnographic practice and theory-building from the appropriating centre and situating them in the destabilising periphery. As such ethnographers frame their research and collecting as forever coming from without and operating beyond the limits of the disciplining centre. This can be accommodated within the widely documented bush-village model. What emerges from this construction is the ethnographer as bush creature and his knowledge as untamed but under constant threat of being appropriated by the centre, whether that was constituted by the colonial administration or early nationalists and is now occupied by postcolonial traditionalists or cultural tourism.

The village-bush model is a classic one in African and African diaspora cosmologies, and the essays in this volume confirm this abundantly. Michèle Coquet claims that the Bwa conceive of the opposition between the indigenous leaf masks and the imported fibre masks with carved heads as equitable to the distinction between the wilderness and the lineage/village. Tania Tribe reports that each *terreiro* (Candomblé house, or 'parish') is divided into two main areas: an 'urban' space, comprising the public and private buildings, and a 'virgin' space with trees, plants, and water; the latter 'forest' area is 'seen as sacred and dangerous and tends to be avoided by most of the inhabitants of the *terreiro*'. In his article on the Bedu masquerade Karel Arnaut equally sees the masks operating within a space oriented by the two poles of bush and village. According to Hein Vanhee the animating spirits that made Kongo *minkisi* 'living things' were essentially 'outsiders,' either originating from the bush, the water or the sky. Herein also seems to reside the religious and aesthetic appeal and potential of Mammy Wata as presented by Jill Salmons. Basically, Mammy Wata are entities from beyond the immediate environment: water spirits either of local provenance or in the form of the white ship-sailing creatures that emerged from the ocean and were seen as returnees from the land of the dead. Mermaids and Indian snake-charmers reproduce this essential foreignness and elusiveness, and are made to signify other 'things' that appear as sudden as they slip away: money, happiness, and maybe just life itself.

Figure 3: Domesticating town/bush creatures. A policeman mask (imina policier) at Banani, complete with peaked cap, notebook for issuing fines, fake gun and holster. (Photograph: Polly Richards, 1996).

One could make use of MacGaffey's categorisation of *minkisi* as situated in one of two 'cosmological domains', to construct an opposition between the asocial, the untamable and the violent on the one hand, and the disciplined and socially constructive, on the other hand. Hein Vanhee describes how *minkisi* are either 'of the above', associated with violent destruction (like the *khonde*), or 'of the below' and concerned, for instance, with the protection of children. Similar associations are referred to in this volume. Karel Arnaut in the case of Bedu and William Rea in connection with masquerades in south-western Nigeria, testify to the concern of masquerades with children as 'precious element[s] of social life'. In contrast the aspect of violence, destruction, and lewd, anti-social behaviour are equally documented by Keith Nicklin and Karel Arnaut; but perhaps this should be taken more broadly and be extended to aggressive tourists and policemen, to intrusive politicians from the relatively far-away capital, to the ruthless economic realities that pervade and upset village life.

When looking at change in Dogon masquerade, Polly Richards observes how (traditional) villages adapt to 'urban novelty' brought in by their own youth, or by tourists. Van Beek (1991: 70) observed that recent alterations challenge the 'bush symbolism' but that masquerades are nonetheless the sites in which 'new ways of interpreting the world emerge'. In an important article on contemporary dance groups in Cameroon, I believe Nicholas Argenti made the interesting observation that '[The] myths of the liminal, wild or foreign origins of masquerades now equate forest and town, and ... young men returning from ... the coast or the towns outside the polity are said to "bring the masquerades back" with them' (Argenti 1998: 760). It would be unwarranted to claim that this applies wholesale to other masquerades in West Africa, but Argenti's observation at least opens a promising field of enquiry. Karel Arnaut indicates in his essay that this model of conceptualisation may indeed be seen operating in more 'topical' Bedu masquerades such as the one organised during a presidential election meeting. Looking at how urban *terreiros* in present-day Rio de Janeiro struggle with shortage of 'virgin' or 'forest' space where certain rituals are meant to take place, Tania Tribe, following Vagner Silva, describes how the forest space is mapped out onto the surrounding city with 'spaces like streets, cemeteries and crossroads' being attributed certain 'mythical forces through the presence of the deities'. Michèle Coquet observed that 'the bush' in its guise of Bwa leaf masks represents 'humanity's sudden appearance'. Taken together, these observations attest to a concept of the bush as a space of unexpected, sometimes painful, transformations, male violence, novelty, post-colonial strangers, tricksters, etc.

To conclude, the latter observations point out that the rather idyllic picture of the 'new' museum as enlightened art patron and the 'new' curator as cultural broker, is bound to remain ambivalent and subject to power struggles.[6] As relative strangers and 'bush creatures', the travelling curators must remain aware of the fact that their *démarches* bring untamed economic and symbolic (academic, culture-political) forces into play. In his essay Karel Arnaut has tried to come to terms with the attempts of Bondoukou people to 'traditionalise' the Bedu masquerade, to rebuild an 'archaic' Bedu in the face of research which set out to prove the opposite: the dynamics of living tradition. In a recent article Anne Doquet (1999) observed how among the Dogon 'culture tourism' puts up the pressure to stage 'traditional' masks. Aware of the tourists' taste for recognisable, predictable 'tradition' *young* dancers are seen complaining with the elders about too much flexibility in the traditional masquerade.

Having witnessed the double play of village and bush power in performance, it would be surprising if it were not part of the 'celebration' the *African Worlds* gallery is trying to stage. The contributions of 're-visions' may help readers and visitors realise that the taming of art through outsiders' research and collecting both releases and domesticates artistic creativity.

In the final account, this could indicate how the local art patronage and 'forensic' curatorship advanced by the Horniman Museum are very much part of a renewing of ethnographic practice. In a seminal article George Marcus (1999: 98) asked that we recognise 'ethnographers as ever-present markers of "outsideness"' and he further muses that 'it is only in an anthropologist-informant situation in which the outsideness is never elided and is indeed the basis of an affinity between ethnographer and subject that the reigning traditional ideology of fieldwork can shift to reflect the changing conditions of research'. The 'appropriate ethnographic collecting' introduced by Keith Nicklin and pursued by Anthony Shelton has initiated the kind of renewal theorised by Marcus, and this volume reports on how far we have got in revising ethnography and collecting.

Notes

1. This observation reminds us in at least two ways of Lévi-Strauss who, in The *Savage Mind*, saw his 'bricoleur' employ materials and techniques at hand (1989: 16, 20), while on his voyages to Brazil he found 'our' debris thrown into the face of humanity (1955: 36). Phil Cope's Haitian artist is 'throwing' back relics of globalisation, an activity which comes close to what Appadurai (1990: 16) has called the 'repatriation of difference'.

2. But see Lury (1997) and Gell (1998: 251-258).

3. The anonymous 1931 publication 'Instructions sommaires ...' is considered to hold the ideas of several people including Marcel Mauss and Marcel Griaule. Michel Leiris is considered as the scribe rather than the author of this document. Michèle Coquet (personal communication) has pointed out that the text I refer to is Mauss's line. Nonetheless, I follow Jean Jamin (Leiris 1996: 1379) in retaining both here and in the bibliography Leiris as the writer of these lines.

4. For an introduction into cultural brokerage by Africans during the (early) colonial period, see de Moraes Farias & Barber (1990).

5. Cosentino (2000: 102) makes a similar point, quoting David Byrne who described Afro-Caribbean altars as 'visual jazz, constantly reworked and reactivated'.

6. Some interesting, recent attempts to come to grips with the ambiguities of curatorship as cultural brokerage are Gable (1996), Atondi (1999), and Macdonald (1997).

Bibliography

APPADURAI, A. 1990. Disjuncture and Difference in the Global Cultural Economy. *Public Culture*, **2**, 2, 1-24.

ARGENTI, N. 1998. Air Youth: Performance, Violence and the State in Cameroon. *JRAI* (N.S.) **4**, 4, 753-781.

ATONDI, I. 1999. La Violence Muséale: Aux Origines d'un Discours Ambigu. *Cahiers d'études africaines*, **155-156**, 905-921.

BAUMAN, R. & BRIGGS C. 1990. Poetics and Performance as Critical Perspectives on Language and Social Life. *Annual Review of Anthropology*, **19**, 59-88.

COSENTINO, D. 2000. Mounting Controversy: The Sacred Arts of Haitian Vodou. In Paine, C. (ed), *Godly things: museums, objects and religion*, 97-106.

DE MORAES FARIAS, P. & BARBER, K. (eds), 1990. *Self-Assertion and Brokerage: Early Nationalism in West Africa.* Birmingham: Centre of West African Studies.

DOQUET, A. 1999. Les Masques Dogon: de l'objet au Musée de l'Homme à l'homme Objet de Musée. *Cahiers d'Etudes Africaines*, **39**, 3-4, 917-635.

GABLE, E. 1996. Maintaining Boundaries, or 'Mainstreaming' Black History in a White Museum. In Macdonald, S. and Fyfe, G. (eds), *Theorising museums*, 177-202.

GELL, A. 1998. *Art and Agency: an Anthropological Theory.* Oxford: Clarendon Press.

GRIAULE, M. 1938. *Masques Dogons.* Paris: Institut d'Ethnologie.

LEIRIS, M. 1931. *Instructions Sommaires pour les Collecteurs d'objets Ethnographiques.* Paris: Musée d'Ethnographie & Mission scientifique Dakar-Djibouti.

LEIRIS, M. 1996 *Miroir de l'Afrique* [texts edited by Jean Jamin]. Paris: Gallimard.

LEVI-STRAUSS, C. 1955. *Tristes Tropiques.* Paris: Plon.

LEVI-STRAUSS, C. 1989 (1962). *The Savage Mind.* London: Weidenfeld and Nicolson.

LURY, C. 1997. The Objects of Travel. In Rojek C. and Urry J. (eds*), Touring Cultures: Transformations of Travel and Theory,* 75-95.

MACDONALD, S. 1997. The Museum as Mirror: Ethnographic Reflections. In James, A. *et al.* (eds*), After Writing Culture: Epistemology and Praxis in Contemporary Anthropology* [ASA Monographs 34], 161-176.

MARCUS, G. 1999. The Uses of Complicity in the Changing Mise-en-Scène of Anthropological Fieldwork. In Ortner, S. (ed), *The Fate of 'Culture',* 86-109.

MUDIMBE, V. 1988. *The Invention of Africa: Gnosis, Philosophy, and the Order of Knowledge.* Bloomington: Indiana University Press.

SCHILDKROUT, E. & KEIM, C. (eds), 1998. *The Scramble for Art in Central Africa.* Cambridge: Cambridge University Press.

VAN BEEK, W. 1991. Enter the Bush: a Dogon Mask Festival. In Vogel S. (ed), *Africa Explores 20*th *Century African Art,* 56-73.

If You See Ijele Masquerade, You Have Seen It All

1

Emmanuel Nnakenyi Arinze

To the Igbo, especially to those who live in communities like Achalla, Aguleri, Umuleri and Nteje, Ijele is the ultimate in the masquerade tradition. The Igbo in Nigeria are a people who believe very strongly in their tradition and culture and they enact this in a variety of ways and forms, like rituals, ceremonies, dance and music. However, one very significant tradition that is highly regarded and to which the Igbo looks forward to is *iti mmanwu,* that is, the performance of the masquerade. This is an event that enjoys a universal currency in most parts of Igboland. Nonetheless, differences do exist on the scale and size of the masquerade culture that can be observed in Igbo villages and communities. There are small social masquerades which are not fearful and intimidating and there are big spirit masquerades which are terrifying, fearsome and powerful. For this second category, one would have to be initiated into the secret of the masquerade to be able to participate in its performance while there are no initiation ceremonies for the social masquerades. Of all these masquerades, Ijele stands out as the masquerade of masquerades in Igboland for it towers above all others in terms of uniqueness, size, beauty, grace, majesty and elegance. According to an Achalla elder (1998), no masquerade can be bigger than Ijele.

Ijele is not found in all parts of Igboland; it is rather located in the communities around the Anambra River basin of Achalla, Nteje, Aguleri and Umuleri even though, its presence has today spread to other areas that are not traditionally Ijele communities.

The Igbo are particularly proud of Ijele for it is the epitome of the classical Igbo masquerade tradition which blends the antiquities of Igbo iconography and represents the Igbo cosmos. It is no wonder therefore that whenever Ijele appears, one uses the expression 'Ijele oke mmanwu!' ('Ijele the great spirit and masquerade').

The masquerade tradition among the Igbo brings people and communities together during performance. It helps to create harmony and understanding and promote communal dialogue. As an agent of specialisation, it ensures that the young learn the ways of their elders and imbibe the ethics and wholesomeness of their cultural traditions which will ensure that the communal heritage is passed from generation to generation.

Cole describes Ijele as a massive show of human and spiritual forces and resources. To him, an Ijele mask is a multi-faceted symbol of human leadership, ancestral authority and the prolific powers of nature (Cole 1989: 22). Ezekwe states that Ijele is like a mobile art gallery that shows the life of the Igbo in all its complexities. In describing some of these complexities, he says that Ijele is many things to many people as it symbolises the ingenious mind of the Igbo and the social solidarity that makes its constitution possible. The Igbo are generally known not to have kings. However, among those Igbo who have a monarchical system, Ijele is associated with the king. Thus in towns like Achalla and Onitsha, Ijele stands for the stately grandeur of the king who has attained an honoured position in life, splendour, the fullness of life and great economic and social success (Ezekwe 1987: 103). Ijele as a unique masquerade overwhelms the beholder by its size and splendour hence the Igbo describe it as 'Ijele nnukwu-mmanwu' ('Ijele the big masquerade').

I carried out research studying the Ijele masquerade and the artist, Ichie Ezennaya, assembling the materials for the construction of the Ijele now in the Horniman Museum. I followed the construction process and participated in a special performance of Ijele in Achalla in August 1998 to celebrate the successful construction project. In the course of my research, I found that in Achalla, the family of Ichie Ezennaya has a long history of building Ijele masquerade costumes for the community, kings, and neighbouring towns. I followed the entire process from building an Ijele to its performance in Achalla in 1998. It also lead to the commission and construction of the Ijele presently on display in the Horniman Museum (fig. 1).

Ichie Ezennaya (fig. 2) also known as Onuoraegbunam ('the mouth of the people will not kill me') and

Figure1: Ijele on display at the Horniman Museum. (Photograph: Horniman Museum, Heini Schneebeli).

Figure 2: Ichie Ezennaya, the builder of the Horniman Ijele. (Photograph: E. Arinze).

Omenka ('the maker of great things') is the builder of the Horniman Ijele. He comes from Odawa village in Achalla, Anambra State (Nigeria) but lives and works with his family in Ogbunike. According to Achalla oral history, it was one elder known as Duchiozo who introduced the *Igwe* institution (kingship) and Ijele to Achalla. Hence, there, the people refer to Ijele as *Ijele Duchiozo*. The legend of Duchiozo is an important element in the Achalle oral tradition.

The building of Ijele is complex and demanding and the builder must possess skills in designing and tailoring as it takes up to one year to build one. In a traditional setting, the entire community would provide food and palmwine for the Ijele master builder and his workers on a daily basis throughout the duration of their work. As the building of Ijele is in itself a social and historic event which does not happen often, the entire community gets involved in the process as people and families would regularly visit the builders, engage them in conversations and discussions and generally follow, day after day, the progress of the work until it is completed. This fosters the sense of collective ownership and accomplishment as they become proud owners of the big masquerade, Ijele. In return they shower praises, presents and gifts on the master builder and his workers.

Ijele is a massive structure which stands out as a masterpiece of craftsmanship and creative ingenuity. Essentially, the modern Ijele is made of multicoloured cloth of both local and foreign provenance, local cane, bamboo materials, and foam to reduce the weight of the structure. In the past, all the supporting structures were made of wood and the textiles were all made locally. This made the traditional Ijele extremely heavy to carry, yet, men with extra strength did carry it with ease.

According to Aniakor (1978: 44):

> *The basic structure of the Ijele mask is that of a huge cone-cylinder, a form relatively rare among Igbo masks. The Ijele head-dress is basically a cloth-covered cone supported on a circular foundation. Two giant arches span the cone, intersecting at right angles at the apex. A network of secondary poles wrapped with thin stripes of coloured cloth reinforces the structure. Small tassels project fan-like from the two arches visually increasing the size of the construction and a large number of motifs – human, animal and spirit – at once decorative and charged with meaning, heighten the formal complexity of Ijele. Posed frontally, these images are deployed in a frieze-like manner on the horizontal supports around the construction. One can see the sky through the open work which creates a realistic background for the figures perched on the head-dress. The vibrant colours and patterns, the glint and dazzle of small mirrors, and beauty of rosettes further enrich the tableau.*

Figure 3: Eke-ogba (the python), a major motif on Ijele, encircles the entire superstructure. On the left are a number of onye-uweoji Ijele (Ijele police) heads under construction. (Photograph: E. Arinze).

25

The motifs that adorn Ijele are many, different and colourful, and they explain the various happenings in the Igbo world. Prominent among the motifs is the *eke ogba* ('python') which is located in the middle of the structure. The python in Igbo mythology is a great and powerful reptile that can swallow a human being, hence it is positioned centrally on Ijele (fig. 3). Other motifs include *nna-mmanwu* (father of the masquerade), *ogbanibe ezenkita* (dog teeth), *ogbanibe ogene* (metal gong), *aka Ijele* (hand of Ijele), *ogbanibe okuko* (chicken), *ogolo*, *onye-uweoji Ijele* (Ijele police), *ntu ugo* (eagle feather); *iru* or *ihu Ijele* (face of Ijele), *oji-na-ocha* (trouble shooter black and white), and *onyeocha nenu inyinya* (whiteman on a horse) (fig. 4). These motifs add colour to Ijele especially when in performance while some, like the 'Ijele police' who are dressed in police uniform with a mask actually perform with Ijele and help to keep order in the arena. At the apex of the Ijele structure is an equestrian figure representing either *nwa-DC* (colonial District Officer) (fig. 5) or an *Igwe* (Igbo king). The motifs on Ijele represent the interplay of the spiritual, the animal, and the physical worlds in a harmonious community.

Figures 4: (f.l.t.r.) Nna-mmanwu (father of the masquerade), the ogolo, and the aka Ijele (hand of Ijele) motifs.
(Photographs: E. Arinze).

Ijele is the apotheosis of Igbo display masks, the elephant among spirit-creatures, and overwhelmingly, the most expensive to commission and dance. The great expense of materials, labour, feeding of artist and sacrifices meant, until quite recently that Ijele was a communal undertaking (Cole and Aniakor 1984: 139).

When in performance, its majesty, beauty, and monumentality capture the Igbo universe in motion with its colours and its intricately woven motifs playing on the artistic sensibilities of the onlooker. So, when Ijele performs, it carries with it the figure of the supreme mystical authority of Igbo elders and ancestors. According to Ezekwe (1987: 105): 'Ijele dramatises through dance and movements the high status and achievements of the ancestors, thus combining mimetic and display elements with the religious one.'

In spite of its size and weight, Ijele is carried by a man who is usually selected by the community. Before a man can carry the masquerade, certain rituals are performed. He is given a raffia pad mat which he places on his head in the enclosure where the mask is kept before and after the performance. He then expertly, with the assistance of the elders, balances Ijele on his head and shoulders before stepping out into the arena to the prompting of the *Igba-eze* drums and the cheers of the crowd. While in motion, the carrier of Ijele does not feel its weight as he dances, moves, twirls, turns, runs and breaks suddenly, defying gravity, and displaying breath-taking agility while the sound of the flute continues to guide his steps and movements. Ijele is usually about 4 m. high, over 2 m. wide, and weighs 227 kg; and yet it is carried with ease and dexterity.

Ijele dances to the sounds of *igba eze* (music of the kings) and its dance steps are in keeping with the regal dance steps of Igbo kings and elders. The Ijele orchestra is made up of several drums of different sizes, *ogene* (metal gong), *oja* or *opi* (flute) and *ekwe* (wooden slit drum). In addition, there is always a lead vocalist who intones the songs that the musicians will respond to as Ijele dances. While the orchestra sings and performs in harmony, they are under the authority of the *Nna-igba* (father of the drummers and musicians). As a result of its size and weight, Ijele does not perform continuously for a long time. Rather it performs for between ten to twenty minutes, after which it retreats to the enclosure. This is repeated several times before it finally retreats to the thunderous cheers of the crowd and gunshots while the elders nod their approval.

Ijele usually performs in an open clearing or sandy track which is either circular, oblong or rectangular and generally situated at the centre of the town. Major routes often lead to this vital centre where sacred trees such as *oji*, *obgu*, and *ofo* provide shade for the audience. In most cases, some shrines, groves, and men's council meeting houses are also sited around this arena.

Figure 5:
Nwa-DC
(colonial District
Officer) figure.
(Photograph: E. Arinze).

Ijele moves his massive body first forward and backward, then from side to side, and then in semicircular turns from left to right. The cloth hangings sway in rhythmic response, the numerous symbols of the head-dress seem to tilt from side to side, the decorative mirrors glint in the sun, and the open-work headers seems to revolve in shifting scenes of colour and design. Each movement of the Ijele is slow and majestic, ennobling his image as the king of masks and a figure of supreme mystical authority. Ijele dances around the arena in this dignified fashion then, as if urged on by escorts, the rhythm of the music and the audience's admiration, he quickly changes to another pattern of dance. Seeming to be borne aloft by the spirits of the winds, Ijele goes into full motion, followed by his entourage, the new pace belying his monumental size. The audience is spell-bound. Suddenly he stops and returns to the rhythmic swaying of the massive body from side to side, forward and backward, and in half circles from left to right and back again. The mask takes a few measured steps and then goes into full motion again, and the music keeps with his quickened, light step. The orchestra becomes a polyphony of sound: flutes, drums, gongs, singers, performs in counterpoint, extemporizing variations and weaving sounds at once majestic, mysterious, and entertaining. In the same way, Ijele dances around the arena like a king, combining stateliness of bearing with swift and dramatic dance movements before he finally returns to the enclosure. In the first dance mode, Ijele displays the high status and achievement associated with the ancestors he embodies in the second, he provides the audience with visual, spectacle, for his execution of clever, swift dance steps is awesome considering his massive size (Aniakor 1978: 44).

In keeping with tradition, Ijele generally performs last when other smaller masquerades have to share the same arena with it. This tradition pays tribute to Ijele as the biggest of all big masquerades in the Igbo world.

Unlike most Igbo masquerades, the identity of the carrier of Ijele is known. At the end of the performance, he emerges from the enclosure to a hero's welcome where he is praised and blessed by the elders while his age-grade members, young maidens, and women dance with him for his manly achievement of successfully carrying the big masquerade.

As Cole (1989: 22) noted, dancing Ijele embodies the complex lives of art. It is a gift of the gods to man a costly sacrifice by man to god. Dynamic, alive, defiant of gravity, it twirls and pulsates, projecting the powers of nature and the ideals of human kind. In spite of its monumentality and massive structure, Ijele never falls and has never fallen. (fig. 6) Ijele is a delight to watch in performance. Ijele is a masquerade of peace that is

Figure 6:
Ijele in performance. Two 'Ijele police' dressed in police uniform perform with Ijele and help to keep order in the arena. Achalla, August 1998.
(Photograph: E. Arinze).

performed for the collective good of all in the community. Therefore I stated that *Ijele bu onyinye Chukwu Ndigbo* (Ijele is a gift of God to the Igbo) (Arinze 1998: 5).

In Igbo tradition, no individual can own Ijele. An *Igwe* can commission an Ijele in the name of his community which he uses during special festivals, like Ofala. Ofala is an important festival in Igbo communities that have kings. Ofala is celebrated during the enthronement of a new king, and subsequently every year, to mark the anniversary. Ofala is used for 'counting the years' for the *Igwe* and the community. It is a great community festival where all the titled chiefs dance, pray, and publicly pay homage and renew their total loyalty and submission to the *Igwe* and the larger community. Ofala is generally a very colourful ceremony that can go on for a week, and Ijele features prominently in it – its appearance marking the climax of the festival. If an *Igwe* dies, his final Ofala must be performed before his death can be officially announced and a new *Igwe* enthroned. This process can take up to one year in some cases.

Prosperous communities can commission an Ijele to be built for them; it will be owned by the entire community. Also enterprising age-grades (*otu-ogbo*) can order an Ijele which they can use in accordance with the standards set by the elders. In Igbo society the age-grade is an important element in governance. People born within a given period (five years or less) form an age grade; each age grade adopts a name and a form of greeting by which it can be identified. As people grow older and die, their age-grade gets smaller until the last person in the age-grade dies and it ceases to exist. In most Igbo communities, if you do not belong to an age-grade you are not recognised as a true member of the community and you can be denied certain rights and privileges.

Ijele is a masquerade of the elders and not for younger people who are yet to acquire the wisdom of the elders or appreciate the myth and spirituality of Ijele. Thus, the elders perform Ijele while the youth enjoy it, as it is only the elders in the community who can command, give the order, approval and authority for Ijele to perform. According to Achalla elders, the reason for this is to ensure that the feet of Ijele are firm on the ground as it takes dignified steps in response to *Igba-eze* music.

In traditional Igbo society, Ijele is on display only when in performance. After performance, it is dismantled and packed into boxes and kept away until such a time that it will be used again. Ijele being the 'big masquerade' that it is, cannot be found in an art shop like other objects. As a grand artistic display born of the economic fruits of the soil and as the highest manifestation of an Igbo community, the mask unites the people in their pride and in their sense of historical continuity with the ancestors (Aniakor 1978: 42). This assertion confirms the words of an Achalla elder who, during the August 1998 performance at Achalla, said: 'Ijele will live forever, it will never die'.

Bibliography

ANIAKOR, C. 1978. The Igbo Ijele Masquerade. *African Arts,* **11**, 4.

ARINZE, E. 1998. *Ijele Nnukwu mmanwu Ndigbo.* African Worlds Information Booklet. London: Horniman Museum.

COLE, H. and ANIAKOR, C. 1984. *Igbo Arts, Community and Cosmos.* Los Angeles: Museum of Cultural History.

Emmanuel Nnkenyi Arinze

COLE, H. 1989. *Icons: Ideals and Power in the Art of Africa.* Washington D.C.: National Museum of African Arts.

ENEKWE, O. 1987. *Igbo Masks: The Oneness of Ritual and Theatre.* Lagos Nigeria Magazine.

The Lobi People of the Upper West Region of Ghana in September 1999

Michael Pennie

This paper is a product of my most recent visit to Ghana – a trip that has become for me an almost annual event, the latest of many excursions to West Africa which began more than a decade ago. My interest in, and curiosity about, African sculpture inspires these journeys. The vague preoccupation with the carvings and the people who make them, has become increasingly focussed over this period. At first I travelled throughout West Africa, visiting different countries, looking for sculpture, but returning most often to *Pays lobi* and in recent years to the Lobi who live in Ghana. This convergence on a specific people and art form – figure carving, as I too, carve wood – has broadened to include other artefacts and presently my curiosity directs me towards the entire material culture of a group that is not well known. My association with the Ghana Museums and Monuments Board encourages these endeavours. Our joint projects are the exhibitions 'Lobi' (and the proposed museum of local art and craft in Wa) and 'West African Journeys'. I write as a travelling sculptor and not as an ethnographer. Following my small book *Adventures with Lobi – an abc. Part one: the wood sculpture*, which as the title suggests describes earlier excursions to *Pays lobi* and features 26 carvings from our collection. I am presently working on *More Adventures with Lobi – another abc*. This companion volume, which is more photographs than text, includes everything but the carvings and allows this paper to describe journey number eleven, which tells of the Lobi people at this time.

South of the Sahara and roughly bounded by the 15th parallel live settled agricultural communities. They grow cereals (guinea corn, millet and maize), cultivate shea nuts, and herd cattle. In the dry season a dust-laden wind – the 'harmattan', drives down from the desert across an arid landscape. In the 18th century the Lobi people emigrated to Burkina Faso and Côte d'Ivoire from the region that is today Northwest Ghana.

They have been expanding southwards ever since, either searching for more fertile land and for game, migrating from farms that become exhausted, or moving because of strife between clans. In Ghana they are moving closer to Kumasi encouraged by the comparative affluence of the southern cities.

Today the population of the Lobi and associated peoples is approximately 300,000. In Burkina Faso *Pays lobi* stretches 350 km from Diébougou south to Bondoukou in Côte d'Ivoire. It covers the province of Poni and the southern tip of the province of Bougouriba in Burkina Faso and includes the administrative divisions of Tehini and Bouna in Côte d'Ivoire. Across the Black Volta into Ghana there are Lobi settlements from around Nandom in the Upper West Region continuing as far south as Bole in the Northern Region. The term Lobi has come to be both a linguistic and cultural designation used by observers, not members, of a mixed population. It is an oversimplification not restricted to the 'true' Lobi, but the appellation of a cluster of peoples: the Birifor, the Dagara, and to a lesser extent the Gan and others. The name 'Lobi' covers diverse groups of people who speak very different but related languages and share a common artistic tradition and social organisation.

The Lobi have no formal political assembly, no leader, no village chief. The headman — a descendant of the first man to settle — is the only real holder of authority. They live under the umbrella of a neighbouring people, such as the Wala in the Upper West Region.

The Lobi community is structured on a system of double filiation, every subject, including women, belonging to the patriclan of his/her father and the matriclan of his/her mother. It is a society divided into 4 matriclans which are associated in pairs, such as Kambou – Hein and Da – Some or Pale, who entertain joking relationships ('*plaisanterie*' in French).

Lobi life is regulated by the subtropical climate: a Fahrenheit temperature in the 90s and two seasons. It rains from April or May until September or October when farmers — almost all Lobi men are farmers – pursue subsistence agriculture, followed by a severe dry season. The lengthy remainder of the year is the time to practice ritual, ceremony and storytelling, drumming, dancing and singing. It is also the time of year when the younger men are encouraged to go south, to the cities to find temporary jobs. The young are given money to buy sandals and trousers – clothes that will enable them to work on the cocoa farms and banana plantations for 3 or 4 months in order to earn enough to take money home and perhaps buy a bicycle or a radio.

My visits to Lobi country have always been during December and January, for short periods in the middle of the dry season which is also the coolest part of the year. I travel to as many places as possible in *Pays lobi* in search of an overall picture, looking for truths that apply to all Lobi people. Proper researchers I know, have tried to convince me that seeking such generalisations especially about the Lobi is a foolish quest. Their ceremonies and rituals vary from village to village and across any distance Lobi customs are multifarious and regional differences make it impossible to generalise. However, although my knowledge is fragmentary, my experience is with the whole, the Lobi in Burkina Faso, Ghana and Côte d'Ivoire, from Bondoukou to Lawra.

This year I flew from Heathrow by Ghana Airways on a DC10 that took off 12 hours late at 5 minutes to midnight. The passengers were mostly African, Ghanaians returning and a few Europeans going to Kotoka Airport. Was there among them I wondered, an amateur ethnographer/sculptor returning to a university in Ghana after a research trip to Britain?

My first destination was capital city Accra, my second to travel by some means, as yet undecided, to Wa in the Upper West Region – a town unknown to the two Ghanaian women sitting beside me in the plane.

Figure 1: Abdulai and Sam and the Mitsubishi in the market place at Wa.
(Photograph: Michael Pennie, 1999).

Once in Accra I spent the next two days trying to arrange transport to the Upper West. In past years it had been possible to fly some of the way north to Tamale, but Fan Air was not operating the weekend I arrived. The State Transport Coaches were fully booked for some days ahead. I was in Ghana for less than three weeks and did not have the time to wait – even so hire cars were neither affordable nor practical given the state of the roads in the north. I had been warned that although the rains were ending in the south, they were still in full pelt in the northern regions, with some weeks to go. Disconcerting news, I had hoped to avoid the worst of the rainy season. If I managed to reach Wa I would be there during full spate. My heart sank – not for the first time I felt overwhelmed by Africa – frustrated, and inadequate for the task I had set myself.

Miraculously, on Monday morning I was rescued. I approached a friend and told my tale. He offered to lend me a Mitsubishi pick-up that he had for sale; a 4-wheel drive R 300, with air conditioning, and Sam as driver (fig. 1). All this for a reasonable daily rate, excluding the fuel and the driver's expenses which I had to pay for as well. Next day our adventure began – early in the morning, the best time for journeys. Sam had brought some Lucky Dube tapes – township reggae – so we were all set for a long haul. The road to Kumasi was jammed with heavy traffic, enormous tankers belching black oily smoke. These monsters avoided the potholes that pock-marked the mostly tarmac road by driving on whichever side had the best surface, right or left – ignoring the on-coming traffic, which had to go off-road.

At Kumasi we stopped to fill up with diesel and buy sandwiches from the Shell Shop. We did well on the good roads to Bamboi but from there our way was tedious and terrifying. I could almost hear Sam's heart sink as he engaged with the demands of the bumpy and broken dirt road. The surface was being washed away by the rains, the remaining outcrops of rock were dangerous, impeding our progress. Sam was constantly changing gear as well as braking – slowing the pick-up almost to a stop and then accelerating away, for a few metres before encountering another obstacle; at a speed rarely more than 20km. Our approach to the north was presaged by a darkening sky, threatening rain; I was all the while anxious that this would stay as drizzle and not a downpour. It was an interminable journey. I had expected a 4 o'clock finish but by then we had travelled less than half of the 150 km along the road that wasn't a road! It was just after 6 pm when we arrived at Bole, one of the most southern Lobi towns. The settlements were just visible in the dusk, the houses strung out at the side of the road. We moved on to the high plains of Wa, the grain and livestock region of Ghana, with the wettest rainfall (approaching 125 cm) in the country. We were on a tarmac road at last, but in the dark with the rain obliterating the illumination provided by the headlights, this was as frightening as driving on the ungraded dirt road with pot holes, broken terrain and flooding.

We reached the outskirts of Wa and the Uplands Hotel (now with South African Cable in every chalet) at 8.30 pm, after 14 hours of being constantly on the move and being bounced around in the cab of the Mitsubishi I was exhausted as well as hungry. I ate an omelette and slept.

Next day, Wednesday, the morning light was brilliant, the sky blue with high clouds, and a gentle breeze blowing fresh. With high hopes I was up early and set for my first day's work – Sam was there before me and had already washed off the red mud covering the pick-up. Saving his daily allowance he had slept in it. My first call was as usual, at the village of Vieri, on a road meandering for 30 minutes out of Wa and to the southwest, passing Nakori and its mosque on the way. Vieri is the gateway to the Lobi people living in this region and the place to find Abdulai, my guide to settlements near and far since 1993. But protocol required that I greet Pusu Daari, Abdulai's father, a man of nearly ninety, who was reclining under the mango tree next to his house. He is the local Wala chief, with some responsibility for the inhabitants of the district: the Wala, Dagara and Lobi.

However Abdulai was not there. Pusu gave us directions to where we might find him. But following these turned out to be a wild guinea fowl chase into the bush. We had been persuaded to take two passengers, Abdulai's wife and his sister. We drove miles in the direction of Bulu looking for Bulingin, Abdulai's new village, where he is the teacher of sixty Lobi schoolchildren. This was my first experience of the bush during the wet season. I had not seen the lands of the Lobi green – lush with maize, with millet blocking out the sky. Instead of corn stubble and red earth, at this season the vegetation was hiding the *soukhalas*, the houses made of brown earth. After an hour or so of bumping and sloshing we stopped, i.e. we were unable to go further, as the waterlogged trail had dwindled to nothing – letting Hawa and her mother proceed the rest of the way on foot. Reluctantly and with difficulty we turned the Mitsubishi around – we were completely surrounded by corn – and retraced our tracks to Vieri.

Fruitless excursions were by no means unusual or even unexpected. Most of my time and money was spent on actually looking for the Lobi. By comparison, the time spent with the Lobi over the years had been quite short. Their tolerance with strangers was limited – access was not always granted. If I was received then the first hour of discussion was good, during the second a degree of impatience crept into the proceedings. The third was most often spent haggling over how many cedis the principals deserved for allowing me to look, listen and take photographs

We eventually arrived back at Vieri and to my astonishment Abdulai was waiting for us – how come?

Having already greeted his father, I now had to visit his sick mother, a tiny desiccated figure lying alone on her bed mat in a room warmed by a brazier of glowing charcoal. This was providing comfort for the blackened abscess disfiguring her chest. Abdulai was upset – 'She is dying' he said. Outside the sick room, we talked of other things; arranging our programme. I was anxious to make up for this first morning when work had been curtailed by the rain. We agreed to begin again and to start our village visits next day. The 9th of the 9th, 1999 – a week since I left home and I've only just begun. I was up at 6, breakfasted before 6.30, we were on our way by 7. Going to Ponyentanga and a second attempt to reach Buligin to rendezvous with Abdulai, this time going the long way round on a good road south (the only one). At the junction of the track west, calamity – our way was flooded, a pond and impassable. But meeting Abdulai was no problem, once again, amazingly he appeared at the exact moment we came to a halt.

Thus inundated we changed our plans once more and we went further along the main road, to Ga and there finding a clearer path to Wechiau. The area in the Upper West where I practice is as three sides of a square bounded on one side by the Black Volta. The Lobi I was looking for inhabit the centre, approached by tracks crossing from corner to corner, which were at this time more or less washed out.

Wechiau is a small town with a palace (fig. 2). A single storey edifice built of *banco* in the Sudanic style –
recently painted white with a deep black border rising one metre from the ground. The front elevation has ten buttresses, each with a pinnacle topped by a black-painted egg; back to back crescent moons with stars above, decorate the entrances; one to the interior the other into the courtyard. Sam parked the truck in the square and I went inside to pay my respects to the present incumbent, the Na

Figure 2:
The palace at Wechiau.
(Photograph: Michael Pennie, 1999).

and to congratulate him on his three new solar panels – two that illuminate the town and one lighting the palace.

One of those men sitting with the Na in his reception room, was Assemblyman Abraham Sey. He told us how, on Friday afternoons some of the children of Wechiau, he called them *yum yum* boys and girls, walked the 3 km to the Black Volta and the Hippopotamus Sanctuary. At the river bank this young choir began to sing, and clap as an accompaniment. Singing to the hippos submerged in the deep water. As the song ended the female hippos rose to the surface to show off their children – the babies were being held gently in their mouths.

Michael Pennie

Before leaving Wechiau I took some photographs of the Na's residence and across the square, the 'Girls Are Bad' tailor's shop. Next stop was Nirikuyiri – together with Ladayiri and Lasiatuolo one of the three places that made up the triangle of Lobi villages I visited regularly. Abdulai had been eager to add Buligin to this list and had been disappointed when we failed to reach it. It was raining again and the house at Nirikuyiri seemed to float in a sea of mud and water. Using the umbrella that went with the pick-up, I made a dash for the dry and warm interior. This was the home of a man I had known for some years only as Nyuor's brother (Nyuor is his neighbour) – he had recently gone blind. I sat with him and his son. The younger women and children were eating from a plastic bowl, a brown dog was waiting patiently nearby for scraps. One of the children was wearing a tie of woven grass encircling her neck, going down her back and around her waist. We talked, the two men going through my abc with me – an older woman listening, commenting and being active, an amanuensis, showing me things and places around the house. I was asking about amulets and adzes, beds, chairs and cats as well as tobacco and snuff. The Lobi roll their own *taba* from home-grown tobacco leaf. Abdulai cautioned me: 'It makes the heart race and has an effect you cannot stop'. My host was neither a cigarette nor a pipe smoker, but he ground his tobacco to snuff – snuff is made of thoroughly dried leaves mixed with the ashes of burned plantain skins, and pounded into powder. The mortar – a granite boulder with an inside worn to a hemisphere and polished with use – and the pestle – a ball the size of a tomato and also of granite – were brought out to me and the process was demonstrated by the woman. The prepared snuff is kept in a small calabash.

Asking about beds, I was told that in this household most people slept on animal skins. The senior wife showed me a black and white cowhide. I sat on this for a while before being taken through an elegant oval-shaped doorway, past a discreet shrine at floor level and into the kitchen to view a double-size bed-mat made of long corn stalks and rolled up when not in use. Another mat, one of larger canes, hung down over the entrance to the sleeping rooms. In the kitchen the day's water supply stood in three lidded jars on an earth shelf, below this steam was rising from a

Figure 3: At the entrance to Nyuor's house. (Photograph: Michael Pennie, 1999).

cooking pot over a fire. A clothesline carried everyday wear but special items were kept in two stacks of storage jars piled six high and supported by the wall. I was shown a treasure basket (but not the contents) and the senior wife posed for a photograph amongst her possessions. Leaving the room, keeping my eye on the low roof timbers, to avoid banging my head for the umpteenth time, I saw clearly written on one of the beams, in chalk: 'This woman is bad, I warned my father.' The perpetrator of this possible slander was safe from discovery – the older generation could not read English. The writer was probably a son or daughter attending Senior Secondary School. Abdulai, Sam, and I hurried through the rain, splashing along a winding path across a field of corn, the flight of an arrow's distance to Nyuor's house (fig. 3). *Soukhalas* are built some way from each other – the Lobi like to see what is coming.

Nearing the outside wall I caught sight of two mysterious objects, like filled socks, hanging together from the end of a stick high above the roof. Up close, I was none the wiser until I was told that they were the skins of fishes (from the nearby reservoir) which when boiled in water and taken as soup, makes giving birth painless and quick; this was said by a man. These cods were packed with ashes to preserve them.

Nyuor's house was quite different from his brother's, a radical departure from the traditional plan of a Lobi dwelling which is a complex mass of rectangular rooms clustered around a granary. Recently built – this was a quadrangle, an open space completely enclosed by small living spaces, except for a narrow entrance. The walls were of clay, built as usual in layers, with a narrow platform and a wall and posts supporting the expensive zinc roof. Washing; T-shirts and trousers and print wraps – hung out to dry under the projecting canopy, it remained soaked by the driving rain and goats, dogs and guinea fowl gathered together to keep out of the wet (fig. 4). Plastic buckets, large clay pots and aluminium cauldrons i.e. every available container was strategically placed to catch the rain off the corrugated roof. I was asked to take shelter and elbowed a goat aside so that I could sit on the stool

Figure 4: Nyuor's household catching rain. (Photograph: Michael Pennie, 1999).

provided and perch my camera bag on the balustrade out of harms way. One of the dogs began licking my salty arm, as I paddled in the mixture of rainwater and goat shit that covered the concrete floor. The Lobi consider cats to be useful, they catch mice; but dogs are called *dobibe*, which means 'what is that for?'

I was surrounded by this large extended family that had emerged from the many rooms that made up the house, babies and children of all ages – not at school – and young men and women, their work curtailed by the weather, old women but not old men. One elder, she was blind, too, was wearing a beautiful pendant – a carved figure about 15 cm long, cruciform except that one arm was missing, the details obliterated with use, a protective sculpture polished with age. Her age presumably as she had worn it all her life – she was delighted that I took a picture.

I also photographed the shrine that Nyuor had built outside the entrance of the house, to protect his family, with tomatoes and gourds growing around it and also Nyuor feeding his chickens. He enjoyed having his picture taken, every inch the head of the household, smiling, showing teeth that had been filed to a point. I bought a catapult from him, not that it had been used as such, as it was without its red rubber sling. Nyuor had made it, as usual an upside down figure with legs apart, carved from a small forked branch, with one hand to the mouth. When I asked the significance of this gesture, Nyuor explained that it depicts a man who became too friendly with another's wife. Consequently the husband and his friends ganged-up to give him a beating. They surrounded him and there was no escape. So he put his hand to his mouth and vanished. To re-appear, almost immediately, at his home, safe behind the closed door of his room.

I expressed my incredulity, however as everyone around me vociferously affirmed the possibility of this happening. I was soon persuaded. Being there, in *Pays lobi,* I was easily convinced that certain people have the ability to disappear and reappear at will. Next stop was Vieri on market day (one that takes place every five days) busy with traders and their customers. A community checking out the aluminium basins of rice, enamel basins piled high with charcoal, containers filled with mounds of under-ripe tomatoes, as well as each other. There were flip-flops neatly arranged; these were mostly blue, bright against the overcast sky. The bicycle repairman wasn't too busy; nor was the girl selling kola nuts. There were baskets of chewing sticks (imported from Côte d'Ivoire – the Lobi use a local product) and sweeping brushes; grasses bundled together and laid out on the ground for inspection and mortars of turned wood shaped as a diabolo for crushing salt crystals. Several *cabarets* displayed pots of foaming *pito* to tempt the thirsty – I carried bottled water but I was hungry and shared some deep fried batter cakes with Abdulai. (Sam declined, in fact during the ten days I spent with Sam I never saw him eat anything). Instead of pyramids of dawadawa seeds, (from the tree of the same name or *Parkia filicoidea,*) that had been boiled and handmade into balls, for making soup, it was dawadawa stock cubes, wrapped in bright yellow paper, that were neatly arranged on a table and offered for sale.

Figure 5: Jeweller at Vieri market. (Photograph: Michael Pennie, 1999).

I bought some jewellry, every day wear and not 'old', selected from plates of rings, dishes of beads and bracelets laid out on plastic sacking over the wet earth (fig. 5). I chose strings of florescent green and blue plastic beads and some of white plastic, cylinders rather than spheres and strings of tightly packed discs, almost tube-like, predominately red with yellow and black. These are the fashionable equivalent to the white glass and unfired clay beads of indeterminate age that I bought some years ago for the 'Lobi' exhibition. From one shop I selected examples of tin earrings; the pendants – stars or hearts – glittering pink or blue against shiny gold.

A metalworker wearing padded jodhpurs – to clamp between his knees the metal buckets and enamel bowls that he was repairing – spent his day sitting on the ground surrounded by the tools of his trade, riveting patches and soldering splits. The women selling yams refused for some time to agree to a photograph – until Sam's decided to buy Lobi yams. He eventually negotiated a price that included a photo. These Lobi women were aggressive and argumentative, the Dagara traders were not difficult, on the contrary – they entered into the spirit of the proceedings and were pleased to be involved. (Twelve albums of photographs taken throughout West Africa over the last decade are to be deposited with the National Museum in Accra in 2000.) Sam took a very long time to select his preferred yams, having the truck gave him the chance to buy cheap in the north, particularly yams and charcoal, transport, and re-sell these at a good profit in Accra.

My journal records that I had a bad night, for three reasons, an upset stomach, constant rain drumming on the corrugated tin roof of my room, and the night being cold. The discomfort persisted – on Friday morning I needed fresh air. In spite of the heavy rain I sat outside for my breakfast, in a small pavilion, protected from the downpour – the black sky like a roof; recalling *Fridays Rain Takes A Long Time To Stop* (Pennie 1994). The cook successfully delivered my tea and toast, a tray in one hand and a large sunshade held tight against the storm in the other.

After this, to Vieri again where Abdulai appeared once more right on time – even while Hawa was telling me that he was not there – what is going on? We drove to Nirikuyiri, to Nyuor's house – another of Nyuor's names is Sorkpere, or 'witches please leave my last son alone' (the several children born before him had died at birth). This was a dismal place in the wet but I sat among people pleased to see me and eager to contribute to the conversation – again going through the *abc*.

To my surprise – I was shown a shrine room – rather I was allowed to peep into a place a few metres square. Although I had met, talked and shared *pito* with Nyuor each time I had been in the Upper West, until this trip I was unaware of him as a soothsayer. Earlier in the year I had seen a group of clay figurines that apparently Nyuor had made, built in an open space not far from several Lobi dwellings. On this occasion there was *pito* for sale and batter cakes too. This was a shrine made to keep the peace at a Lobi party and to stop the celebrations from getting out of hand. According to Abdulai, Nyuor and I had become friends and it was this status that would allow me access to the place of Nyuor's gods – on my next visit, on Sunday. I asked Nyuor to make me 'something.' I was deliberately vague to see what he came up with and prepared to be surprised. Although he did ask me to buy some lengths of coloured string from a market, necessary for whatever it was he intended to make. As I had little time left with the Lobi, buying this material became a priority.

Leaving for Wa, it had stopped raining and the sky was a cloudless blue. Two monkeys ran across the road and into the trees. If Sam had had his gun he would have shot them, to skin, cook and eat them.

On Saturday morning my first call was to the chemist in Wa, for a prescription for diarrhoea. He gave me twelve large pills; one to be taken four times a day, for three days and then and he banged his hand on his counter as he said this: 'It would be gone' – such confidence! (I took all the tablets – sulphur, they made little difference to my bowels and my predicament continued until I was out of Africa).

In the gun shop almost next door I asked to see a shotgun of the type a Lobi hunter would use; a Russian Baikal was brought from under the counter and unwrapped. This is a gun which is called a Simplex by the Lobi (apparently they call all makes of shotgun by the same name) and used with Red Star Hi-Speed cartridges; these were expensive. Lobi men are often armed; they carry their guns everywhere to protect their property (including costly brides) and to deter confrontations, especially at funerals.

I took the first dose of my medicine and thus primed we began our journey to reconnoitre Nyoli. Here the Lobi are known as Pwalba and originate from Mali and then Gindabo, further away still, where the Lobi are named after the people of Miu in Burkina Faso. Augustin Safi, the secretary of the Wa Assembly, had recommended these two places to me as true Lobi villages – rather than Lobi people mixed with Wala or Dagara. The Lobi in and around Lasiatuolo have Birifor names and also originate in Burkina. On this trip I was looking for those commonplace articles used and consumed by the Lobi. At Gindabo market I photographed shea butter and bought a black plastic comb; an item no longer delicately carved in wood. From baskets of seven different sizes Sam bought two of the largest, to carry home his goods.

Fati Banda, the local chief's daughter, was at the hairdressers – her hair in rollers; will she have straight hair when I return to deliver her print? I was looking for cotton threads or strands of wool; natural fibres (synthetic threads are said to provide paths for witches) – as Nyour had requested - but at Gindabo, there were none.

So to Wechiau again, another market and a caged canary for sale. Throughout *pays lobi* I have sometimes seen these small cages suspended, usually empty, above a house. I had thought that the birds played some part in a ritual. At Wechiau I was told that they are kept as adversaries, to compete with other canaries, captives in other houses. The first bird to sing at the beginning of the day brought prestige to its owner's household.

Many shoppers were sorting through mountains of clothes, heaps of T-shirts, trousers, dresses and tops for adults; children's clothes too and old shoes and sandals. Cast-offs donated somewhere in the world, which have found their way to Wechiau.

I had decided to buy examples of the most popular cotton prints worn by Lobi women. So from each market (Gindabo, Wechiau, Vieri, and Wa) I collected pieces of cloth. These included the design I'd seen most often being worn by Lobi women: a cloth, deep blue with black stripes and spotted with a white oval, inside this an image of a black bird in flight – a print called 'Excellence'. At last from a haberdasher, some black and red and white wool taken from his polythene bag of bits – for Abdulai to deliver to Nyuor. Sitting at one shop was a man in black, brushing antimony, known locally as *yombo,* from a coal black bottle into a woman's straightening hair, which had been burnished by the grooming. He looked to me like a chimney sweep – wearing rubber gloves and an apron, these and his clothes were black leaded by the dye.

The road back to Wa was flooded, we were quickly surrounded by boys who gleefully encouraged us to take a chance; to drive the pick-up through the pool behind those who were happy to walk ahead of us; demonstrating the depth – the water well above their knees. My relief at our safe passage was short-lived as a hundred metres further on, it was a lake that obliterated the road. This time we got our feet wet – the boys had fun, but I didn't. I was feeling beyond crap and missed a great photo opportunity – a floating Mitsubishi!

That night I slept without disturbance – perhaps because of the rain and the consequent power-cut there were few weekend visitors to the Uplands and the hotel was quiet.

In the morning there was sun as well as clouds as we drove the long way round to Ga – turning right to meet Abdulai at Vieri. He was waiting for us with his bicycle – it was this machine that was the reason for his mysterious mobility. Abdulai was a cross-country cyclist, up earlier than I and following his paths to be in the right place at the right time.

Today we had no problems with flooded tracks, to my delight we met three chameleons! Beautiful creatures, luminous green against the red laterite surface, walking across the road from left to right. According to legend to see chameleons going in this direction is good and means a gift of food or money will come to you. Whereas crossing from right to left is bad and signifies that something will be taken from you.

We arrived at Ladayiri to find the sortileger Nuri, an old acquaintance, supervising his wives making *pito* – beer for the impending festivities to commemorate his father's death one year ago. Nuri's family and friends were coming to eat and drink but not to dance (there would be no xylophone music at this party). Fowls were to be killed and sacrifices made until the deceased had signalled his satisfaction with the provision of meat and beer to be shared and enjoyed. Nuri will do the same for his mother who had more recently died, at the appropriate time. I commiserated with him and agreed that this was an expensive period for him. Over the years I have taken photographs of Nuri as a builder, a hunter, and as a soothsayer more than once. I have photographed him roasting a pig, smoking an evil smelling roll-up and now as a brewer.

I bought two large pots, made by one of his wives; selected from a group of storage jars incised with patterns that were the signature of the potter. These stood waiting to be filled by calabash from the twin cauldrons of steaming, guinea corn. A porridge that had been simmering for at least a day to ensure fermentation in aluminium boilers blackened with smoke. And supported on six stones and over a fire fed by a miscellany of branches; creating enough of a draught to maintain the blaze.

Finally to Nirikuyiri, to collect my 'thing' – a big day. With mixed feelings I entered Nyuor's room – not the shrine room but his bedroom – ignorant of what was about to take place. I expected a carving, but would I like it? How much would I have to pay? What had I let myself in for? Perhaps I should have been more specific in my expectations two days ago. So it was with some trepidation that I sat on Nyuor's bed – to find that this was neither carved wood, cane nor cowhide but a spring interior mattress with a baseboard, its newness preserved by polythene.

Nyuor sat on the floor with his back to the wall; next to him, his nephew; both were barefoot (fig. 6). Flip-flops had been left outside the door. Nyuor was holding his nephew's (the blind man's son again) right hand, who, with head on his chest, seemed to sleep through the whole proceedings. On the floor in front of the soothsayer were two carved and painted figures, the largest lacquered black with a floral wrap, the other of stained wood. Beside them were a heap of cowries and three red plastic cartridge cases. Nyuor began by explaining the procedures to Abdulai who nodded his comprehension, while some very small children outside the room repeated each phrase – mimicry or learning? He continually punctuated his litany by shaking the

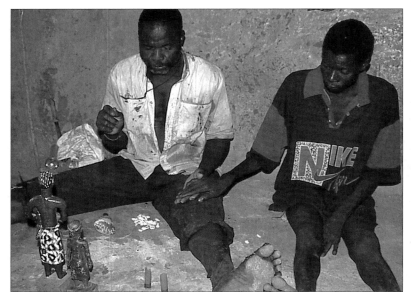

Figure 6: Nyuor and his nephew as soothsayer and medium.
(Photograph: Michael Pennie, 1999).

Figure 7: Nyuor in the room of his gods.
(Photograph: Michael Pennie, 1999).

cowries, throwing the shells on the ground as if they were dice. All this was going on while I was desperately replacing the batteries in my flashgun. Once I was ready to take pictures the conversation with Abdulai took a more serious turn. The incantations began in earnest accented by Nyuor's slaps on his right thigh and turning the hand he was holding; palm up or palm down to the accompaniment of short staccato phrases, as if he was addressing a wayward child.

Abdulai's problems were the first to be reviewed – here was a man who was remiss, in that he did not consult soothsayers. Nyuor advised him that if he wished to reverse his fortunes he must choose a different god. Hey presto – he would be safe and prosper; no more lost jobs, an end to those ventures that had lost him money and he would live a decent life. Abdulai listened to this intently, although his eyes glistened with moisture, he had the look of a man determined to do better.

'Driver you are wanted' called out Abdulai; it was Sam's turn. He was summoned into the room. 'This man has trouble' the hand being held had pointed in his direction as he waited, unsuspecting, outside the room – 'Is it a new woman or an old one? Or is it two?' There was general satisfaction that this conjecture was right, Sam confirmed that he did have woman trouble, specifically an unfaithful wife. 'Go home' he was instructed, 'take five of these cowries, buy some kola and throw them (i.e. the shells and nuts) towards the sunset, and you will be saved'. Sam picked up the shells, apparently intent upon doing as he was told. 'What about me?' I asked 'You are free and peaceful' was the answer; 'The spirits are around here, if there is a problem they will tell you!' I felt at once relieved to escape scrutiny and disappointed to be left out – I was obviously beyond the spirit's jurisdiction.

We moved next door into a room that had little space for four people. It was already overcrowded with an accumulation of modelled and constructed objects; built out from the walls towards the centre of the room. In

Figure 8: Clay figure with a plastic beaker and a small calabash for snuff, another figure and a larger calabash with cowries. (Photograph: Michael Pennie, 1999).

every direction were powerful, visually exciting sculptures; creatures made from the raw materials and natural additions that were available to the shrine builder (in this case Nyuor) (fig. 7). Closest to me were two sticks planted in the earth floor, each topped with three branches supporting an earthenware pot with a lid. A configuration repeated at intervals around the room. There were numerous clay figures of different sizes with varying amounts of descriptive detail. Although all were complete bodies – with head, torso, lower body, and limbs – layers of dust and the dark and light stains of sacrifices and libations obscured their features and the details of their gender. Teeth, eyes, and nose were accented with cowries and neck encircled by the white shells.

These figures were constrained by the clay they had been modelled with, made with proportions determined by the material and only as high as the red earth could support itself without an armature. The parts: head, body and limbs had been manipulated by two hands, the fingers moving, squeezing and positioning the soft material; clay creatures impressed with harder objects to provide detail. A familiar equivalent in this sense might be a figure made from sand on a beach, with shells and pebbles or a snowman with added pieces of coal, a pipe, and a scarf. This small room was a place of action and not of display, a workshop or a studio, premises where assemblages were made and events happened. A room of apparent chaos; nevertheless with every part a contributing ingredient: making the whole effective and authentic (fig. 8).

Nyuor took a black fowl, folded the wings to the body and with the head back between them, slit its throat – dark blood, but surprisingly little – spurted from the incision. The bird was thrown down and I watched grimly as it took an appallingly long time to die. Wings fluttering and legs, frantic to take off for safety, knocking over my recorder – after minutes it was dead. To everyone's relief and an expiration of satisfaction – belly up! This signified that the gods had accepted the sacrifice and sanctioned the commission. Nyuor took a brass ring – decorated with two chameleons one on top of the other – from where it lay near the foot of a lion-like earth figure and handed it to me, as a keepsake.

Surrounding these large modelled images were carvings, made by Nyuor or his father, innumerable wood figures – those I could distinguish were in a standing position. Most were embedded in the clay as otherworldly acolytes around a chimera. The detail of the carvings; such as hands, head and features – evidence of the sculptor's skill was hidden by layers of added material, giving the objects a disembodied presence. I was confronted with this paradox: I knew these to be sculpture – the creation of unknown beings from elements that are always present but not apparent (according to Duchamp-Villon). These were objects endowed by the sculptor with expressive form – but they were not to be seen. The visual aspect, that most vital experience was inhibited in these dark places and subsumed by those rituals that eventually obliterate the carvings. Remarkably, what remains is an enriched presence – these shrines cannot be seen, but their power is overwhelming. The sculpture utilised as intended – an intermediary between the diviner and the world of the spirits; working – effective as they are fragments of the whole and not as we know these objects – separated from each other, cleaned, sterilised, exposed and displayed.

My excitement at being there was too much; the impact of this room was almost suffocating. After a short while I struggled out – for air and for light – to leave, as if my interference was a transgression. I was over-anxious that the event would be summarily curtailed before I had made a record of it.

And now to the *zuuri*, a lump of matter out of which hair from the tail of a cow, and long strands of black, white and red wool emerged. Hanging from one of two 'pots on posts' by a suspension loop. Nyuor addressed this object at length and then he turned to me. I was given instructions as to the *zuuri's* nourishment, in the absence of kola in my home, alcohol was recommended. I was told how to use it, instructed in the procedure necessary to recover a debt, for example, how to safeguard my family and prolong my existence. Talking about money led to some discussion as to Nyuor's fee. I agreed to the amount asked, although it was much more than I had bargained for, a sum from which Abdulai was given 10.000 cedis by Nyuor 'for his translation' services.

So I took the *zuuri* – as I had been told, and without speaking or looking back, walked out of the room across the courtyard and through the gateway. I left Nirikuyiri. That was the end of my time with the Lobi – until next year.

This particular glimpse of Africa, of the Lobi, follows in footsteps of a short but distinguished list of scholars that includes Henri Labouret, Madeleine Père, Piet Meyer, Cécile de Rouville, and Daniela Bognolo. All of whom have made a more rigorous scrutiny of Lobi material culture than I, although their research has most often taken place in francophone Burkina Faso and Côte d'Ivoire and not in Ghana, except for the work of Jack Goody.

At the beginning of this century the Lobi were one of the 300 or so African peoples who made sculpture – the Lobi people in Ghana continue to do so, not for display or status or commercial reasons, but for their own use.

What does my sight-seeing reveal? The gradual absorption of change and the continuing adherence of the Lobi people to their beliefs and social structures. In the Upper West the mixed blessings of tourism are increasingly evident. At Lasiatuolu there is now a secondary school and at Vieri a new Methodist church – institutions that will transform the Lobi, accelerating development, increase learning and their understanding of a modern world that is very close by. The commonwealth of developed nations could alleviate the harshness of their lives – the cancellation of debt, increased aid, and fairer trade would bring the necessary investment in agricultural technology and the production of food, improved sanitation and better living conditions, health care and protection from killer diseases – so that the Lobi people might prosper and their remarkable way of life – where their art is central to their spiritual and physical well-being – would continue.

Bibliography

BOGNOLO, D. 1990. Le Jeu des Fétiches. *Arts d'Afrique Noire,* **75**.

BOGNOLO, D. 1991. Le musée du Poni. *Arts d'Afrique Noire,* **78**.

GOODY, J. 1956. *The Social Organisation of the LoWiili.* London: Her Majesty's Stationery Office.

LABOURET, H. 1931. *Les Tribus Rameau Lobi.* Paris: Institut D'Ethnologie.

MEYER, P. 1981. *Kunst und Religion der Lobi.* Zürich: Museum Rietberg.

PENNIE, M. 1994. *Fridays Rain Takes a Long Time to Stop.* Bath: Artworth.

PENNIE, M. 1998. *Adventures with Lobi: an abc.* Bath: Artworth.

PERE, M. 1988. *Les Lobi Tradition et Changement.* Laval: Editions Siloe.

PRUSSIN, L. 1969. *Architecture in Northern Ghana.* Berkeley and Los Angeles: University of California Press.

ROUVILLE DE, C. 1987. *Organisation sociale des Lobi.* Paris: L'Harmattan.

SOME, R. 1993 A propos de "Fetiches Lobi". *Arts d'Afrique Noire,* **85**.

WARIN, F. Statuaire lobi: question de style. *Arts D'Afirique Noire,* **69**.

Phil Cope

Haitian Vodou
Shrine, African
Worlds gallery
Horniman
Museum.
(Photograph: Horniman
Museum, Heini Schneebeli).

When Ghede met Barbie: Syncretism in Haitian Vodou Culture

3

Phil Cope

Le syncretisme n'est pas seulement, pour les esclaves, un simple melange de divinites chretiennes et vaudou; c'est aussi une forme de resistance des esclaves contre la domination culturelle de l'exploiteur. In: 'Syncretisme Catholique – Vodou', Bureau National d'Ethnologie, Port-au-Prince, Haiti, 1997.

Introduction

The history of Haiti is one of the most contradictory, instructive and – with the notable exceptions of short periods when Haitian interests are seen to collide with those of our own in the overdeveloped West – one of the least known of all the countries of the underdeveloped world.

Haiti is one of the poorest nations on earth, with levels of deprivation more often associated with countries of the Asian and African continents. The roots of this poverty are sunk deep within a devastating colonial history, a 200-year dependence on the major Western powers and a narrowly-based and corrupt oligarchy. During the past 150 years, the United States of America has played an increasingly significant role in perpetuating this unequal partnership of poverty between the richest and the poorest countries in the Western hemisphere.

In Haiti, life expectancy is just 55 years and 14% of all children die before the age of five. 85% of the population is illiterate and per capita income is a mere US$260, while 61% of Haitians subsist on an average of US$60. Only 10% have access to clean drinking water. There is only one doctor for every 5,556 people;

there is only one nurse for every 5263; and there is only one hospital bed for every 667 within a malnourished and poorly-housed population. In 1994, the US National Labour Committee reported that:

> *If you enter a state-run hospital in Haiti, you must bring your own sheets and purchase your*
> *own food while you are there. Often more than one person is in a bed. Patients have to buy*
> *their medicines as well as any needles that might be used ... at the state-run hospital in*
> *Hinche, Haiti's fourth largest city, there is blood on the floors and sheets, and the stench is*
> *unbearable* (quoted in Ridgeway 1994).

According to UNICEF, 70% to 80% of Haitians are living below the absolute poverty level. And in the words of Jean-Bertrand Aristide, the liberation theologian who was to become Haiti's president for a short period before being ousted in a US-supported coup in 1991:

> *The poor are not gifts from the sky. They are the products of the structures of exploitation and*
> *those structures have their roots since those months when Columbus arrived in America*
> (quoted in Ridgeway 1994).

But Haiti is also the country where the only fully successful slave revolt has been recorded; where the first black republic of the modern world was established, where, in the words of Martiniquan poet, Aime Cesaire (1938): 'negritude rose for the first time and stated that it believed in its humanity'; and where lessons about how to stand up against a vastly more powerful force were learned and then forgotten and are having to be learned again.

Vodou

Vodou is one of the greatest achievements of people of African descent. The word means 'spirit'. It offers to its believers the same benefits as other world religions: an access to healing powers, a connection with relatives and friends who have died, and a confirmation of identity through tradition and history.

The *lwa*, the gods or spirits of Haitian vodou, appear by taking possession of their subjects. The most important *lwa* require great diligence and worship from their devotees, for only in this way will they provide a suitable 'mount'. The ceremonies' colourful ritual, officiated by a *'houngan'* (priest) or *'mambo'* (priestess) involves the drawing of symbolic patterns or *'veves'* on the floor in flour; the incessant, rhythmic beating of drums; and the sacrifice of animals and the drinking of their blood. These and other practises are intended to achieve the intense condition which enables possession to take place, at which point initiates may fall into a trance, speak in tongues, and mediate between the spirit world and the present.

Syncretism

Stripped of all personal possessions, the slaves, who were brought to Haiti to work in the sugar plantations from the mid sixteenth century onwards, brought with them the vast mythology and customs of their original beliefs. These, infused with a heady mixture of Catholic imagery imposed on the slaves by their masters, were modified to fit the new harsh realities of life in the West Indies.

This adaptive nature has had to become one of the most prominent characteristics of the Haitian personality, reflected most clearly in its religion and in its art, both of which demonstrate the possibilities of the simultaneous existence of different levels of meaning and understanding.

The vodou religion offers its adherents a rich and tolerant pantheon of sometimes complimentary and sometimes opposing spirits. A synthesis of the deities of the traditional religions of the tribes of West Africa and Amerindia, and the more contemporary *lwa* manifested through the worship of their ancestors sits comfortably alongside those of the Christian faith. And most surprisingly, these are often further embellished by popular secular images from all corners of the world.

This complex syncretism is at the heart of any understanding of vodou, both its historical development as a response to the need to survive culturally and spiritually against all the odds of an oppressive dominant presence, as well as its continuing effect on the character of the Haitian people today.

Haitian syncretism has today gone beyond the borrowing of the beliefs, images and artifacts of other religions, as – alongside the Christian (and other) saints – Haitian vodou altars now also borrow and incorporate images from the West, often prioritising those of our popular TV culture. Or perhaps it is that consumer culture is the new religion of the affluent West. Richard Avedon's naked, snake-draped photograph of actress, Nastassja Kinski – made famous in a popular poster of the 1981 – has been incorporated into shrines to Damballah, the *lwa* of water and wisdom; Barbie dolls are seen as images of ideal beauty and as such conscripted to represent Erzulie Danton, the *lwa* of beauty and love; Darth Vador from *Star Wars* is associated on Haitian altars with the warrior attributes of the Ogou family; and even Fred Flintstone manages an appearance, transmuted into the god he never could become in his limited cartoon world!

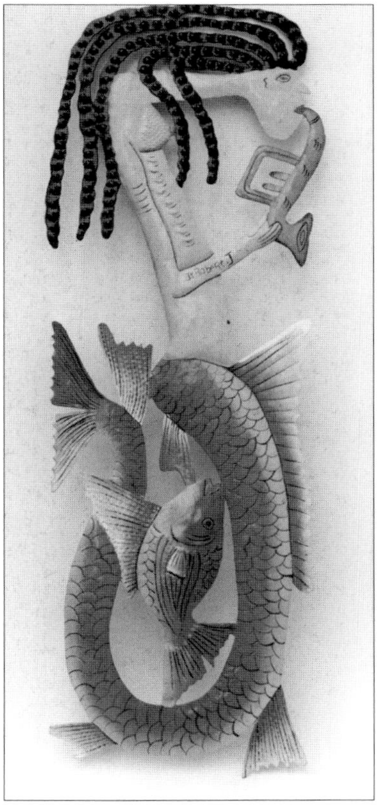

Figure 1: 'La Sirena' from the workshop of Jacques-Jean Hubert. The Sirena traditionally blows a conch but in this contemporary ironwork she plays the saxophone.
(Photograph: Phil Cope).

Poverty

People who have had everything taken from them, have little choice but to make the best of what is thrown in their direction, to adapt, to borrow and to recycle. Haiti's poverty has meant that its people have often had to make imagination their principle possession, creating in the process, what Donald Cosentino (1996) described as, 'working models of heaven'.

The magnificent ironworks of Jacques-Jean Hubert and others, constructed in and around Croix des Bouquets, representing the lwa of the vast vodou pantheon are cut out of discarded oil drums (fig. 1). Pierrot Barra's *'mojo board'* sacred vodou constructions utilise thrown away

Phil Cope

objects from Port-au-Prince, Haiti's capital's mountainous dumps of rubbish. But, deeper than this economic imperative, Haitians' belief in the omnipresence of spirits means that they are bound to respect even those images and beliefs that have been forced upon them by the sword and those objects that others have discarded.

The syncretic nature of Haitian culture predates our much more recent debates about postmodernism by centuries. Acceptance of and adaption to new images and ideas is central to the Haitian psyche in direct opposition to the reductionist nature of much of modern life and religion.

Places

Amerindia

'Hayti' was the native Arawak Indian word for 'high land'. Christopher Columbus, though describing the native people as 'lovable, tractable, peaceable, gentle, decorous', set in train their wholesale destruction (quoted in Ridgeway 1994: 6).

Least well explored of all the influences which make up Haitian vodou is the important Amerindian influence, particularly on the Petwo branch of vodou, from Haiti's original Taino and Carib inhabitants. Papa Zaca, the agricultural god has no African equivalent, although his name is similar to the Amerindian word for corn, hoeing or maize (fig. 2). The 'asson', the rattle sacred to the *houngan*, is to be found in Taino culture and its beaded decoration is clearly Amerindian. The Ghede spirits of the cemeteries have more in common with the Mayan, Inca and Aztec civilisations and the Mexican 'Day of the Dead' than anything originating from Africa. The designs drawn on the floor at the start of a vodou ceremony (the *veves*) have no African equivalent, although the idea is common in Amerindian sand paintings.

Africa

Driven by the promises of the island's riches, by greed and by ambition, the Spanish approached their generous hosts, in the words of Las Casas, 'like ravening wild animals ... killing, terrorising, afflicting, torturing, and destroying the native peoples' with 'the strangest and most varied methods of cruelty, never seen or heard of before.' (quoted in Ridgeway 1994: 6). James, in 'The Black Jacobins' (1938), observed that 'All the natives received as wages was Christianity'. As a result of the Spanish invaders' sadistic approach to the native people, Las Casas reported that in 1552 'the population is barely 200 persons ...' (from a pre-Colombian population estimated at perhaps as high as 5 million individuals.). The colonists' solution to this unfortunate absence of free native labour was, as throughout the new empires, the wholesale importation, by force, of slaves gathered from the continent of Africa, a journey which usually left a woman sterile for two years. By 1789, the island was the wealthiest European colonial possession in the Americas, producing three-quarters of the world's sugar and leading the world in the production of coffee, cotton, indigo and rum. It was also the largest individual market for the European trade in people, 'absorbing' 40,000 new African men, women and children a year.

The subjugation of the slaves, who were brought from Congo, Angola, the Republic of Benin, Nigeria, and Cameroon was practiced through psychological means as well as physical, as described by the French Minister of Colonies in 1771: '... it is in the interest of good order not to weaken the state of humiliation congenital to the species, in whatever degree it may perpetuate itself; a prejudice all the more useful for being in the very heart of the slaves and contributing in a major way to the due peace in the colonies...'. In direct opposition to this force, as the religion of the oppressed, vodou offered the possibility of some kind of continuation of an independent African identity and acted as a powerful common language between slaves of different ethnic origins.

In August 1791, the initial act of rebellion of the slaves of the colony of Sainte Dominique was a vodou ceremony, led by the high priest, Boukman. During the Revolution, according to C.L.R.James, 'Voodoo was the medium of the conspiracy'. The struggle lasted for 12 years and the slaves defeated in turn their white masters and the soldiers of the French, an invasion by the Spanish, a British expedition of some 60,000 men, and finally, a French expedition of similar size led by Napoleon Bonaparte's brother-in-law, Leclerc. It was the defeat of Bonaparte's expedition in 1803 that resulted in the establishment of the Negro state of Haiti which has lasted to this day.

The belief in a cosmic continuity at the heart of vodou transcends the simple demarcations of birth, life and death. Human life is merely the narrow crossroads between emergence from and return to an invisible and watery world, the source of all life. This is Guinea in Africa, the Gulf from which many of the slaves who were transported to the New World were dispatched. Guinea is seen as the birthplace and repository of the spirit world and the last link with the lost home in Africa. 'Here, on the island Below the Sea, the Loa have their permanent residence, their primal location. To it the souls of the dead return, taking marine or insect forms until their reclamation into the world, their rebirth' (Deren 1953: 36).

It is from this place that vodou ceremonies attempt to attract the spirits to return to communicate with the living. In each vodou temple, or *ounfo*, is a *peristyle*, the space where the ceremony is conducted. At its centre is the *poteau-mitan*, the post down which the spirits travel from the heavenly to the earthly worlds. Although clear demarcations are often difficult to discern, there are three main rituals of the vodou faith: Rada ceremonies originating from Dahomey (what is now the Republic of Benin) and Yoruba, and honouring *lwa* from Guinea, are thought of as being 'cool', 'sweet-natured', and 'civilian', associated with peace and reconciliation; while Petwo rituals, celebrating local *lwa* from the island, are 'hot', 'violent' and 'vengeful', and associated with magic charms and healing; a third and less popular ritual, Kongo, is associated with *lwa* of Bantu origin who demand the sacrifice of dogs. A fourth, secretive ritual, Bizango, is concerned primarily with justice, and is dominated by the powerful presence of Baron Samdi, head of the spirits of the dead, collectively known as *guede*. Each vodou *lwa* can be classified according to its place of origin, its principles and character. And each is associated with one of the four elements, as well as a tree or plant, a colour and a specific ritual.

From Dahomey and the Wedo family came Legba, in Africa a seducer of women and mischief-maker, and in Haiti the chief of all *lwa*, and a much kindlier character altogether. With his guiding principle being the Crossroads, he protects houses and temples and enjoys the sacrifice of goats and roosters; The Rada family couple, Damballah and Ayida Wedo, symbolised by the snake and the rainbow respectively, have as their principle the Heavens, and are responsible for thunder and the sea and the wealth of their patrons (Damballah

Wedo is clearly descended from the Dahomean rain god); La Sirene, the female spirit in mermaid form, is associated with seduction and fertility. (There is a strong tradition of mermaids and water-spirits in the religions of Africa. The Yoruba and Bini people from Nigeria, for example, had Oshun, the spirit of the river and Yemoya, the mother of fish); Ogoun Ferei originated from the Nago nation in Nigeria and has Fire as his principle, and power, war and the forging of iron weapons as his main characteristics: his colour is red and his emblem is a sabre of the Yoruba tribe; Baron Samdi is a Petro spirit of the underworld, the head of the Guede family associated with death, the moon, the night and cemeteries; Simbi, the god of sweet waters' colour is black or grey, his preferred trees are mango, calabash or elm, he accepts offerings of black or grey meat like pig, goat, guinea fowl, turkey or chicken, he is the guardian of springs and ponds and has the gift of clairvoyance. His special days are Tuesday, Thursday and Friday. He demands of his adherents that they throw themselves into a pond or river.

Figure 3: Altar to Black Crow. Voodoo Spiritual Temple of Priestess Miriam and Priest Oswan Chamani, New Orleasn, USA. (Photograph: Phil Cope).

.... and back to America

Recent initial research in Louisiana revealed a glimpse of the continuing spread and development of vodou practices in the USA where images and personalities from native American life and mythology are being incorporated into the ever-growing pantheon. Central to these additions is Black Crow, the Sauk Indian leader of the 1830 rebellion against white domination, whose presence is regularly solicited today to help his mainly impoverished, mostly black, mostly female believers (fig. 3).

> *I feel that Black Crow has always been part of the black spirit. We was took from Africa and that left us – we didn't hear any of those drums. It was the Indians that brought us back to the drums and the music. (Berry 1995: 20).*

By 1809, following the Haitian Revolution of 1804, Louisiana had received some 10,000 French and mulatto planters who fled with their slaves who in turn brought with them their complex systems of belief which continued to flourish in the rich native history of their new homes.

The resurrection of Black Hawk and other native Indian figures in the vodou and spiritualist churches of the southern US states represents significant continuations of both the all-embracing nature of these faiths as well as an important validation of native history, experience and belief of all shades in an America which has marginalised and degraded their significance.

Conclusion

The culture of syncretism bred into the mind of the Hiatian so violently during the colonial period evidenced in the intermixing of vodou, Christian and other imagery at all levels of Haitian religious life – from the huge colourful murals portraying scenes from the New Testament in the Episcopal Church in Port-au-Prince to the smallest family altar – has created a tolerant, truly 'catholic' theology.

While the Christian crusades and slave trade tortured and murdered millions, the vodou religion has avoided fanatical holy wars to convert the non-believer. Theirs is a confident, self-contained, generally-benevolent though dynamic force. It is the perpetually-unresolved and revitalising nature of its practise that retains its relevance for its people, in marked contrast to the closing doors of fundamentalism of many other contemporary faiths.

William Seabrook in his 'The Magic Island' (1929) compares the vitality of vodou with that of Christianity in its early years 'when miracles and mystical illuminations were common everyday occurrences'. Despite a certain degree of discrediting of his work, he writes, I think still pertinently:

> *The high gods enter by the back door and abide in the servants' lodge ... They have shown themselves singularly indifferent to polite company, high-sounding titles, parlors and fine houses ... indifferent indeed to all worldly pride and splendour. We have built domed temples and vast cathedrals, baited with glories of polychrome and marble to trap them, but when the gods come uninvited of their own volition, or send their messengers, or drop their flamescript cards of visit from the skies, it is not often these gilded temples or the proud of the earth they seek, but rather some road-weary humble family asleep in a wayside stable, some illiterate peasant dreaming in an orchard as she tends her sheep, some cobbler in his hut among the Alps...*

It is the great confident strength of Haitian vodou to quietly translate the often limiting meanings of the imagery of the Catholic church and of Western secular icons into the dynamic languages of their original African deities.

The exhibition, *African Worlds* is said to be concerned with the celebration of diverse voices. Vodou shrines in Haiti don't have captions. Nor does vodou have a written code, like the Bible or the Koran to instruct its adherents. The images themselves within Haitian vodou practice offer an almost infinite drama of voices – constantly adapting to a rapidly changing world – clearly articulated for those with eyes to hear.

Catholic-Vodou syncretism

In 1997 the exhibition 'Le syncretisme Catholique-Vodou' was set up at Port-au-Prince presenting the ongoing research of the National Bureau of Ethnology on Afro-Catholic syncretism. Because the kind of research the Bureau is carrying out all too often remains unnoticed by professional anthropologists in the West, I have chosen to present some of their findings and key concepts. First I give a summary of, and comment on the four main terms the Bureau has chosen to analyse syncretism. This is followed by a long quote from the introduction of the exhibition catalogue in which the Bureau's researchers frame their findings within an analysis of, and proposals for social and cultural reconstruction in Haiti.

Four key terms

The first key concept is 'correspondence or equivalence'. There is a clear correspondence between the African spirits and the Christian saints. Such correspondences were constructed when the images forced upon slaves in the colonial epoch in the form of statues or chromolithographs were (and still are) reinterpreted to African realities, unbeknown to their white masters (fig. 4). This is illustrated in table 1.

Figure 4: Christian chromolithographs at the shrine of houngan Lesley Egalité, Port-au-Prince, Haiti. (Photograph: Phil Cope).

Furthermore, the Catholic festivals of Ash Wednesday and Lent have become the vodou ceremonies of Mardi Gras and Ra-Ra on the same days in the calendar. Also, the Holy Trinity has been translated beyond recognition into the three principle powers of vodou – 'les Mystères' (the spirits), 'les Morts' (the dead) and 'les Marassa'(the twins). The important vodou pilgrimage to Saut-d'Eau in July to bath in the waterfall of the watergod, Simbi, suggests a Christian inspiration – although baptism also has clear pre-Christian African roots.

The second key concept is that of 'resistance against domination'. Slaves were punished severely if discovered in acts of *lwa* worship. Article 2 of the *Code Noir*, the slavers' charter, stated that all slaves had to be baptised into the Catholic faith. Aristide, the liberation theology priest and one-time president of Haiti stated that: "If we take Haiti as an example, in that time, when a priest baptised a slave, if that slave continued to fight for freedom, they baptised him once again. They told him: 'You have to be quiet. If you fight for freedom, that means you have a horse in your head' and they can baptise him a third time. That's why a lot of slaves were baptised more than 10 times ... to use religion to keep people in slavery." (Aristide 1992).

In addition, Article 3 forbade any exercise of religion other than that of the Catholic church. Vodou was,

Lwa	Catholic saint
Agoue T'Arroyo 'the master of the sea and all islands'	St Ulrick 'a fish in his hand'
La Sirene, the wife of Agoue T'Arroyo	Our Lady of the Assumption or St Philomene
Damballah Ouèdo 'a cosmic snake from whose egg the world has hatched, the god of procreation, fecundity and force'	St Patrick, and his serpents, in the Petwo rite; Moses, the law-giver, in the Rada rite
Loko Atisson 'the lwa of forests and curative plants'	St Joseph
Erzulie (Erzulie Freda Dahomey) 'a water godess of Dahomean origing, maitresse, the goddess of love, romance and dreams'	Maria Dolorosa, the Virgin Mary 'she is married to three husbands: Ogoun, the beautiful Damballah and Agoue'
Papa Ogou 'the spirit of war'	St Jacques Majeur
Ogou Badagrl 'the patron of warriors'	St George (fig.5) 'dragon slayer'
Les Guedes 'divinities associated with death and the cemetery'	St Jerome
Legba 'the gatekeeper and protector of the home'	St Peter 'keys for opening the way to another world'

therefore, not just a melange of the two faiths – a confused, undisciplined hotchpotch as it is so often described – but rather a structured, intentional and powerful form of resistance to white colonial rule.

Adopting the imagery and the ritual calendar of Catholicism was not a matter of free choice; supplementing this with hidden entities and meanings however was.

Thirdly, the 'syncretic work' (Dozon 1995) consisted in 'reinterpretation'. During colonial times French Catholic priests distributed images of saints among the slaves. In itself ownership of these images was a proof of faith. Forced to share their rooms with these religious incentives, the process of reinterpretation by Haitians commenced. The house altars as well as the passionate dancing during Catholic feasts were meant to be seen by the colonials as exotic, somewhat exuberant expressions of religious zeal. In the process a parallel universe of religious experience and meanings was being created. Sites and times of religious oppression where thus turned into places and moments of freedom (cf. Fabian 1998).

The fourth and most encompassing is the key concept of 'marronage'.[1] Above all syncretism is predicated on an emerging awareness of subjugation by an omni-present, unassailable power. Any direct confrontation with the authorities was impossible. The reinterpretation of the Catholic imagery and ceremonial meant the creation of a parallel universe of experience and moral rules. This experience has left a deep impact on Haitians up to now. Haitians are said to prefer to speak in tongues, to cover up their ideas, to exhaust themselves in giving good impressions. In negative terms this is called mendacity and deceit. In whatever way you look at it, 'maronnage' is a way of escaping the dominant system while staying in place; it is a case of religious delocalisation.

Figure 5: Vodou sequined flag of St Jacque/St George. Workshop of Pierro Barra, Port-au-Prince, Haiti.
(Photograph: Phil Cope).

Marronage: the way out

The aspect of marronnage that is revealed in syncretism leads us to certain characteristics of Haitian thinking. Above all, we are facing here a dialectic of 'yes' and 'no', of 'right' and 'wrong', of 'acceptance' and 'negation'.

a. The behaviour of a survivor and a 'pillager'.
[...] This clearly shows this mentality of pillaging (getting what you can get) when, in a relationship of unequal power, the Haitian invents strategies of survival that are very close to lying, bluff, the mask. He compromises with Catholicism, the dominant religion. He compromises with capitalism and the big plantation to develop his own economy of pillage.

[...]When they [the Haitians] get near power they reproduce systematically the model of the coloniser. One wants to have everything quickly. without much effort or the necessary investment. Every notion of collectivity disappears. It has merely become a question of 'zanmitay' (friends) and 'fanmitay' (family).

This behaviour of the survivor is a legacy of colonisation. Franz Fanon said that the oppressor is the model for the oppressed. One needs to escape this logic of oppression in order to invent and create another logic.

b. The problem of authenticity and truthfulness.
Are the Haitians condemned to live a life of lies and bluff? Must they always be 'mèt dam', black skins with white masks, like Fanon once said? Are the Haitians well or badly masked 'mardi-gras' in an eternal carnival?

We answer and affirm frankly that we are not condemned to survive but to live 'tankou moun' (like any other human being). In order to reach that ideal, the conditions that have given rise to this double personality must disappear. That means the end to the society of exclusion which marginalises the majority of the people by putting them in a situation of economic exploitation, political oppression and ideological manipulation.

Since the beginning of the 1980s Haiti is in crisis. The main demand of the Haitian masses is a different society 'kote totu moun se moun' (where everybody is somebody) and where do not reign this discrimination and this secular apartheid.
[...]

Conclusion
Here we have studied and interpreted the phenomenon of Catholic-vodou syncretism. Undoubtedly there is interesting work to do on Protestant-vodou syncretism. [...]"

In the views of the Bureau of Ethnology, the Haitians are in a perpetual state of carnival, not in the sense of a colourful and enjoyable celebration of life – hardly an apt description of most Haitian's existence – but rather as a people still hiding behind cultural and religious masks, devised during years of submission. Tactics of deception, the creation of facades, and the reluctance to reveal one's true identity are seen as perpetuating a fundamental national insecurity, reproducing systematically the colonial scheme. This dialectic of acceptance and negation is seen in this explanation to stifle collectivity and offers a radical historical explanation as to why Haitians have never been free, in an interesting though highly controversial view.

Notes

1. 'Marronnage' is derived from the French word 'marron' and refers to fugitives or runaway slaves. 'Etre marron' means 'be had', being the victim of deception. Interestingly enough, 'marronnage' as used by the Bureau of Ethnology intimates a higher degree of agency: the victim strikes back with acts of deception.

Bibliography

ARISTIDE, J-B. 1992. *Jean-Bertrand Aristide: An Autobiography.* Paris: Editions de Seuil.

BERRY, J. 1995. *The Spirit of Black Crow: the Mystery of Africans and Indians.* Jackson.

BUREAU NATIONAL D'ETHNOLOGY. 1997. *Syncretisme Catholique – Vodou.* Port-au-Prince.

CESAIRE, A. 1938. Notes on a Return to the Native Land. Trans. from Cahiers d'un retour au pays natal. In Eshleman, C. and Smith, A. *Aime Cesaire: The Collected Poetry.* Los Angeles: University of California Press.

COSENTINO, D. (ed), 1995. *Sacred Arts of Haitian Vodou.* Los Angeles.

COSENTINO, D. 1996. On Looking at a Voudou Altar. *African Arts.* **XXIX** no.2. Spring 1996.

DEREN M. 1953. *Divine Horsemen: the Living Gods of Haiti.* London.

DOZON, J.-P. 1995. *La Cause des Prophètes: Politique et Religion en Afrique Contemporaine.* Paris.

FABIAN, 1998. *Moments of Freedom: Anthropology and Popular Culture.* Charlottesville.

FANON, F. 1991 (1961). *Les Damnés de la Terre.* Paris:

HURBON, L. 1972. *Gods in Haitian Vodou.* Paris.

HURBON, L. 1995. *Voodoo: Truth and Fantasy.* Paris.

JAMES, C.L.R. 1938. *The Black Jacobins: Toussaint L'Ouverture and the San Domingo Revolution.*

RIDGEWAY, J. (ed), 1994. *The Haiti Files: Decoding the Crisis.* Washington.

SEABROOK, W. 1929. *The Magic Island.*

Recontextualizing the Horniman's Collection of Benin Bronzes

O. J. Eboreime

The redisplay of the Benin bronzes in the *African Worlds gallery*, was turned into an occasion to advance iconographical and historical research on pieces in the Horniman Africa collection. In this paper I mean to present some of the material which was generated from fieldwork aimed at eliciting contemporary interpretations of bronze plaques and pieces. For this I drew on my familiarity with Edo historical and ritual discourse. Photographs of the Horniman collection of bronze plaques were analysed by comparing elements of their iconography with living traditions and rituals, such as the annual *Igue* festivals. The burial rites of the Queen Mother in 1999 and the centenary celebration of 1997 at Benin City provided a wealth of comparative material. Further data were obtained through interviews with chiefs, priests and women.

The aim of the interpretative enterprise was a historical iconographical reconstruction which was intended to illuminate the central question of how the bronze plaques reflected the history of the Benin Kingdom and court life from about the middle of 16th century to the beginning of 17th century.

Monarchical chronologies

The Benin Empire with Benin City as its capital lay almost completely within the subtropical rain forest belt. Between Benin City and the sea there is a thin belt of mangrove while much of the vegetation to the north, within 100 km, is derived forest with savannah.

Today, the city of Benin is the capital of Edo State, one of such 36 states within the nation-state of Nigeria. Edo State is coterminous with what used to be the core of the Benin kingdom within which the authority of the Oba held sway. Evidence from territorial arrangements (the city walls and village earth works), corroborated by oral traditions and historical linguistics, show that the Benin kingdom must have evolved from village settlements through a city state into a kingdom.

The history of Benin is thought of by the people in monarchical terms. It can be summarised as follows:

1. The early period form the 9th – 10th centuries AD up to the early 15th centuries dominated by the Ogiso mythical sky kings: Oronmiyan (1170), Eweka I (early 14th century), Oguola (C. 14th century), Oba Ohen (early 15th century).
2. The era of the warrior kings beginning from Oba Ewuare the Great (mid-15th century), Ozolua, Esigie, Orhogbua and Ehengbuda (late 15th to early 16th centuries).
3. The period of crisis and renewal beginning from the late 16th century with Oba Ohuan through Akenzua, Akengboi up to Ore-Oghene.
4. A period of revival and decline: the late 17th century, beginning with Oba Ewuakpe, with a spell of revival by Akenzua up to Oba Ovonramwen who was taken captive and exiled.
5. A period beginning in 1914 with the reinstitution of the monarchy under Eweka II who rebuilt the palace and revived royal rituals up until Oba Eredauwa, the reigning king installed in 1979.

Four great obas and one queen (Idia) reigned in the 15th and 16th centuries. They are commonly remembered with mixed feelings of awe and reverence for their greatness and contribution to the growth and development of the Benin Kingdom.

1. Ewuare the Great (1440-1472) is reputed to have reformed the structure of the Benin chieftaincy by creating two classes of chiefs: the palace chiefs (Eghaevbo N'Ogbe) and the town chiefs (Eghaevbo N'ore). Thenceforth, the oba appointed the Iyase (prime minister) of Benin.

He increased the number of members of the Council of chiefs from six to seven by creating a new title of Edaiken (duke) of Uselu quarters – a title which to this day is bestowed on the first son and heir to the Benin throne. He consolidated the monarchy by introducing the principle of primogeniture. Oba Ewuare provided a religious base for his political reforms by introducing the annual *Igue* festivals which essentially celebrate the mystical powers of the oba and renews his divine right to rule as a living icon of the collectivity of all Benin (Edo) ancestors embodied in the royal altars, Erinwindu, where the ancestral staff, Ikhure, is preserved and venerated.

2. Oba Ozolua (1481-1504) was a military king who continued with the expansion of the kingdom by military conquest, carried his wars as far to the south west as the Ijebu kingdom. He encouraged internal and external trade. His reign was marked by early contacts with the Portuguese with whom Benin exchanged envoys from 1486 onwards.

3. Oba Esigie (1504-1550). With the assistance of his mother Queen Idia, oba Esigie conquered the western Niger kingdom of Igala. Portuguese missionaries first set foot in Benin City during his reign. The church they left behind was converted into a syncretic indigenous Holy Aruosa Church with the oba as the spiritual head. The church exists till this date.

4. Queen Idiya (Iy'Oba Idia) (1506). Oba Esigie was the first Benin king to honour his mother with the title of *Iy'Oba* (Queen Mother) of Benin, in return for the spiritual and physical help he received from her in his campaign against the Attah of Igala who was defeated by the Benin army.

Bronze totemic cocks, *Ikekogbo* (royal altar) and other staffs of office form part of the paraphernalia of the queen. The 16th century ivory mask laced with images of Portuguese soldiers is one of the principal Benin art pieces dedicated to the queen mother institution which has played a significant role in Benin court life for some four hundred years (Paula Ben Amos 1983). The ivory mask is kept at the British Museum.

5. Oba Orhogbua (1550-1578). Orogbua was the son of oba Esigie who extended the Benin Empire to Lagos and beyond. He had received some education from the Portuguese , something which helped him to broaden his horizon and network of relationships with the Portuguese and other Europeans. Benin exchanged slaves, ivory and pepper for European goods. The first British trade mission under Captain Whyndam visited Benin City under his reign, in 1553.

In addition to the leadership provided by the above kings and the famous queen Idia, other factors also contributed to the rise and expansion of the Benin kingdom in the 15th and 16th centuries.

a. The favourable and accessible location of Benin in a strategic part of the forest zone enabled her to perform a middleman's role in the trade route between the savannah and the coastal communities.

b. The Benin army was a strong and well-motivated body of young volunteers. An army of 20.000 to 50.000 could be raised within weeks. The *Iyase* and the *Ezomo* were respectively the Commander-in-Chief and the Deputy of the Benin museum.

This Army was however humiliated by the British forces who captured Benin on 15th February 1897 with the help of their superior fire power from the maxim machine gun. Hundreds of bronzes of exquisite and unique designs were found in the palace and some of the aristocracy's houses. These were raided and looted by the invading army.

Oba, patron of the arts

The Oba patronises art through the elaborate guild system in which the identity of the individual artist is subsumed within the ideology of kingship, religion and the Edo nation. Bronze is cast on the order of the Oba by the bronze casters guild *Iguneronmwon*, headed by *Chief Inneh*, while the ivory and wood carvers were led by *Eholor of Iguosama* ('God's helpers in the process of creation').

There are six main artists guilds: *Igueromwon* (bronze casters), *Iguematon* (blacksmiths), *Igbesanmwan* (wood and ivory carvers), *Owina N'Ido* (weavers and costume designers), *Isekpokin* (leather workers), *Ikpema* (drummers, percussionists).

The Oba also commissioned art objects for diplomatic gift exchange. For example, a bronze stool was sent to King Alfonso of Portugal in 1520. The King of Portugal reciprocated with a brass bound leather Bible and a crucifix. A bronze horseman was also given as a wedding gift to H.J. Swainton, a British trader, by Oba Ovonramwen in 1890. The bronze horseman is now kept at the National Museums and Galleries on Merseyside, Liverpool

Reinterpretation of the Benin bronze plaques

The production of plaques must have begun in the second quarter of the 16th century and ended in about 1640 (Dark 1973). In 1540 Oba Esigie is said to have ordered a brass crucifix to send to the king of Portugal as a present. In return he was given a copy of a Roman Catholic catechism together with other valuables (Egharevba 1968).

Edo craftsmen and chiefs equate carvings and bronze castings to their olden days photographs which narrate and commemorate scenes in Benin history. Benin arts are primary vehicles for intellectual and aesthetic expressions serving as visual metaphors, image texts and forms of unwritten constitution regulating rituals, social and political relations between the king, the priests and the people. The motifs relate to a vast collection of stories, historical accounts, aphorisms and song-texts that have been preserved orally for many generations (Blackmun 1988). Ritual specialists within the palace and outlying communities interpret the visual symbols, and image texts at different levels of meaning through indigenous readings of dances, costume details, and gestures that are associated with the plaques.

While simple explanations are provided for the general public, access to deeper meanings are obtained through initiation into the hierarchies of the palace associations which in themselves make up the indigenous educational system of Benin society.

Prior to his deposition in 1897, the Oba Ovoramwen like his predecessors had traded with several Europeans including Cyril Punch receiving brass, brocades and beads whose income went into the erection of a large architectural master piece with galvanised iron roofs and walls decorated with bronze plaques. Indeed:

> Benin court art attest to conflicts, contacts and trade with neighbours and foreigners and leads
> credence to oral and historical traditions about the expansion and contraction of the Empire
> and the eventual destruction of the Benin kingdom as an independent polity
> (Kaplan 1993: 37).

As a general interpretative scheme, Benin bronze plaques can be divided into three categories The thin and flattest ones with low relief constitute the earliest group. They have brass heads of high collars with flanged bases. The second category have circles and crosses as background motifs. They are relatively few in number and could have been cast to decorate pillars of small buildings. The third type of plaques have high relief (Dark 1975: 59).

Dark's detailed comparative study of costumes and accoutrements on some Benin plaques with their European counterparts led him to conclude that the armour depicted are cabasset helmets of the 1580s and 1620s.

Interpretation of the bronze plaques and pieces in the *African Worlds* gallery has similarly drawn impetus from my Edo background, indigenous knowledge and cognition facilitated by comparison with ongoing rituals and practices in Benin.

Photographs of the Horniman collection of bronze plaques were taken to the field. With the help of my field assistants who were groomed in the palace, the motifs and themes from the plaques were compared with living traditions and rituals witnessed during the annual *Igue* festivals. The reason for the presence or absence and significance of motifs were explained in detail through private interviews held in the houses of chiefs, priests and women. The burial rites of the Queen Mother in 1999 provided a unique opportunity to witness ancient practices, songs and rituals, made public; while the centenary celebration of 1997 provided a corpus of corroborative materials to help in the analysis of the plaques.

Images, texts, histories

What follows are iconographical interpretations of seven bronze plaques that are in the Horniman collection. They can be said to reflect the history of the Benin kingdom, court life, as well as speak of the contact with immediate neighbours and foreigners, from about the middle of 16th century up to the beginning of 17th century.

1. Oba Orhogbua

Figure 1: Oba Orhogbua (1550-1578).
(Photograph: Horniman Museum, Heini Schneebeli).

Figure 2: The present Oba (right) strikes an ivory gong; the high priest (left) holds the royal ancestral staff at the Emobo festival in 1998.
(Photograph: J. Eboreime).

The figure in this plaque (fig. 1), is Oba Orhogbua. He was educated and baptised in Portugal. On his accession to the throne, he was immediately confronted with the task of having to deal with rebellious villagers who had refused to pay their annual tributes. The authority of kingship over previous loyalties was symbolised by the Oba taking up the *ukhure-oho,* the ancestral rattle staffs. The stick represents the Oba's prime claim to ownership of the land which the village elders had to surrender to him.

The dual acts of subjugation and submission are re-enacted annually at the festival of *Igue*, where the Oba's physical and mystical powers are ritually emphasised and strengthened. Those who originally settled the land surrender their own staffs to the Oba who, as the living representative of their ancestors, is the supreme owner of all land. The icons on the more elaborate *ukhure* distinguish royalty from non-royalty and define power relations between the king, the people, and the nobles at all levels (fig. 2).

The royal tattoos *iwu*, are a mark of Benin citizenship. Before 1929, a Benin man without body markings was not qualified to become a chief. On this plaque, Oba Orhogbua is wearing a heavily embroidered brocade wrapper with a frill overlaid by a waistband sash with tassels. *Iwu* body markings adorn his body. Water leaf *olokun* motifs form the background of the plaque. At the corners are crocodile heads. Crocodiles are servants of Olokun, hermaphrodite god of the seas, wealth, and child of Osanobua, who guards the waters.

2. 'The elusive priest of Ugbor village with four braided hair strands'

Figure 3: Right: The elusive priest of Ugbor village. (Photograph: Horniman Museum, Heini Schneebeli).

Figure 4: Far Right: Ifieto guild member holding a ritual armlet *egb*). (Photograph: J. Eboreime, 1998).

As well as the significant dreadlocks, the priest of Ugbor village wears a stone hand axe, a ritual armlet, *egba* (see fig. 4), and a mystical badge on his forehead with Benin citizenship marks above each eyebrow. He is adorned with body markings and wears a leather strap across his chest which rests on a waistband. The four bundles of hair have a special meaning which can be understood through the story of the priest of Ugbor village and Oba Ewuare.

This priest took advantage of his unimpeded access to the palace to try the Oba's wits and wisdom by posing riddles. He offered to forfeit his life if the Oba could answer any of them. The Oba showered him with beads, cowrie shells and precious ivories, but each time his answers failed. On the advice of a diviner from a northern Ishan chiefdom, the Oba added a pretty woman to the gift items accompanying the failed riddle session. Once the woman had filled him with sweet strong palm wine she extracted the meaning of the riddles and sent word secretly to Oba Ewuare through a stepson of the trickster priest.

Once again the priest embarked on his extortionist riddle mission to the palace but he was

devastated when the Oba reeled off the answers to his riddles. He was thrown into the royal prison to await the executioner's sword.

At the Ogiuwu shrine (dedicated to the god of death) sudden showers of rain led to the postponement of the execution. As the sweet showers of rain lingered on, the executioners fell asleep and the elusive priest sneaked away from the jaws of death. Afraid for their own lives, the executioners killed a hen and smeared their swords with its blood as proof that the Oba's orders had been carried out to the letter.

The Oba was astonished when the Ohen N' Ugbor reappeared after four weeks wearing the symbolic bundles of hair which hold the meaning which he interpreted to the Oba in the light of his perceived betrayal.

Bundles	Proverb
right	Let a woman into a secret at your peril.
left	A step child or adopted child will never be as dependable as your biological child.
top	The gentle shower of rain ruins a day's work.
rear (out of sight)	The power of sleep is so overwhelming that it overrides the strongest desire to work.

3. Chief Uwangue, the flamboyant and proud one

Figure 5: Uwangue, the flamboyant and proud one.
(Photograph: Horniman Museum, Heini Schneebeli).

Figure 6: The Oba's personal ritual officials, Osa and Osuan.
(Photograph: J. Eboreime, 1998).

The Oba has always been more than a divine monarch. He was a political king who was actively engaged in mediating the competition for royal favours between the town and the palace. His ability to exercise personal power had always depended on his ability to maintain a balance between competing groups and individuals and success in keeping open multiple channels of communication with other sectors of the population.

The impact of the Portuguese encounter with Benin is positively reflected in the stylised representation of Chief Uwangue, the new head of the senior society, on this architectural plaque. The Portuguese on the right, hold brass manilla (money), while the one on the other side holds an iron spear, probably cast in Benin. Both figures wear the Benin straw hat, like those worn by the Oba's personal ritual functionaries, Osa and Osuan (see fig. 6). A large fish motif, probably a shark, forms a mutual link between the Oba's representative (Chief Uwangue) and the Portuguese trader on the right. The flamboyant and proud Uwangue Osokhirikpa N'Oslopakhara extends the right hand of friendship to the trader on the left. The trader's staff suggests he is a legitimate official with some diplomatic authority on a trade mission to negotiate with the Oba, through the Chief.

4. Edogun

Figure 7:
Edogun n'ibiwe
n'ekhua.
(Photograph: Horniman
Museum, Heine
Schneebeli).

During the struggle for supremacy between Oba Ewedo and Uzama nobles in 1255, Edogun led the royal forces to eventual victory and firmly entrenched the supremacy of the Oba. This event is re-enacted at the Ugie iron rituals of the annual *Igie* festival. The annual *Igue* festival is an occasion when the beauty and power of royalty are paraded in procession and dance. Each chief dances before the Oba with his sceptre (*eben*, state sword). Dropping the sceptre would invite the wrath of the ancestors through their living representative, the Oba of Benin. His torso is bare, exposing Benin body marks. Two interconnected strings of beads cross his body diagonally. These beads are called *akpa obo 'kpa* (one-sided beads).

On both wrists are the two *ikoro* brass bracelets, while the wrapper is made of embroidered brocade laced with stone beads. The wrapper is topped by a sash and a hip mask holds both sash and wrapper in place. The figure is wearing ankle beads and pea bells. The ceremonial state sword is raised in obeisance to the Oba. The background of this plaque is decorated with *ebeamen*, water leaf and the 'sun never misses a day' motif (*owen I' b' ede 'ku*).

5. The chief priest of the River deity 'Okhuaihe' at Ogheghe

The Ohen Okhuaihe is wearing the high bead collar, (*odigba*), the leopard teeth necklace (*akon ekpen*), and around his neck are two brass bells (*egogo ohen*) of oval shape. A fish eagle feather (*igan oghoghon*) is stuck in his plaited hair and his right hand is gripping a spiked club (*ukpokpo igban*). His left hand grips a broken sword (*umozo*) which symbolises the broken powers of the rebel who had once owned it. His torso is market with the Benin body marks (*iwu*) and above his eyebrows are the Benin marks (*ik'aro*). His wrapper is embroidered and edged with coral beads and he is wearing ankle beads (*ivie owe*).

Figure 8: The chief priest of the river deity. (Photograph: Horniman Museum, Heine Schneebeli).

Figure 9: Dancing with ekpokin, the leather box. (Photograph: J. Eboreime, 1998).

The *avbiogbe* figure also has plaited hair with a long coiled strand of hair holding a fish eagle feather. Around his neck is a single strand of beads; an indication of his status as an emissary (*uko*). The part that is broken off, probably shows this figure holding the leather box (*ekpokin*) that contains the soil of the re-conquered territory and or the head of the ruler (fig. 9). His wrapper is topped by a decorated sash and under it is another wrap-around skirt with tassels (*ebuluku*). The background of the plaque is decorated with ebe amen and olokun water leaf motif.

6. The Oba's Emissary

Throughout the old Empire of Benin, dependent chiefdoms and villages paid yearly tributes to the Oba. They were paid in slaves, leopards, ivory, rolls of tobacco, palm oil, goats, and cowrie shells. Cowries from the East Indies where the currency in pre-colonial times from 900 A.D. to 1897.

Figure 10: The Oba's emissary. (Photograph: Horniman Museum, Heini Schneebeli).

The figures on this plaque carry a tribute of a different kind. The high collar, beaded anklets and bracelets, rounded lead helmet and scabbard, all identify the Imaran, the fourth in the hierarchy of Benin war chiefs. The title was, and still is, usually bestowed by the Oba on loyalists from the northern Edo chiefdom of Ishan. The present Imaran of Benin, for example, is Chief Ojomo, whose Ishan lineage goes back more than ten generations. The Imaran title was created by Oba Eresoyen in 1740.

The other figure has a braided hairstyle, a three-stranded bead necklace and celt stone tied to the diagonal stripe running the length of his apron, and holds the leather gift box (fig. 9). All these elements strongly suggest that the figure is a priest of the royal order. Both Benin historical records and palace oral tradition identify this functionary as either Ohen okheghe, the priest doctor of the royal army or Ohen Odighi N'Udo, the priest of the Udo Lake chiefdom.

7. Ezomo Agban, deputy commander in chief of the Benin army

Figure 11: Right: Deputy commander in chief of the Benin army.
(Photograph: Horniman Museum, Heine Schneebeli).

Figure 12: Far right: The Deputy commander leading a ceremonial attack on royal protectors.
(Photograph: J. Eboreime, 1998).

Although he is standing alone, the Ezomo's posture and ceremonial war regalia suggest that he is dancing the victory dance, Isi' Okuo, at the victory parade after defeating an enemy. Victory dances were also performed at funeral processions to celebrate the military achievements of the person who had died.

Performed at a contemporary war parade, the *Isi' Okuo* enacts significant events such as coronations, burials, and the annual *Igue* festival. *Isi' Okuo* can also enact episodes from military history, and the exploits of war heroes such as the humiliation of rebellious provinces (fig. 12).

Ezomo Agban is in full war regalia. The deputy commander is wearing a high pyramidal helmet with flaps covering the ears (*erhu iy'ewu*) and the leopard teeth necklace encased in a brass base (*akon atalakpa*). A brass pectoral war-bell (*egogo amen u'yan re*), is hanging from the necklace to guarantee a warrior's safe return.

The Ezomo is also wearing leaded brass body armour (*ewu'oze*) engraved with the image of a leopard's face, a royal symbol that invoked awe and reverence. Underneath the body armour he is wearing a leather dress with straps and brass bells. The brocade wrapper is designed in the *guilloche* pattern (*Oba n'urhi*) and edged with coral beads. The background of the plaque is decorated with six 'the sun never misses a day' and water leaf motifs.

According to Benin legend, while Ezomo Agban was relating his war exploits to the new Oba, Ehengbuda N' Obo, he was interrupted by a thunder clap. In vexation, Ezomo Agban declared war on the inhabitants of the sky.

He built scaffolds which where said to be two miles high, tied calabashes of palm oil to them and set the scaffolds ablaze. This action caused a heavy rainstorm accompanied by more thunder claps which Ezomo Agban took as a sign of victory over the Sky. The burning scaffolds fell and scattered over a distance of over three miles. The spots where the various segments of the scaffolds fell, have become sacred sites and shrines to Ezomo Agban. To this day any one conferred with a chieftaincy title, pays homage there.

8. Ekpenede, Iyase of Benin

Figure 13: Ekpenede, Iyase of Benin, in full regalia.
(Photograph: Horniman Museum, Heine Schneebeli).

Figure 14: Once the Iyase left Benin at the head of the army, he was never permitted to return again whether in victory or defeat.
(Photograph: Joseph Eboreime).

Before 1608, every Oba was a political, ritual and military king who personally commanded the army. However, after Oba Ehangbuda's ill-fated expedition of 1608, it was decreed that no Benin king should go to war or undertake voyages over water. The Iyase became the field commander of the Benin forces but once he left Benin at the head of the army, he was never permitted to return again whether in victory or defeat (fig. 14).

In this plaque, Iyase Epenede is in full military regalia, consisting of leaded bronze body armour (*evu-oze*) and an iron helmet (*erhu-egere*), decorated with horse tails. He carries a stabbing spear (*ogan*), a sword (*agdada*) – encased in a scabbard under his armpit – and a decorated shield (*asa*), in his left hand. Hanging below his high collared and beaded necklace and leopard teeth set in brass, is a charmed bell. The bell (*egogo amen n'yan re*), guarantees the safety of the wearer like the one carried by a statue of Oba Ozolua the Conqueror (1483-1504). This statue at the Ozolua quadrangle in the Benin palace is today associated with the military prowess derived from the supernatural agencies controlling the collective destiny of the Edo nation.

The smaller figure is a horn blower, apparently celebrating a major victory with his overlord. He is also wearing full military regalia; full body armour made of interlocking leaded brass plates. Earlier armour was made of iron (*ew-ematon*) but this is no longer used because the humid climate caused it to rust.

Brass plaques were the appropriate medium and mnemonic commissioned by various Obas, for one or a combination of the following reasons: To commemorate significant historical events and enshrine the past in the present and the present in the past. To glorify the Oba as well as the awe and the glamour of kingship. As altar and shrine pieces, to lend meaning, and visual support to shared beliefs, myths and traditions.

Bibliography

BEN-AMOS, P. 1980. *The Art of Benin*, London: Thames and Hudson.

BEN-AMOS, P. and RUBIN, A. 1983. *The Art of Power the Power of Art: Studies in Benin Iconography.* University College of Los Angeles: The Museum of Cultural History.

BLIER, S. 1998. *Royal Arts of Africa: The Majesty of Form.* London: Lawrence King.

DARK, P. 1973. *An Introduction to Benin Art and Technology.* Oxford: Clarendon Press.

DARK, P. 1975. Benin Bronze Heads: Styles and Chronology. In McCall, D. and Bay, E. (eds), *African Images and Essay in African Iconology.*

EBOREIME, J. 1999. Towards Museum Education in a Multi Cultural Context: Indigenous Voices, Cognition and Re-interpretation of Benin Art. Paper presented at the Annual MEG Conference *Glimpses of Africa.* London: Horniman Museum, May 1999.

EGHAREVBA, J. 1968. *A short history of Benin.* 4th ed. Ibadan: Ibadan University Press.

EWEKA, E. 1992. *Evolution of Benin chieftaincy title.* Benin City: Uniben press, University of Benin.

IRABOR, I. n.d. *Benin: a simple historical perspective.* Benin City: Maidson & Maidson.

UGOWE, C. 1997. *Benin in World History.* Lagos: Kosaya.

Siren Seductress of the Seven Seas: Mammy Wata in the Global Village

Among the Ibibio and Annang peoples of southeast Nigeria's Palm Belt, an indigenous belief in water spirits, *ndem mmo*, is virtually universal.[1] This is not surprising in view of the vicinity to coast and river of many of their settlements, situated in territory drained by the Cross River and innumerable smaller watercourses. To the west, peoples of the Kwa Ibo estuary and the eastern Niger Delta such as the Andoni and Ogoni hold annual ceremonies in honour of water spirits called *owo*. They share this cultural trait with the Ijo people of the Delta, among whom the *owo* occupy a dominant role in cosmology and ritual. Among the Kalabari the men's *Ekine* or *Sekiapu* association stages an annual festival in honour of the water spirits, who for a time visit the terrestrial world of human beings in the form of figures wearing carved wooden masks of stylised human or animal form on top of the head (Horton 1965).

In this part of the world there also exists the concept of a beautiful woman with the lower part of her body in the form of a fish, luring hapless souls, especially men, to a watery lair. The mermaid myth is of course found in many parts of the world. It is not inconceivable that the myth owes its origin to sightings of a large herbivorous aquatic mammal, such as the manatee (*Trichechus senegalensis)*, which was formerly common on the Guinea Coast.

In West Africa such a being is often called Mammy Wata in pidgin English. It is believed that Mammi Wata appears only fleetingly to human view: in the market crowd, whilst fetching water or bathing at a stream, whilst lying in bed or travelling by canoe anywhere. Typical victims chosen by Mammy Wata may experience nightmares, usually involving snakes, or convulsions, and at times enter altered mental states such as trance. Amongst the Annang and Ibibio it is the general practice both for Christians and for adherents of the indigenous belief system (often there is no strict dividing line between the two) to refer psychological problems to a diviner, a male or female *Abia Idiong*. It is the role of this practioner to ascertain the cause of affliction and to help the patients take a positive course of action. Mammy Wata may or may not be found to

Jill Salmons

Mami Wata
Shrine at the
African Worlds
gallery
(Photograph: Horniman
Museum, Heini
Schneebeli).

be the cause of the problem. It is equally likely to be attributed to another supernatural cause such as witchcraft, or to a physiological disease. However, should Mammy Wata be recognised as the source of affliction, elaborate rituals, including the giving of gifts to her have to be undertaken under the guidance of a Mammy Wata priest or priestess. Attitudes towards Mammy Wata are ambivalent, as a person in her embrace, although offered potential sexual gratification and great material wealth, runs the risk of impotency and early death, especially by drowning. In some cases the afflicted eventually become Mammy Wata practitioners themselves.

Mammy Wata is commonly believed to have some, or all, of the following characteristics: great beauty, long flowing hair , pale skin, brightly coloured and bejeweled attire. In local depictions she often has a comb for her locks, and a hand mirror in which to admire herself· In other versions she is adorned with serpents. It is with the latter category that this paper is largely concerned.

For many years, artists in southeast Nigeria have produced wooden representations of Mammy Wata which have been strongly influenced by an imported chromolithograph, originally printed in Germany, of an Indian snake-charmer picture which has been available in this part of the world since the early 1900s (fig. 1). In an account of my fieldwork primarily among the Ibibio and Annang peoples I pointed out

Figure 1: Imported snake-charmer prints have influenced representations and concepts of Mammy Wata in southeast Nigeria and elsewhere. (Photograph: Jill Salmons, 1976).

> *It appears...that the introduction of the foreign print served to gel ...visual concepts of [the water]spirits... the print and carving [having] been agents in the diffusion of the belief in a particular kind of water spirit, Mammy Wata* (Salmons 1977: 14).

Regarded by British colonial officers as 'truculent', the Annang, western neighbours of the Ibibio, are the most productive and talented of southeast Nigerian wood sculptors. Akpan Chukwu of the settlement and clan of Utu Etim Ekpo, near Abak township, was possibly the greatest 20th century Annang carver. Living something of a 'Bohemian' lifestyle, Akpan is reputed never to have worked without a bottle of gin secured between his legs. Kenneth Murray, Nigeria's first Surveyor of Antiquities, visited him in 1944 and made the connection between a Mammy Wata sculpture in Akpan's workshop at the time and the German print. Murray believed this artist to be the innovator of 'the new style of carving', and although his notes (Murray n.d.) indicate that he intended to acquire a Mammy Wata sculpture from Akpan, he did not actually do so.

Akpan Chukwu died at a relatively young age in 1952, according to some of my informants, victim of sorcery or poisoning by one of his many jealous rivals. In due course, one of the three village locations which I

Jill Salmons

selected for intensive field study was Utu Etim Ekpo. In 1974 I moved into the compound of Joseph Chukwu, one of Akpan's brothers, then in his seventies. Among the many pieces which I commissioned from Joseph were some multifaced masks of the type worn in masquerades of the *Ekpo* (male ancestor spirit) association. (see Nicklin & Salmons 1984: 29, pl. 3) I was also able to acquire from him an exceedingly complex headdress in which the central serpent-bearing half-figure is flanked by seated figures and paddlers, with a kneeling trumpeter in the prow. The paddlers' arms can be made to imitate genuine paddling motion by pulling a string leading from the figure, through the body of the vessel. This represents an extraordinary artistic *tour de force,* combining in a single work multiple figure sculpture with puppetry technique.[2]

In the making of the headdress Joseph Chukwu (who died in the early 1980s) followed the process which Akpan had taught him, first sketching the design in pencil on the wood prior to carving, with the aid of measurements made with a ruler. Joseph carved the head and trunk of the central figure himself, whilst segments of remaining figures and the snakes were made by apprentices under his supervision, and then assembled and afterwards painted by him (fig. 2).

Most wood sculptures in West Africa are monoxylous, but among the Annang many of the larger masks and figures, including puppets, are carved from a number of pieces of wood, jointed and held together by wooden pegs or modern steel nails. As in the case of the *duein fubara,* or ancestor screens, of the Kalabari people of the Niger Delta (Barley 1989), some authorities suspect that this mode of manufacture indicates European influence, possibly from the slaving ships of the days of sail dating back to the 15th century. In order to examine the process of Mammy Wata manufacture in detail, to maintain a material record and for future didactic and museum exhibition purposes, I requested Joseph to make a carving sequence in respect of the central female figure. This he adroitly did (Salmons ibid.: 10-11; figs 2 & 3).

An interesting example of the failure of the artist accurately to 'read' the Mammy Wata print lies in a curious excrescence attached to the lefthand side of the central figure, first noted by Murray in respect of Akpan Chukwu's carving. This is present not only in respect of Joseph Chukwu's version, but also occurs in those made by Akpan's son, Akpan Akpan Chukwu. According to the latter artist, also living in Utu Etim Ekpo, the lump in question is Mammy Wata's purse, a reasonable supposition as she is a water spirit possessing plenty of cash. The lump, however, is the artists' rendition of a miniature picture of a snake charmer at work, inset at the bottom left of the print.

Joseph Chukwu informed me that before the Biafran War he had made a Mammy Wata carving equivalent in size to a real person. This was for the shrine of an *Abia Idiong.* To my knowledge, no such sculptures survived the ravages of war. The work of another Annang artist whose household I shared, Matthew Udo-Nwa Ekpe, of Ikot Obong, near Ikot Ekpene township, was rather different. He was an illiterate artist who carved in a more traditional way, by eye rather than measurement producing remarkably neat and crisp carvings of great originality and flair. As a young man, Udo-Nwa had worked alongside Akpan Chukwu, and it was in Chukwu's workshop that he first came across a Mammy Wata carving.

Figure 3: *Mammy Wata* group as figures in a canoe, made by Annang artist Matthew Udo-Nwa Ekpe of Ikot Obong, for the National Museum Oron.
(Photograph: Jill Salmons, 1977).

Leaving artistic interpretation to the carver, from Udo-Nwa I commissioned a sculpture of the type he had previously made for *Idiong* priests in the neighbourhood (fig. 3). Riding in a canoe the two principal figures of this piece are female and comprise a standing young woman with snake triply encircling her upper body, with another snake suspended between outstretched arms; the second figure is seated, and wears a pink skirt. Both have non-African-type hair of attached natural fibre, and the face and legs have decorative motifs executed in a dark pigment upon whitened skin. This mode of decoration is characteristic of that worn by women during the 'coming-out ceremony' (rite of incorporation) following the period of seclusion associated with the Annang pre-nuptial fattening institution, *mbobo* (Salmons 1981). Similar modes of adornment are also adopted during initiation into the Mammy Wata cult. The seated woman is a bearer or 'handmaiden' to the standing neophyte. Five smaller figures in the canoe tableau are as follows: a youth in the bow of the canoe, blowing a horn; a young woman, with arms held to the fore, as in dance; two male paddlers; and a man holding a staff and wearing the cap of a titled elder, a man of seniority, probably the sponsor of the ceremony depicted.

In the rainy season of 1992 I conducted a survey of Ogoni artists of the eastern Niger Delta, with special reference to wood sculpture. This was the season of the annual harvest rites, the New Yam Festival. The Ogoni are an agrarian people who occupy the fertile hinterland of the modern city of Port Harcourt, growing a large variety of crops in addition to yam and plantain staples. My aim was to conduct research relevant to the interpretation of a large number of Ogoni pieces held by the Barbier-Mueller Museum in Geneva (Martin *et al* 1997: 277-79) and, by so doing, extend my understanding of cultural exchange between certain Palm Belt and Niger Delta peoples. A major part of the project involved the commissioning of wooden masks and figures from more than twenty sculptors interviewed, which became the core of two Ogoni ethnographic collections, for the Port Harcourt Museum and the Horniman Museum respectively.

My research situation was very different from that previously undertaken in respect of the Annang and Ibibio, about whose societies and art a reasonable amount had already been published, particularly through the work of John Messenger (1975). Very little indeed had been published about the Ogoni, though access to Murray's notes on Ogoni art (Murray n.d.) and Dr. Sonpie Pongwe-Tonwe's doctoral thesis on Ogoni history provided me with invaluable direction, especially at the beginning of my Delta fieldwork.

Much of my time was occupied in attending masquerades directly connected with the New Yam Festival, and also with witnessing the taking of honourific titles by men and boys which also happened to take place in this season. But it would also be true to say, that in the course of many interviews with carvers and performers, and certainly in discussions with most indigenous diviners, Mammy Wata often reared her beautiful head.

Among Niger Delta peoples, there are those, like the Isoko and the Ogoni, who look primarily for material and spiritual sustenance to the land rather than to the water. Given their more watery environment there are also those like the Ijo and Kalabari whose way of life is dominated by the exploitation of fish and whose deities tend also to occupy sea and stream. Among the latter category, water spirits dominate the spiritual universe, and from time to time these *owo* are believed to tread *terra firma* in the interests of living communities. Understandably, due to the network of streams and rivers that traverse Ogoniland, and the proximity of Ogoni settlements to the coastal areas, water spirits, *owo,* also figure in the cosmologies of the Ogoni. Significantly two Ogoni Mammy Wata priestesses interviewed claimed that the spirits who affected them 'were not juju [sic] of this area' but had come from the Delta, and that all of the rituals and songs are conducted in Ijo or Kalabari (two major Delta languages). Another priestess informed me that while her husband had been working in Tiko, coastal Cameroon, he had discovered a box containing a comb as he walked along the seashore. On bringing it home he warned his wife not to open it, but she did so, and since that time the 'juju' had taken control of her. The name of this spirit is *Owu Mini* and the woman has to address him in the Kalabari language.

Most Ogoni villages have at least one devotee of the Mammy Wata cult, though in one village, Gwara, I was informed that their own village goddess, *Gbenebege* was too strong to allow any Mammy Wata spirits to enter the community. Devotees of Mammy Wata, usually women, have shrines containing images of the spirit, either carved in wood, made of clay, or painted as murals. Mammy Wata is also depicted in headdress form, for example in South Khana clan a recreational play called *Owu Ikina* is performed at Christmas and Easter. In this case she is depicted as the upper half of a woman holding a Coca Cola bottle, or sitting in a canoe. A cap mask known as *Birabii,* representing two male Mammy Wata, can be worn only after offerings of incense, an egg, a bottle of spirits, another of mineral water and a lighted candle have been given in appeasement.

A half-figure Mammy Wata sculpture was made by Court Finema of Nyokwiri Boue, Babbe Clan, in August 1992, and shortly afterwards displayed at the Horniman as a new acquisition (see *African Arts* 1995: 74) (fig. 4). This piece, with the depiction of a delicate face with retrousse nose is typical of Ogoni human mask and figure sculpture style. The upraised arms are entwined with a snake, and another snake around the waist with head pointing upward towards the woman's chin is in the manner of the imported print and the Chukwu Mammy Wata sculptures described above. Although Finema's carving shows a vertically striped garment on the upper part of the body, no jewellry is represented, and in this feature is similar to that made by Udo-Nwa. Further variations of the Finema piece from the print include the lack of any carved head in respect of the serpent supported by the arms, and the depiction of braided hair in the style of many Ogoni female face masks. These variations might indicate that the artist was influenced by seeing another Mammy Wata carving rather than the print.

Ethnographic fieldwork conducted by Keith Nicklin in the Republic of Benin (former Dahomey) in 1997 confirmed that cheap reproductions of the originally German snake-charmer print, some of which were printed in Cairo, are common in markets, homes and *Vodun* altars of the coastal part of the country. In addition, he noted that some of the wealthier priestesses sometimes travelled to other West African countries, especially Togo, Ghana and Nigeria, to obtain furniture for their shrines and undergo further initiation into the cult. The impression that he gained was that of a mobile coastal sisterhood of Mammy Wata priestesses, called *mamissi,* in these countries, dispersing sacred objects connected with an ever-changing beliefs inherent among its devotees and adepts. As Dana Rush has suggested (1999: 66).

Along coastal Benin and Togo, Mami Wata is much more than a single spirit: she is an entire pantheon. For any new problem or situation needing spiritual intervention or guidance, a new Mami Wata spirit arises from the sea.

In recognition of this impressive internationalism, together with the wish to acknowledge the existence of a large camp of Ogoni political refugees in Benin Republic, during Nigeria's recent military dictatorship, Court Finema's Mammy Wata figure was placed in a reconstruction of a Benin *Vodun* altar in honour of the Mammy Wata deity, in the new *African Worlds* gallery at the Horniman. Placed in this shrine, too, were carvings whose inspiration come directly from prints of various Hindu deities which are now also commonplace in Benin and Togo (fig. 5). The backdrop to the altar in question, however, comprises a large velveteen cloth bearing the popular snake-charmer image executed in coloured sequins and seashells, by a team assembled by Ouidah artist Apollinaire Gouvide and his wife Martine de Souza.

Nicklin noted that another frequent element in Mammy Wata altars in *Vodun* shrines in Benin Republic was a representation of the Rainbow Serpent, painted on

Figure 4: Ogoni artist Court Finema with a *Mammy Wata* sculpture which he made for the Horniman Museum, at his home in Nyokwiri Boue, Babbe Clan.
(Photograph: Jill Salmons, 1992).

Figure 5: Ouidah artist Apollinaire Gouvide painting a carving which was copied from an imported print of a triple-headed Hindu deity, in Benin Republic referred to as Densou, one of *Mammy Wata's* male manifestations. This piece is currently displayed in the Horniman Museum's *African Worlds* exhibition, in a Vodun altar reconstruction in honour of Mammy Wata.
(Photograph: Keith Nicklin, 1997).

the wall over a framed print of the snake-charmer. Suzanne Blier (1995: 83) refers to one of the Fon *Vodun* 'supernatural energies' (so called because they combine diverse elements), as *Dan*, the 'serpentine wind god'. Among the Yoruba *orishas,* both in Yorubaland and in the Brazilian *Candomble* tradition, the same deity is known as *Osumare*. In Benin *Dan* or *Osumare* has been absorbed into the Mammy Wata belief system either as her husband or consort, depicted as an *arc-en-ceil*, with or without the head and tail of a snake, above various representations of her.

In Henning Christoph and Hans Oberlander's photographic study (1996) of *Vodun* in the Republic of Benin, as one of *Vodun*'s pantheon, Mammy Wata is described as 'the laughing water goddess', less strict and violent than other gods. The authors' comment that in Benin Mammy Wata is often depicted as a mermaid was corroborated by Keith Nicklin's observations in *Vodun* shrines in 1997, in and around Cotonou and Ouidah, with reference to wall paintings and carved figures. Other representations were obviously derived from the snake-charmer print.

After encountering a number of *mamissi* in this part of the world, both female and transvestite male, Nicklin (1999: 6) wrote:

> *Mammi Wata... likes to eat a lot and enjoy life in every way. Gifts to her include the most powerful of drinks (Martini Bianco and White Horse whisky), the most red of lipsticks (Cobra brand), the most advertised of cigarettes (Marlboro) and the strongest of perfumes (Chanel) and body rubs (Vicks). Mammi Wata is to be obeyed and indulged.*

During the 1970s, much of which was spent in remote field locations, I was unaware that a significant number of fellow Africanists had also been researching Mammy Wata at many Guinea Coast locations. Soon after my 1977 publication the results of this work started appearing in print. Two further examples of Annang carvings influenced by the German print, one of which was reported to have been probably carved by 'an Ikot Ekpene master during the second quarter of...[the 20th] century' are illustrated in a catalogue of the Arnett Collection, Atlanta (Wittmer & Arnett 1978: 62-3). Also illustrated in this catalogue is a Mammy Wata painting showing influence of the German print, by a contemporary Urhobo artist (Ibid.: 62) as well as an Ibibio wooden figure undoubtedly drawn from an unknown image of the Hindu deity, Hanuman (ibid.: 60-61).

In his book on the art of Eastern Nigeria, G.I. Jones (1984: 86-92) discusses the occurrence of Mammy Wata imagery which he had seen in the 1930s in the context of *Mbari* earth sculpture built by the Oratta and northern Etche Igbo peoples in honour of their tutelary deity. Although Jones had seen church mission oleographs of the saints in the area at this time, he had not seen any resembling a mermaid. Importantly, Jones states:

> *The Oratta mythology might consider Mammy water to be a European water spirit and indeed their mythology derived all Europeans from the deep water. But the attributes of Mammy water came from Nigerian sources and derived from the Ijo Delta.*

Jones (1984: 92), maintains that Mammy Wata became a 'stock character' in *Mbari* shrines only after World War I, although she had already appeared in the area by 1914, when Talbot saw an Etche earth sculpture of what an Ijo informant informed him represented a woman being crushed by a python.

The impression of Mammy Wata in modern Igboland as a powerful and enigmatic serpent-controlling temptress is fully conveyed in Della Jenkins' account (1985: 75-77):

> *Seductress by night and kidnapper by day Mamy Wata leaves her watery home to roam the land on foot or in a taxi, in many guises: butterfly, child, man, snake, woman... She wreaks havoc in markets. She talks to and steals children playing near rivers, capsizes boats, and as a python, swallows goats and ruins houses.*

Signboards advertising Mammy Wata shrines in Igboland incorporate images derived both from the snake-charmer print and others from India. Jenkins (Ibid.: 75) observes that 'Indian people evoke mystery and awe today, and may have done so for many generations.' One thing is certain, icons drawn from such sources are perceived to aid local priests to cure 'all diseases such as gonoria [sic]' and provide 'protection against poison, touch and follow, hit and fall...' (idem: fig. 132).

As the imported image spread into the forest region northeast of Calabar, new meanings, not necessarily connected with a belief in water spirits, sometimes developed. For example, recent work by Ute Roschenthaler (1998: 38-49) shows that among the Ejagham of southwest Cameroon, carved images of a woman with upraised arms, holding a python, are used in dances held in honour of female ancestors. The central feature of these headdress tableaux incorporate smaller figures wielding staffs, machetes and swords, elements which suggest influence of the snake-charmer print via other carvers. Roschenthaler(Ibid.: 46) maintains that the Ejagham insist that 'it is not Mamy Wata, because she lives in the sea and not in their part of the country' and that such headpieces depict idealised feminine beauty.

Among the Idoma of the Benue Valley there exists a belief in a spirit called *Anjenu,* which, like Mammy Wata emerges from beneath the water from time to time, visits people in their dreams and induces trance states among her victims. However, *Anjenu* spirits possess neither the siren qualities or powerful imagery of Mammy Wata. Writing of her fieldwork during 1976-78, Sidney Kasfir (1982: 51) refers to the Mammy Wata cult spreading into Idoma and Tiv country, and of an Annang Mammy Wata face mask having been acquired by a Tiv *Kwaghir* (openair puppetry theatre) group in Katsina Ala. She writes in summary:

Thus one finds Mammy Wata in one part of the Benue operating as a purely secular symbol, alongside actual beliefs in spirits such as anjenu, aljanu *and* alijenu, *while in another part of the Benue, Mammy Wata is being incorporated into the existing belief structure as a variant of* anjenu *spirits.*

According to Henry Drewal's investigations in Igboland (1988: 38-45) the earliest evidence for the influence of the German print in Africa is a photograph taken by a J.A. Green of Bonny in the Niger Delta in 1901. The photograph shows a half figure wooden headdress which he believes was unmistakenly influenced by the print, among an assembly of Annang and Ogoni carvings. Drewal points out that the original chromolith was printed in Hamburg around 1885, and illustrates (Ibid.: 39, fig. 2) a 1955 version produced in Bombay. However, whereas the Ogoni. Annang, and Ibibio have largely remained faithful to this print in their visual interpretation of Mammy Wata, the Igbo, along with many other groups, have since been influenced by many other prints. In Drewal's view,(Ibid.: 39):

The enormous popularity of the snake-charmer lithograph has led to a growing African market in Indian prints of Hindu gods, goddesses, and spirits over the last thirty years. Africans interpret these as a host of Mami Wata spirits.

In his book on *Vodun* in Togo, the photographer-journalist Gert Chesi (1980: 253 ff) had earlier drawn attention not only to the role of the snake-charmer picture (identifying the artist as Hamburg painter Arnold Schlesinger) in the dissemination of Mammy Wata imagery, but refers to prints imported from India performing a comparable role in the case of the three-headed male Mammy Wata spirit, Papa or Nana Densu. A splendid figure of Nana Densu, with triple-faced head and five arms, painted white-pink-and-gold and identified as 'Mami's husband', is illustrated by Chesi (Ibid.: 252). Elsewhere, Chesi refers to *Densou* as 'an intermediary between the believers and Mami Wata' (Beumers 1996: 118). A similarly decorated half-figure 'Mami statuette'. finished in glossy car varnish, by the same Togolese artist, Agbagli Kossi (1934-92), is also shown (Ibid.: 245). The latter figure has the serpent supported by upraised arms, with snake around the waist of the figure, pointing upwards, associated with the snake-charmer print. However,the left hand of the figure grips a carved axe of the type usually associated with the *Vodun* deity *Heviosso,* a Dahomian manifestation of the Yoruba god of thunder and lightening, *Shango.*

Two Mammy Wata sculptures made by Kossi for Chesi were exhibited in the *Africa Meets Africa* exhibition at the the Museum of Ethnology, Rotterdam. According to the exhibition catalogue (Beumers 1996: 117-18), Agbagli Kossi,

in Ghana and Togo... was considered the most significant voodoo sculptor. He was also a priest, healer, diviner and proficient in astrology... [He used] images of Buddhist and Hindu gods... [to produce works which help] dismantle the stereotypic view of Africa.

Observations by Chesi and Drewal concerning the influence of prints of Hindu deities are endorsed and amplified in an exposition by Dana Rush (1999: 60-75) of the absorption of Mammy Wata into the *Vodun* religion of the Republic of Benin, Togo, Ghana and Haiti. For Rush coastal Benin Republic is a cultural *vortex*, eclectically and perpetually drawing in 'just about anything that crosses its path' (Ibid.: 61). This of course includes chromolithographic imagery in the form of the famous snake-charmer print and a wealth of those showing Hindu deities, which nowadays include copies from Nigerian presses. In no uncertain terms we are informed by Dana Rush that the Hindu gods shown in the prints 'have not been combined with local gods, they *are* the local gods' (ibid.: 62).

In addition to the snake-charmer chromolithograph Rush (op.cit.: 64) lists the following print subjects associated with Mammy Wata and 'incorporated into her artistic lexicon: the Pope, Eve, Jesus Christ, the Virgin Mary,

Figure 6: Mammy Wata masquerader wearing costume influenced by the imported snake-charmer print, with her consort dressed as Ollie, as in the classic "Laurel and Hardy" comedy films; de Souza family festival, Ouidah, Benin Republic.
(Photograph: Keith Nicklin, 1997).

and numerous Christian saints; Hindu deities are likewise popular, as well as images of Hare Krishnas and of Shirdi Sai Baba (an Indian guru) and Islamic images of al-Buraq, the winged horse.[4]

In the former Benin slave port of Ouidah a masquerader's entire costume serves as an accurate evocation of the snake-charmer print. This was witnessed by Rush at the coronation festival or *Bouriyan* of the eighth head of the de Souza family held in 1995 and again by Nicklin (personal communication) at the annual de Souza festival held there in 1997 (fig. 6). At the latter event, Mammy Wata's consort was a masquerader dressed as the fat character, Ollie, from the Laurel and Hardy comedy films. In addition, many Hindu images have become identified as avatars of Mammy Wata, no longer conceptualised as a single water spirit, but now regarded in coastal Benin and Togo as a pantheon. For example, the Hindu monkey-king, Hanuman, familiar to *Vodun* adepts through the imported print, is commonly known as a Mammy Wata manifestation called *Gniblin* (op. cit.: 66-7).

Using a wide range of field data collected in 1990 and 1991 at nine sites in several southern states of Nigeria, Charles Gore and Joseph Nevadomsky (1997: 60-9) present a critique of previous Mammy Wata studies (e.g. Salmons 1977; Drewel 1988) in which the water spirit is analysed as 'an externally imposed phenomenon'. Such an approach, they maintain, has served to obscure 'local configurations' and erase 'specific traditions' (Ibid.: 61-2). Gore and Nevadomsky's description of the southern Nigerian shrines clearly demonstrates that

> *Mammy Wata is a configuration of social practice and material culture that can vary radically among different groups or in different contexts within the same group.*

The co-authors cite examples of Mammy Wata imagery and ritual in Edo contexts as diverse as the following: in the Edo court at the shrine of *Oshodin;* as covert practice associated with witchcraft; within the generally accepted Christian church tradition; and ensconced in a pantheon of local deities.

In many parts of Africa contemporary artists, especially painters, have been influenced by Mammy Wata imagery. One such artist is the Annang artist Imeh Fabian Udo Idiong of Ikot Esse, near Ikot Ekpene, aged about 25 when I knew him in the mid-1970s. Using commercially made paints, and in a modern, realistic style quite unlike the figures formerly painted by older artists such as Matthew Udo-Nwa Ekpe, he was employed to decorate funerary memorials and community halls in his home area. The Mammy Wata open-air mural which he was commissioned to paint at the Oron Museum in 1976 was an accurate rendering of the snake-charmer print.

It was Susan Vogel's ground-breaking exhibition held at New York's Center for African Art in 1991, *Africa Explores: 20th Century African Art,* however, that revealed the extent to which Mammy Wata has entered the repertory of contemporary expression elsewhere in Africa. For internationally renowned Zairian painter Cheri Samba of Kinshasa (b. 1956) it is a popular theme to which he returns 'whenever the market or his own preoccupations suggest it' (Vogel & Ebong 1991: 18-19). Many of his interpretations of Mammy Wata or *La Sirene* under the title 'La Seduction' (Ibid.: figs. 3 & 76) depict a seated or recumbent voluptuous woman with long hair, sometimes with comb or mirror, and with an inset portrait of the author reading the biblical text Luke 6, verse 24: 'But alas for you who are rich; you have had your time of happiness', which is written in French on the painting. This is Samba's warning of the dire consequences of enjoying Mammy Wata's sexual favours and wealth. Cheri Samba, and other Zairian painters often combine the fishtailed woman holding comb and mirror of the classic European mermaid image, together with the coiled snakes of the snake-charmer and many prints of the Hindu deities.

In Zaire also appear paintings of *Papi Wata,* a man, sometimes bearded, with the lower part of the body in fish form (ibid.: 18) and shown by Samba in his 'La Seduction' series. Keith Nicklin saw paintings of *Papi Wata* executed by roadside artists on the outskirts of Cotonou, and collected one example for inclusion in the Mammy Wata altar at the Horniman Museum. He also interviewed a male transvestite *papissi*, Hounon Atonkasse of Zogbohoue, Cotonou (Nicklin 1999: 6). Although most Mammy Wata devotees and priests are female, some men do participate in the cult at all levels.

Cole & Ross (1977: 189-90) describe examples of mermaids among the cement sculptures adorning some *posuban* (military company shrines) in Ghana, which though showing no obvious visual evidence of influence from any specific imported print, are called by elders 'Mammy Water' or 'Queen of the Sea'; the one illustrated (op. cit.: fig. 369) shows a half-fish, half-woman figure with long dark hair, lacking snakes.

Water spirits abound also in the New World in the beliefs of many black and creole communities in the Americas. For example *Yemanja,* a stately and coldly beautiful Yoruba ocean goddess, has become syncretised in the *candomblé* belief system of Brazil with the Virgin Mary, whilst *Oshun,* mystic ruler of a central Yorubaland river of the same name, has become a 'beautiful, vain, acquisitive, deceitful' *candomblé* spirit entity or *orisha* (Omari 1988: 21). In Haiti the water spirit *Lasiren,* iconographically, seems to owe inspiration to the classic European mermaid image. Metal artworks, cut and beaten out of old oildrums and featuring representations of *Lasiren* and other *Vodun* deities, originally made for indigenous ritual use by Georges Liautaud and his imitators, have for many years constituted collector items in Europe and the USA (see Morris 1998: 382 ff). Haitian *Vodun* beliefs posit Queen *Lasiren* as the partner of King *Agwe,* who together control the sea (Mintz & Trouillot 1998: 148-52).

It has even been suggested that Mammy Wata may have originated in the New World. According to Chesi (1980: 59) 'it is conceivable that returning slaves took... [Mammy Wata] along to Africa from Haiti, where she is venerated.' The argument in favour of New World origins of Mammy Wata and subsequent diffusion of the concept by way of liberated slaves returning to Africa during the 19th century, is best presented, however, by Barbara Paxson (1983) who examines evidence from the Caribbean area and South America, as well as from Africa.[5]

She describes a calabash from Surinam incised with images of 'Watramamma'. The calabash is dated 1831, which predates known African Mammy Wata carvings by at least eighty years.(Ibid.: 418-20). There is also a Surinamese legend of 'the Great Mother of the Inland Waters' who is said to have delivered slaves to freedom, in a boat with six paddlers. Citing several authorities, she points out that the name 'Mammy Water' is in fact Krio, a *lingua franca* created by slaves speaking mutually unintelligible languages (ibid.: 421).In Paxson's view, Mammy Wata in her myriad manifestations,

> *traverses the barriers of language, culture, race ethnicity, time and space. and unites rather*
> *than separates the hemispheres through her watery medium, as a true spirit of liberation and*
> *unity.*

Perhaps even more unexpected than the data from Surinam is Nelson Graburn's assertion that 'a figure looking very much like Mami Wata was revered by the Eskimos' (Cosentino 1992: 12). Donald Cosentino wisely advises us that 'the same ships that visited the shores of West Africa visited Iceland and Cuba too' and that such vessels were the vectors of very many things, from new cuisine to new diseases.

Virtually every commentator, on the subject of Mammy Wata, including Cosentino, remarks on the eclectic manner in which this water spirit absorbs and restructures religious belief, ritual and all manner of artistic expression, from wood sculpture to painting and dance into her exuberant orbit. She consumes yet enriches every aspect of being. In both living life to the full, and sometimes taking it, in Nigerian pidgin English idiom, she literally "chops life." Many altars built in her honour must constitute some of the greatest examples of *assemblage* in existence. In Mammy Wata, a truly global spiritual *bricoleur,* perhaps lies hope of a necessary salve for - in Joanna Pitman's words (Pitman 2000: 41) - the "artistic alienation, provocation and paranoia" of the western world in the new millennium.

Acknowledgments

I should like to thank the Commonwealth Scholarship Fund for sponsoring my fieldwork in Nigeria,1973-75, and Jean-Paul Barbier for that on the Ogoni in 1992. My work was also greatly assisted by many kinds of help from various members of staff of the Nigerian National Commission for Museums & Monuments and the University of Port Harcourt. Fieldwork would have been impossible without the cooperation and hospitality of a host of Nigerian artists and other individuals, only a few of whom are mentioned in the above text, as well as my field assistants, Friday Ettuk-Udoh and James Bubara. I am also grateful to Keith Nicklin for allowing free access to his own field data, and for assistance in writing this paper, and to Janet Stanley, Chief Librarian, National Museum of African Art, Smithsonian Institution, Washington, for promptly forwarding a a copy of her *Select References on Mami Wata*, and a replacement copy of Paxson's paper (1983).

Notes

1. The Nigerian Civil War of 1967-70 caused a great deal of disruption to the activities of indigenous artists and the institutions for which they had produced artefacts such as wooden masks and figure carvings. In the course of my investigations among communities in the Palm Belt, Cross River forestlands and eastern Delta regions of Nigeria (see Nicklin & Salmons 1997: 146-168),in the carvers' workshops and shrines which were among my foci of study, various representations of Mammy Wata repeatedly materialised. During the early 1970s, in order to document methods and materials of manufacture and to gain an accurate impression of the range of works which surviving carvers could produce, I was asked by the then Nigerian Department of Antiquities to commission examples of their work. Apart from the valuable research insight which I gained, the exercise also had the advantage of providing a literally 'state of the art' well-documented collection for the National Museum at Oron, at an important historical juncture. Oron Museum was then undergoing rehabilitation after its destruction and loss of collections during the recent hostilities. The carvers, too, appreciated the new source of income from this unanticipated source of patronage.

2. A photograph of a Mammy Wata half-figure which I commissioned from Joseph Chukwu on behalf of Dr. Pamela Brink appeared on the front cover of *African Arts* (1977). The same piece was again illustrated in this journal (1993) after it had been donated to The University of Iowa Museum of Art.

3. As well as producing a number of masks, figures, puppets and the Mammy Wata piece described here, Udo-Nwa made a further major contribution to the Oron Museum (Nicklin 1978). As part of the permanent displays there, Udo-Nwa was invited to give instructions for the erection of an Annang female funerary shrine, called *nduongo*. After this had been done, he agreed to decorate it in the manner which he had employed for his mother's *nduongo* very many years before. At the time of the public opening of the Oron Museum in 1977 he was the sole living practitioner of this art. Matthew Udo-Nwa Ekpe died a few years later.

4. A link between Mammy Wata and the al-Buraq image in northern Nigeria was confirmed to me by the Director-General of the Nigerian National Commission for Museums & Monuments, Dr. Yaro Gella, and his wife, during the Horniman conference at which a version of the present paper was presented.

5. She was alerted to this theory by Peter Neumann's paper (1961) on the decorated calabash from Surinam.

Bibliography

The references given here, representing only a fraction of the immense literature now available on Mammy Wata, relate specifically to this article.

ADAMS, M. 1998. Review of *African Material Culture*. In Arnoldi, M. and Geary, C. (eds), *African Arts,* 31:1, pp. 91-2.

BARLEY, N. 1989. *Foreheads of the Dead: an Anthropological view of Kalabari Ancestral Screens.* Washington and London: Smithsonian Institution Press, .

BEUMERS, E. 1996. *Africa meets Africa.* Rotterdam: Museum of Ethnology.

BLIER, S. 1995. *African Vodun: art, psychology, and power.* Chicago and London: University of Chicago Press.

CHESI, G. 1980. *Voodoo Africa's secret power.* Worgl: Perlinger.

CHRISTOPH, H. and OBERLANDER, H. 1996. *Voodoo secret power in Africa.* Koln: Taschen.

COLE, H. and ROSS, D. 1978. *The arts of Ghana.* Los Angeles: Museum of Cultural History, University of California,.

COSENTINO, D. (ed) 1998. *Sacred arts of Haitian Vodou.* Los Angeles: Fowler Museum of Cultural History, University of California.

COSENTINO D. 1992. First Word. *African Arts,* 25:2 pp. 1-12.

DREWAL, H. 1988. Mermaids, Mirrors and Snake Charmers: Igbo Mami Wata Shrines. *African Arts,* 21:2, 4pp. 38-45.

DREWAL, H. 1996. Mami Wata shrines: exotica and the construction of the self. In Arnoldi, M. et al. (eds), *African Material Culture.* Indiana University Press. 308-333.

ECKHARDT, U. et al. 1979. *Moderne kunst aus Afrika.* Berlin: Berliner Festspiele.

GORE, C. and NEVADOMSKY J. 1997. Practice and agency in Mammy Wata worship in Nigeria. *African Arts,* 30:2, pp. 60-69.

HORTON, R. 1965. *Kalabari Sculpture.* Lagos: Dept. of Antiquities.

JENKINS, D. 1985. Mamy Wata. In Cole, H. and Aniakor, C. *Igbo arts community and cosmos.* Los Angeles: Museum of Cultural History, University of California,. 75-7.

JONES, G. 1984. *The art of Eastern Nigeria.* Cambridge: Cambridge University Press.

KASFIR, S. 1982. Anjenu: sculpture for Idoma water spirits. *African Arts,* 15:4, pp. 47-51.

MESSENGER, J. 1975. The role of the carver in Anang society. In Azevedo, W. (ed), *The traditional artist in African societies.* Bloomington: Indiana University Press.

MINTZ, S. and TROUILLOT, M.-R. 1998. Water spirits Agwe and Lasiren. In Cosentino, D. (ed), *The sacred arts of Haitian Vodou.*

MORRIS, R. 1998. The style of his hand the iron art of Georges Liautaud. In Cosentino, D. (ed), *The sacred arts of Haitian Vodou.*

MARTIN, J-H. ET AL. 1997. *Art du Nigeria.* Paris: Réunion des Musées Nationaux.

MURRAY, K. n.d. Unpublished notes. Nigerian National Commission for Museums & Monuments, Lagos.

NEUMANN, P. 1961. Eine verzierte Kalebassenschussel aus Surinam. *Veroffentlichungen des Stadtischen Museums fur Volkerkunde zu Leipzig.* 11: 481-98.

NICKLIN, K. 1977. *Guide to the National Museum Oron.* Lagos: Federal Dept. of Antiquities.

NICKLIN, K. 1978. The Utilization of Local Skills and Materials in a Nigerian Museum. *Museum Journal,* **78.**

NICKLIN, K. 1993. New acquisitions: the Horniman Museum. *African Arts,* 28:3, p.74.

NICKLIN, K. 1999. Benin Vodoun altar for Mammi Wata. In *Altars.* Information booklet, *African Worlds* exhibition, pp. 6-7. London: Horniman Museum.

NICKLIN, K. and SALMONS, J. 1984. Cross River Art Styles. *African Arts,* 18: 28-43.

NICKLIN, K. and SALMONS J. 1997. Les Arts du Nigeria du Sud-Est les Ogoni et les Peuples de la Cross River. In *Arts du Nigeria Collection du Musee des Arts d'Afrique et d'Oceanie.* Martin, J.-H. et al. Ch. 3, pp. 147-68. Paris: Reunion des musee nationaux.

OMARI, M. 1988. *From the Inside to the Outside: The Art and Ritual of Bahian Candomblé. Monograph Series, 24.* Los Angeles: Museum of Cultural History, University of California.

PAXSON, B. 1983. Mammy Water: New World Origins? *Baessler-Archiv, Neue Folge,* 31: 407-445.

PITMAN, J. 2000. Artistic Licence Jay Jopling's Expanding Vision for Britart. *The Times Magazine.* April 15 issue, pp.38-44.

ROSCHENSCHALER, U. 1998. Honoring Ejagham Women. *African Arts.* 31:2, pp. 38-49.

ROY, C. 1993. New Acquisitions: The University of Iowa Museum of Art. *African Arts.* 26:2, pp. 78-9.

RUSH, D. 1999. Eternal Potential Chromolithographs in Vodunland. *African Arts.* 32:4, pp. 60-75.

SALMONS, J. 1977. Mammy Wata. *African Arts.* 10:3, pp. 8-1; see also front cover.

SALMONS, J. 1981. Fat is Beautiful. *Art Links,* Sept. issue, pp. 22-5.

VOGEL, S. and EBONG I. 1991. *Africa Explores 20th Century African Art.* New York: Center for African Art.

WITTMER, M. and ARNETT, W. 1978. *Three Rivers of Nigeria.* Atlanta: High Museum of Art.

Agents of Order and Disorder: Kongo Minkisi

Hein Vanhee

At the late nineteenth-century international expositions fanciful displays of selected 'primitive' objects and curiosities backed up the celebrations of the great western civilising mission in Africa. The first explorations into the African interior had, in the words of de Haulleville (1910: 225), opened up for Europeans 'an immense horizon for moral, material and social activity' and it was the task of the first ethnographic museums to fill visitors with this 'most noble passion.' The advance of colonisation and exploitation of the conquered African lands brought a whole range of more and less systematic studies of African societies. The key to understanding Africa was to rationalise it as a jigsaw of 'tribes' each having their own distinct customs and material culture production. This piecing together of 'Africa' with material objects in ethnographic museums contributed in an important way to the domestication of an unknown world (Schildkrout & Keim 1998: 31). The development of modern anthropology after the Second World War marked an important step towards correcting some of the ethnocentric biases of the first intellectual engagements. However, the way of composing 'Africa' with material objects in an ethnographic museum changed only very slowly. Most often the objects were left to speak for themselves and preference was given to visually strong material and to the pretty anecdote. Collectors and curators shared a general sense of what should not be missed in order to be 'complete' and this in large measure determined their collecting and buying policies.[1] Besides Benin bronzes, Senufo masks, Kuba royal art objects, Luba sculpture, etc., a number of Lower Congo 'fetishes' were among the indispensable items.

This chapter discusses indigenous theory about the Lower Congo 'fetishes,' nowadays most often labelled 'power figures' in museums, but best referred to as *minkisi*,[2] a Kikongo term that has no equivalent in European languages (MacGaffey 1993: 21). Though aspects of the philosophy behind *minkisi* and elements of their visual appearance can be found in other parts of Central Africa, we will focus on *Kongo*, being the homeland of Kikongo-speakers and an area covering part of northern Angola, Lower Congo-Kinshasa,

Figure 2: The
worshipping of
idols
(Stanley 1885: 128).

Cabinda and part of Lower Congo-Brazzaville. The first Kongo *minkisi* entered western private and museum collections around 1900. They were mostly *minkisi* of the *nkondi* or *khonde* type: tall standing anthropomorphic wooden statues having numerous nails and blades studded in them and a large medicine packet on the belly.[3] Their naturalistic features, their threatening pose and outfit, and the related scraps of narratives noted in the margin of accession records made them dovetail with the paradigmatic western idea of the African 'fetish'. The anthropomorphic fetish figure indeed epitomised the African's irrational propensity to personify and worship material objects arbitrarily composed of worthless materials and thus motivated very well the European 'humanitarian' task to lead Africans to civilisation. The African collection of the Horniman Museum in London illustrates well this collecting and exhibiting of 'Africa' by a wealthy family in the beginning of the twentieth century. Actually five anthropomorphic *nkisi* figures and one zoomorphic piece are on display while at least another four are kept in the storerooms. As with most collections of *minkisi* there is no information about where, when and by whom they were collected, let alone how they were called and what they were used for. However, by comparing them with *minkisi* from better documented collections we may retrieve something of the identity they lost while making their way to Britain where they first became 'fetishes' and later 'traditional African Art.'

A drawing in Stanley's 1885 account of his explorations in Central Africa, portraying a man worshipping a *nkisi* figure, illustrates well the western construct of the 'African fetish' as an object of worship (fig. 2).[4] Wyatt MacGaffey examined the relation of the fetish idea to the Kongo reality of *minkisi* and pointed out that even though in Kongo theory *minkisi* were more than just material objects, no worship, prayer or adulation was offered to them (MacGaffey 1994: 126). The interpretation of *minkisi* as idols and other misconceptions continued to frame ethnographic descriptions of Kongo culture until a few scholars in the 1970s discovered and started studying a forgotten but rich archive of indigenous texts dating from the second decade of the twentieth century (Janzen 1972, Janzen & MacGaffey 1974a, Dupré 1975). Most of the texts had been produced in response to a detailed ethnographic questionnaire distributed by the protestant missionary Karl Edvard Laman among literate Kongo teachers and catechists. Laman collected up to ten thousand manuscript pages dealing with every aspect of Kongo culture, including *minkisi*, and with a geographical focus on Manianga north of the Congo River, though some of his collaborators worked in northern and eastern Mayombe and south of the river too (MacGaffey 1991: 1-2).[5] Laman did not only collect texts but also an important collection of objects, which was sent to the Swedish Ethnographic Museum in Stockholm. While most ethnographic museums indeed have a number of Kongo *minkisi* in their African section, the Laman *minkisi* constitute one of perhaps three collections which are exceptionally well documented and therefore of great anthropological and historical interest. The Laman collection has been studied in detail by Wyatt MacGaffey who established correspondences between Kikongo texts describing specific *minkisi* and actual objects in the collection (MacGaffey 1991).

In this chapter I focus on two other well documented collections of *minkisi* that were built at Catholic mission stations in Mayombe, an area located to the west of where Laman was working.[6] During recent research I conducted in mission archives in Italy and in Congo-Kinshasa, I studied a related collection of Kiyombe notes and texts, holding important information on the composition, the uses and functions of *minkisi*. Part of this material originated simultaneously with the Laman material, however quite independently from it. The other part dates from the 1930s and adds an important historical dimension to the study of twentieth-century Kongo culture.

Missionaries and minkisi

It was not before 1895 that the engineers of the Congo Free State began to show an interest in the immediate interior lands of the capital city of Boma. The first explorations and studies in preparation of the agricultural colonisation of Mayombe date from 1896. As fearless and efficient agents of Leopold's policy of occupation, Catholic Scheut missionaries founded in 1899 their first mission post in Mayombe at Kangu, 90 km north of Boma.[7] For seven years Kangu was the only catholic mission station in Mayombe and also later it would remain a major missionary centre. A photograph published in a journal of the Scheutists in 1902 shows a small collection of 'idols given to the missionaries by the newly converted' (fig. 3).[8] As missionary activity in Mayombe in 1902 still concentrated merely on the immediate vicinity of the Scheut mission, all objects shown must have come out of the villages around Kangu. We don't know whether these objects ended up in an unknown Western collection or rather in the flames, as was the destiny of most *minkisi* abandoned by converts. When from 1911 onward the Scheut mission of Kangu received an annual sum of money from the colonial administration with the request to collect and buy 'ethnographic objects,' missionaries became less

Figure 3: Minkisi brought to the mission of Kangu (Missiën in China en Congo, November 1902 – Reproduced with permission).

inclined to burn whatever smelled like fetishism or superstition.[9]

The aim of the government was to encourage the further development of the collections of the Congo Museum of Tervuren and in 1914 an important collection of *minkisi* left Kangu with this final destination. Though a number of 'masterpieces' from this specific collection have been exhibited the world over and published a number of times, their true identity and history – as for most ethnographic objects – remained obscure. When the collection arrived in Tervuren after the First World War in 1919,[10] it was accompanied by 23 typewritten pages in French, giving the names of all *minkisi* and further information about the 'diseases sent by each of the fetishes.'[11] This anonymous typescript was mentioned by Maes (1935: 5) in a first general study of Kongo *minkisi*, but the information was treated carelessly and his numerous mistakes were unfortunately taken over by many later writers. A careful reading of the document reveals that it contains the answers to a number of questions and eventually the original Kiyombe manuscript was found back in the archives of the Scheut missionaries in Rome. It appeared that the original Kiyombe text was written by Aloïs Tembo, a young man working as a catechist at the mission of Kangu. Aloïs Tembo had couched local knowledge about *minkisi* into a detailed text whose structure clearly derived from a missionary questionnaire. For example, under the heading 'taboos of the *minkisi*' we read:

> *But I cannot give all the taboos that the fetish priests and the people have to observe towards the fetishes because they are too many in this region, every fetish has his minor and major taboos.*[12]

Tembo was an important informant of Leo Bittremieux and Louis De Clercq, two missionaries who wrote extensively on Yombe culture. We know from his own letters that Father De Clercq commissioned Aloïs Tembo to write down what he knew about the *minkisi* collected at the mission.[13] Afterwards one of the missionaries apparently translated part of Tembo's notes into French. The Kiyombe original shows that after the first 69 objects left Kangu in 1914, the Scheut missionaries went on collecting *minkisi*. Aloïs Tembo carefully completed his notebook on *minkisi* listing up to 180 items. What happened to the objects that did not leave Kangu in 1914 is unclear though it is possible that a number of them became part of the later established '*Musée des Fétiches*' at Kangu.

In the 1930s Scheut counted among its missionaries in Mayombe another few ethnographers who brought together a remarkable collection of *minkisi* at the mission of Kangu, with the occasional help given by doctors from the local hospital. Meanwhile catechists, teachers, and students were occasionally asked to answer questions about *nkisi* cults, chiefship, clan histories, witchcraft beliefs and family life. The era of the exciting ethnographic discoveries had by then somehow passed and as Scheut missionaries were working in relative isolation, nothing of this material was ever published. Together with a small collection of notes by Scheut missionaries, the original Kiyombe notebooks still rest at the mission of Kangu. By the 1950s the 'Museum of Fetishes' had nevertheless become an attraction for the passing tourist.[14] Unfortunately in 1973 the museum was looted and most objects were lost. Two documents, however, were found back in the archives of Kangu, giving the indigenous name for each *nkisi*, details about their uses and functions and even occasional information about where and when the pieces had been collected. More documentation about the objects is found in the Kiyombe notebooks, which give us an idea of the importance of *minkisi* in the organisation of Yombe society after 35 years of missionary activity.

What are minkisi?

According to Kongo theory, *minkisi* consist of a material container, activating 'medicines' or *bilongo* and a named ancestor or spirit from the world of the dead for which the container serves as a habitat. They could do things that ordinary people could not, like fighting witches and healing, but only at the command of the priest or *nganga* who operated on behalf of individual clients. *Minkisi* were morally ambiguous as the nature and direction of their actions depended largely on the intentions of those who paid the *nganga*. The material container of the *nkisi* could be a wooden anthropomorphic or zoomorphic statue, as with most specimens now in western collections. Perhaps more often *minkisi* were composed in a basket, a bag, a ceramic pot, a calabash, a case or a bottle. Most *minkisi* were made of several more and less portable objects, which were all considered part of the material apparatus of the *nkisi* cult. Commenting on a *nkisi* called *Mpanzu Mbongo*, collected at the mission of Kangu shortly before 1913, Aloïs Tembo wrote:

Figure 4: Nkisi Matombe, Kangu, December 1999. (Photograph: Hein Vanhee).

> *This fetish takes various shapes. He lives in a case, in a small parcel, in a bag, in a statue or still in other guises. In addition he has many musical instruments and lots of clothes but this one is the statue. Mbongo gives [its owner] the ability to discover hidden things among the people.*[15]

Mambuku Mongo was a *nkisi* used for divination; the 1913 collection of Kangu held two of them: an anthropomorphic statue and a basket filled with 'medicines'. Another *nkisi* contained in a basket is *nkisi Matombe* (fig. 4), which was formerly used for the ritual investiture of chiefs of the Phudi-clan around Kangu and was still found *in situ* in 1999. Maes (1935: 9) thought that 'Kongo fetishes' fell into four classes according to morphology and function. He classified the statue of *Mambuku Mongo* in the '*mpezo* class' which supposedly consisted of 'nail fetishes' that had white clay in the bulge on their belly and feathers in their headdress. Together with the '*khonde* fetishes' they chased wrongdoers and witches, but whereas a *khonde* killed its victims, a *mpezo* only made them ill. The two other categories Maes distinguished were called '*na moganga,*' for healing, and '*mbula,*' for protection against witches (Maes 1935: 22-34). Maes' arbitrary division was taken over by Olbrechts (1946: 44) in his effort to map out artistic production in the Belgian colony following a one-tribe-one-style logic, and in later work by connoisseurs of Kongo art.[16] The main problem with these classifications is that they take for granted certain contrasts that do not exist in Kongo thought (Janzen & MacGaffey 1974b: 87). Divination to detect witches, fighting them, healing victims of witchcraft and further protecting them are the main functions of *minkisi* but cannot be considered as separate. Witches were supposed to 'eat' or 'imprison' the soul of their victim leaving behind an empty body that would become ill and die if the witch could not be forced in time to release its prey. As the BaKongo understood it - and still understand - to heal is to succeed in dispelling or killing the witch who causes the illness, after which a successful recovery and good health will remain dependent on a continued efficient protection against witches. Paul Mpanzu from Kavuzi wrote in 1934:

> *Our ancestors protected their body by composing nkisi Nsungu, by making a statue and taking horns of animals, gunpowder and brilliant stones. But one has to ware Nsungu at ribs height, take the statues and put them under the bed, dig a few pits by the door and put the horns in. When the witch arrives at night or during the day, Nsungu and the horns will shoot! That is what protects the human body as not to be eaten quickly by the witches.*[17]

BaKongo did recognise certain groups or families of *minkisi* who more or less fulfilled the same functions or whose empowering spirits were related in Kongo myth. *Nkisi Nsungu* for example clearly belonged to the family of *zinduda* (sing. *nduda*) or *minkisi* who protected their owner against the (mostly nocturnal) attacks by witches. Other well known *zinduda* from Kangu as listed by Tembo were *Pfula Nkombe, Muana Mvaku, Kongo, Manuana, Mbambi zi Luenda, Nzumbi, Tiete* and *Kutu Matu*. Informants like Aloïs Tembo, when asked by European ethnographers to sort out a collection of *minkisi* would put these together and distinguish them from, for example, *minkisi* for hunting. It is clear, however, that these loose categories overlapped and that many *minkisi* fitted in more than one group. A provisional conclusion could be that it is not the outward shape - statue, basket, bag or bottle - of a *nkisi* that determined its identity. Each *nkisi* was known by its proper name, which stood for a particular history of origin, the complex procedures of its composition and the services it rendered to its owner or to the local community. The total number of *minkisi* known in a given region could be read as an inventory of the most current problems and afflictions (MacGaffey 1993). Africanists nowadays no longer adhere to the tired ethnic labels and the idea of supposedly corresponding distinct ethnic styles. In reality a ritual specialist or *nganga* wanting to compose a *nkisi* would buy his material from a local sculptor or from a passing trader, or he would go to an established atelier.[18] The 1902 photograph of a small collection of *minkisi* allegedly abandoned by the newly converted of the mission of Kangu is illuminating in this regard. As we know that all these objects were collected in the immediate vicinity of Kangu, they can hardly be assigned to different 'tribes.' Perhaps more than half of the total number of figurative *minkisi* now preserved in western collections were collected in Kakongo and Mayombe. One explanation for this is the fact that this area was the most thoroughly colonised part of Lower Congo and another one is no doubt the western predilection for realism, characteristic of the sculpture of this region.

The composition of minkisi

The statue, basket or bag chosen by the priest or *nganga* remained 'empty' and powerless as long as he or she did not properly add the activating medicines or *bilongo*. According to Father Van Leuven (1903: 198) BaKongo took 'as protective devices against illnesses and all kinds of mischance gunpowder, leaves, stones, driftwood, heads of snakes, beaks and paws of birds, hair from the tail of an animal, eggshells, clay, bark or whatever you can imagine!' The composition of *minkisi* indeed seemed absurd but only so to those who did not understand the principles governing the selection of materials, which are metaphor and metonymy (MacGaffey 1994: 126). Probably all *minkisi* contained white clay from riverbeds and earth taken from graves, which metonymically adduced the presence and power of the dead in the *nkisi*. Sometimes hair and nails of a deceased *nganga* or relics from a notorious witch were incorporated:

> When [the people] see that someone has died because of [the poison ordeal] khasa, then they
> will go and burn [the corpse] at the foot of a liana. The entire body burns up, but not the
> malicious power [of the witch]. They will look and take this power with them and conserve it.
> This is what they will use for their nkisi Dipomba.[19]

Other elements were used because they evoked linguistic or visual associations with the sort of capacities and skills the *nkisi* and the *nganga* were expected to have. One of Laman's informants listed a number of ingredients usually employed because their name suggested, by a play on words, the attributes and functions of the *nkisi*. Thus a *luyala* fruit was taken so that the *nkisi* would rule (*yaala*), another fruit called *nkandikila* so that the *nkisi* would interdict (*kandika*) and *lutete* (gourd seed) so that it would cut down (*teta*), just to name a few examples (MacGaffey 1993: 62). Other ingredients were included because of the visual metaphor they conjured up. The basket of *Mambuku Mongo* (fig.5), one of the major *minkisi* from around Kangu, contained among many other 'medicines' the beak of a bird (*koto ki phata*) known for its skill to defend itself against aggressors and a cocoon made from little twigs (*ntiaba khuni*) by a short green hairy

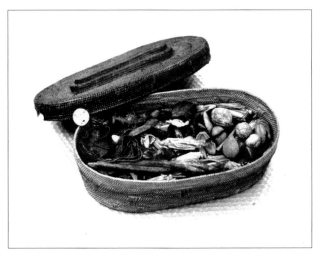

Figure 5: Basket of nkisi Mambuku Mongo. Collected at the mission of Kangu before 1913 (Photograph: RMCA Tervuren, nr. 22472).

caterpillar (*kitsa*).[20] Such ingredients stated metaphorically the skills and intelligence *Mambuku Mongo* had to command to be able to do its job properly. Still other ingredients were incorporated or added to the exterior because they provoked curiosity and astonishment and thus lended authority to the rituals led by the *nganga* (MacGaffey 1988: 196). This is no doubt the reason why we find pieces of dark fossilised resin in *Mambuku Mongo*'s basket. Bittremieux (1913: 91) explained how lightning was conceived as a celestial dog that urinated on earth leaving behind a kind of foam at the foot of a palm tree, which stiffened to a dark glasslike substance. This was called *ndingi* or 'piss of lightning' and considered as a precious ingredient for *minkisi*. Some of the *nkisi* statues were defective and missed an arm or leg. This was done, one of Laman's informants wrote, 'so that if [the *nkisi*] attacks someone he will become like the *nkisi* itself,' and thus worked as a strong visual metaphor.[21] The realistic elaboration, particularly of the head, and the threatening pose of many anthropomorphic *minkisi* were aimed at commanding attention and respect. 'European influence' is easily put forward as an explanation for the realism characteristic of Kongo sculpture. Yet one can hardly assume that sculptors would have adapted to European taste since late nineteenth-century *minkisi* certainly were not made for a European market. *Minkisi* with apparent European features (clothing) did not represent Europeans but rather included by metonymy some of the powers of the whites that were seen as coming from the other world.[22] To that effect also scissors and chains were used in *minkisi*, and they were sometimes sprinkled with gin or whisky (*malavu ku Phutu*).[23]

The animating spirit

The ritual process of properly arranging a whole series of ingredients or *bilongo* in the chosen material container was accompanied by much singing and music. During this ceremony a spirit from the world of the dead moved into the material container. This could be an ancestor known by name, who after having lived for a while in the other world decided to renew his engagement with his living kin and become a *nkisi*. The ancestral being inhabiting the *nkisi* could also be more abstract and designated as a *simbi* or *khita* 'nature spirit' who lived in rivers and pools but also on the land in massive rocks and in the forest. Marie-Claude Dupré (1975: 13), looking at the data collected by Laman, has worked out a classification of *minkisi* according to the original abode of the animating spirit, being in the water, on the land or in the sky. Interesting to note is that though we have some very informative accounts of how *minkisi* were composed, myths of origin of major *minkisi* are likely to reverse the direction of the originating impulse (MacGaffey 1994: 126). The story often goes that it was the animating ancestor or spirit who presented the object to become *nkisi* to its eventual owner:

> *Kingu Masunda [is] a nkisi from above. When he wants to, he will fall, after he has chosen the region and the village where he will fall, and the man who will own him. So on a day with heavy rains, he falls on the courtyard, close to the house, or behind the house. Then the man he has chosen will pick him up and keep him.*[24]

> *When somebody is ill and the nganga explains that it is a subterranean nkisi that is making him ill then one will call for the nganga whose job it is to dig up subterranean minkisi, to dig*

up the nkisi. When the nganga arrives he will go to sleep in order to learn in a dream where the hidden nkisi is located: either in the village, or in the forest, or at the entrance of the village, or somewhere else. The next morning he will go and sniff (konga) [to know] where the nkisi is. He takes his [own] nkisi in his hand and his rattle, which is a [metal] bell or a wooden bell, or a small gourd with pebbles in. When he has searched and found where the nkisi is then he says 'dig here!' and he starts digging together with his apprentices. When they uncover and see the nkisi, then it is usually a beautiful stone, which glitters and shines. They bind him in a piece of cloth or in a raphia fabric. The minkisi which are under the ground are the bottle of Ntonzi, in which they have hidden sleeping sickness so that the entire village will be infected with it [and] another one is Khita, a beautiful stone.[25]

Descriptions left by indigenous writers from Mayombe seem to confirm MacGaffey's (1990: 50) conclusions that *minkisi* basically operated in two cosmological domains and could be sorted in those of 'the above' and those of 'the below,' though a number of them were active in both spheres. *Minkisi* of 'the above' were associated with violent destructive action and conditions of the upper part of the body. *Minkisi* of 'the below' with carefully observing a number of prescriptions and taboos, in order to avoid contracting one of the diseases they controlled, being mainly skin diseases and others affecting the lower part of the body.

The most important *nkisi* of this last group in Mayombe was *Mbenza*. When a man for the first time in his life had engendered a child, he was initiated in the cult of *Mbenza*. The ceremony took place on a special site in the forest and involved marking the body with white clay (*phezo*) and red earth (*ngunzi*), accompanied by music and dancing. One form of chiefship was also initiated this way, whereby the eventual chief would have to stand on a stone painted with white *phezo*. Those who had been initiated to *Mbenza* could eat previously forbidden food like the pangolin (*khaka*) and the civet (*nzobo*) but had to observe a new set of prescription and taboos, mostly to do with sex regulations. *Mbenza* punished those who violated its rules with swellings of the belly and the limbs (*khufu, bioma*).[26] The Kiyombe notebooks from Kangu make it clear that in the 1930s *Mbenza* was still important. Other names for Mbenza or closely related *minkisi* were *Lubingu, Nsavu, Mbumba, Tsiesi Phungu* and *Bunzi*.[27] Another family of *minkisi* of 'the below' were those that protected pregnancies and young children. They received considerable attention from catholic missionaries whose activities in the early period concentrated on children. The practice was referred to as *loba muana*, 'to devote a child [to a protective *nkisi*],' and required accepting a number of rules, some for the mother, others for the child. Vincent Malonda noted in 1933:

The minkisi often used for the protection of children in this part of the world are the following: Malonda, Mvumbi, Mbadu, Makunya, Muaka, Umba, Kiusi, Nsasi, Ntedika, Nsulu, Kobo, Nkembi, Nsengidi mbele, Nti yaka [...]. The prescriptions for nkisi Umba are: a mother who has a child devoted [to nkisi Umba] has to avoid wearing an apron so that the child will not die. On the contrary, she has to take a bag or a blanket, and to cover her head she has to use a towel. A goat may not [be allowed to] enter the house where a child devoted [to nkisi Umba] lives in order that [the child] would not die. A cock may not [be allowed to] crow under the shelter of a house where a child devoted [to nkisi Umba] lives in order that he will not die.[28]

The destructive powers of minkisi

Violent *minkisi* associated with the sky and celestial waters and with diseases of the upper part of the body are particularly those belonging to the *khonde* or *nkondi* family. Many of these are made of a wooden statue and readily recognisable by the nails, blades, screws and other hardware driven in them. Probably all the *minkisi* on display in the Horniman museum belong to this group (fig. 6). In trying to explain the practice of hammering nails into wooden statues manifold speculations have been put forward: nailing *nkisi* figures would heal corresponding affected parts of the body (Gilmont 1899: 186), or would remind the *khonde* of a favour asked, or was done merely to improve the aesthetic quality of the statue (Struyf 1910: 369). The true meaning of this ritual, however, lies in the expression *koma minloko* or *koma mianda* which means to curse an unknown thief or witch by a *nkisi*, to incite the *nkisi* so that it will search the guilty thief or witch and make him ill or kill him. This stirring up of a *nkisi* could be done in different ways. Bittremieux (1910: 288) described how a man who had been robbed went the next morning to *nkisi Khonde Mamba*:

While he was squatting before the horrible wooden statue complete with a mirror and nails, he hammered a nail into the body and mumbled silently but determined: "Ah Khonde Mamba, listen carefully! A thief has stolen my jar! Will he sell it? Will he use it himself? Kill him, hit him, chop him into pieces! Put him in the fire!

Not all *minkisi* of the *khonde* type, however, were nailed or had an anthropomorphic statue that could be nailed (MacGaffey 1990: 54). Another common way to incite the *nkisi* was by shaking and insulting, or by blowing up quantities of gunpowder, as was done in front of *nkisi Maluangu*. People would take the *khonde* and carry him around the village square while crying out loud his name and cursing the witches so that he would make them ill. They would pour out *khonde* potions so that those who walked over it would die. One way to help the *khonde* find the guilty witch or thief was, for example, by putting some of the stolen palm nuts in the *nkisi*. Or as Armand Phongi described:

When somebody dies, the relatives (and mostly the women) take scraps of the clothes of the deceased and go with this to a region where there is a powerful nkisi, and then they go to another nkisi and attach a rag of the clothes until everything is used up.[29]

Minkisi of the *khonde* type were nightly hunters whom one activated in various ways against thieves and witches. In any region people were familiar with a number of them. From the two Kangu collections and the related notebooks of Aloïs Tembo (1913) and Armand Phongi (1934), we know that some 36 *minkisi* of the *khonde* type were known by name in central Mayombe. Some of them were well known over a larger region and may have been older, like *Mabiala ma Ndembe, Kozo, Makwende, Mavungu, Mungundu* or *Mbola*. One of

Figure 6: Standing anthropomophic nkisi of khonde type. Collected in Mayombe, early 20th century.
(Photograph: Horniman Museum 33.123, Heini Schneebeli).

the oldest known *minkisi* is perhaps *Mbumba Kindongo*, first described by Luca da Caltanisetta in 1697 as the central shrine in communal rituals to cope with an epidemic (Thornton 1983: 61). *Mbumba Kindongo* was still known in Kinkenge in the early twentieth century (MacGaffey 1991: 179). Other *minkisi* may have been of a later date, like *nkisi Nguima* which originated in French Congo and swept over Mayombe first between 1914 and 1918, and later again in 1923-1926. *Nguima* provided protection against diseases and against aging, and the *nganga* of *nkisi Nguima* could be invited by a chief to clear the village of witches.[30]

Agents of order and disorder

Displays of *minkisi* in ethnographic museums can be misleading. Recently curators have made attempts to replace the old labels saying 'Congo fetish' by more accurate ones, sometimes providing the vernacular name and a few lines about local usage and meaning. However, the careless visitor is still given the impression that he or she looks at a remote Africa, at the material relics of a 'traditional African society.' Not confined to the limitations imposed by too much ethnographic information, the public is left entirely free to imagine his or her 'Africa.' Since early collectors generally did not bother to make further inquiries about their treasures, the most essential information is usually missing from the museum's accession records. We do have an idea, however, about the general circumstances in which Kongo *minkisi* were either taken away by force or abandoned by BaKongo themselves. Yet presenting them as 'African art' conceals these complex processes by which objects left their supposedly traditional setting to end up in museum showcases. Rightly there is a growing body of opinion that it will be important in the future to integrate something of the 'often unsettling history of collecting' in our representations of Africa through material objects (Schildkrout and Keim 1998: 31). The documentary value of *minkisi* lies perhaps herein: rather than illustrating a traditional past, they document by their dislocation the gradual establishment of colonial rule and African responses to these developments. They are not just discarded relics but they actively participated in the transformation of Kongo society.

The first Kongo *minkisi* were brought to Europe by merchants who traded at Landana and Cabinda and in the estuary of the Congo River in the ports of Boma, Katala, Ponta da Lenha, Malela and Banana. Arnold Ridyard, one of these merchants who were fascinated by the dramatic 'nail fetishes,' wrote in a letter to a friend:

> *When bringing two of the fetishes from shore sometime back, there was a body of men working on the road where my men and I had to pass. On seeing the fetishes, one of them called out Cawso [Kozo], Coangi! and they immediately stopped work and took off their caps until we had passed. The Portuguese and French governments are taking these fetishes away by force as they stop the trade of the country.*[31]

Nkisi Kozo in the form of a double-headed dog was one of the major *minkisi* in Mayombe and the Congo estuary in the beginning of the twentieth century. *Kozo* was stirred up against a thief or a witch by hammering a nail into the statue after which the *nkisi* would go and punish the guilty by making him or her mad. The double-headed dog on display in the Horniman Museum is almost certainly an exemplar of *nkisi Kozo*. The efforts of the French and Portuguese to destroy *minkisi,* mentioned by Ridyard, were paralleled in king Leopold's Congo. After his description of a number of *minkisi* collected at the mission of Kangu in 1902, Father Van Leuven remarked that 'these horrors and hideous customs' fortunately had become restricted to the more remote areas of the interior because, 'they will no longer venture to commit those cruelties where Europeans are, as they know this would cost them dearly' (Van Leuven 1903: 199). Van Leuven who merely saw the work of the devil obviously did not understand how *minkisi* could be an effective instrument in the hands of a local indigenous elite to control commerce. A set of strict rules governed trade in Kongo. Important commercial agreements between chiefs who controlled trade routes and others who checked markets were often sealed with an oath before a *nkisi,* on the assumption that the *nkisi* would severely punish those who dared to break the rules. One well-documented example is *nkisi Lulendo* who was notorious in the 1880s in the region of modern Luozi. Lunungu, one of Laman's collaborators who recorded some information about *Lulendo,* noted that it was not used for healing people but for chiefship, and that its power was to execute people for breaking market rules. The offender would be physically executed by the chief but the chief could only do so because of the extraordinary powers he obtained from *nkisi Lulendo.* After the chief stroke the victim with the little knife of *Lulendo* on the forehead, others would throw him alive in a hole and drive a lance through his body (MacGaffey 1987: 342). A similar ritual endorsement of an agreement was recorded from Boma where in 1873 a slave was decapitated in the marketplace, his cranium speared on a long lance and the sacrificial knife afterwards planted in the ground, all in order to state clearly the rules set out and the consequences of any violation (Bontinck 1979: 310). Decisions affecting commercial transactions in the interior and on lesser markets were no doubt also occasionally sealed with an oath before a *nkisi.* It is not surprising therefore that in the 1890s Europeans who were trying to take over and monopolise trade, found *minkisi* an obstacle to their projects and so ordered that they should be destroyed.

In their crusade against *minkisi* colonial agents and entrepreneurs were greatly helped by the missionaries. This happened in two ways: instances whereby missionaries themselves took away *minkisi* 'by force' are surely documented, but many more objects were willingly destroyed by their converts. The Scheut missionary and ethnographer Bittremieux, for example, described how he destroyed with his own hands the material relics of the *Bunzi* cult near the mission of Muanda (Bittremieux 1930). Such incidents, however, seem to have been rather rare. Most *minkisi* were burnt by BaKongo themselves, however often in response to the mission's appeal. Native catechists made bonfires of 'pagan objects' far out of sight of the missionaries. It is not our aim here to discuss the multiple and complex motivations of early converts, but lots of *minkisi* were discarded by BaKongo complying with the new prescriptions of the Christian church. A number of *minkisi* of the 1930s-40s collection of the mission of Kangu were abandoned by individuals after their conversion to Christianity or after recovering from an illness thanks to a missionary or a European doctor.[32]

Not only the missions effected the mass destruction of *minkisi.* In the early 1920s, heaps of ritual objects were destroyed in order to meet the demands of the new prophetic movement led by Simon Kimbangu and his followers. Kimbanguism was never as strong in Mayombe as elsewhere in Lower Congo, but other cults on a lesser scale that equally demanded the destruction of all *minkisi* had popped up almost every other year since

Figure 7: Nkisi made from two bottles with an angel figure on top of it, Kangu, December 1999.
(Photograph: Hein Vanhee).

the beginning of European penetration in the interior. 'In the history of fetishism,' wrote a Scheut missionary,[33] 'there is a quite spectacular manifestation that revives from time to time: a fetish that is said to be able to make all witches disappear.' *Nduku Bakisi* was the first of this sort of *minkisi* mentioned in the mission records as a cult in which most people around Kangu in 1898 engaged, one year before the foundation of the mission of Kangu. The journal of the mission of Kangu in 1915 speaks of a general discarding of *minkisi* by the people,[34] and elsewhere we read that in 1915-16 all the *nkisi*-stones of the cult of the earth spirit and of chiefship were excavated and thrown away with the approval of the chiefs.[35] This appears to have been the result of the prescriptions that *nkisi Nguima* imposed on those who participated in purification rites. These typically included music and dancing, and a potion prepared by the *nganga* from which all members of the local community had to drink in order to be cleared from witchcraft. *Nguima* was followed by *nkisi Babongo* in 1928 and *Kalatanga* in 1929, and in 1936 everybody had to participate in a ceremony called *Tsusu Mayangi*, whereby all ate from a chicken (*tsusu*) in order to be saved.[36] Maia Green (1997: 338-39) has argued convincingly how such witchcraft suppression movements, as found all over Sub-Saharan Africa, were in essence political undertakings staged on behalf of a chief in order to reassert control over a local community or by others challenging established authorities. Such movements in Lower Congo typically demanded the breaking of all rules imposed by other *minkisi* (often including those of Europeans). One Scheut missionary noted that it was especially during the frenzies of *Nguima* that most major *nkisi* statues had been burnt.[37]

'New' *minkisi* arose from time to time and often metaphorically appropriated some of the powers of Europeans in the elaboration of the ritual objects and communal rites. A *nkisi* that recently came out of one of the villages around Kangu shows this clearly. It is made up of two old European gin bottles firmly tied surmounted by a little angel-like figure with a mirror on the belly (fig. 7). We can only guess at the specific use and function of this *nkisi* but obviously the winged angel figure brought some of the white man's magic for disposal by the indigenous ritual specialist. The same is at hand in the activities of the various prayer groups known in Mayombe today. Most popular among young people is the cult devoted to the female Catholic saint Rita whose prayers are thought to be very effective if recited correctly. Initiates need to set up a personal shrine for the saint at home by properly arranging a number of prescribed items, including a crucifix and statuettes of the Virgin Mary, images of Christ and Sainte Rita, candles, rosaries, plastic flowers and more (fig. 8). The powerful prayers that circulate among the initiates address all sorts of problems like passing exams, finding a job, success in love, healing illnesses and protection against witches. The way in which such a shrine is composed and the animating saint invoked, makes these home altars function in much the same way as *minkisi*.

Minkisi provide us with additional source material for the study of the twentieth-century history of relations between Africans and Europeans. By their dislocation some of them mark the advance of western colonisation and the loss or the end of indigenous control over trade and regional politics. *Minkisi* had produced and maintained order in Kongo society but many of them were defeated and taken away by European colonists who by their own means gradually imposed another order, which long before Europeans would fully realise BaKongo got to know as colonialism. Other *minkisi*, however, by their relatively late collection mark both Kongo resistance to colonial domination and an attempt to act on the new order imposed by Europeans. The material from Catholic mission stations in Mayombe shows how in the 1930s and 40s, *minkisi* were still well known and important in the organisation of society on the local level. Certain *minkisi* were revived from time to time and new *minkisi* arose to cope with the constraints of the colonial yoke, however tragically interpreted as the

Figure 8: Personal Shrine for *Sainte Rita,* August 1998.
(Photograph: Hein Vanhee).

consequences of the uncontrolled activity of too many witches. Today BaKongo no longer make *minkisi* in the way they used to do but the underlying principles, however, continue to determine the activities of prayer groups and the preparation of all sorts of amulets and fortune bearers.

Notes

1. The early twentieth-century accession records and the related correspondence in, for example, the American Museum of Natural History in New York or the Royal Museum of Central Africa in Tervuren clearly reveal the sort of exchanges made between museums in order to complete their respective collections.

2. *Nkisi* is the singular, *minkisi* the plural. *Kongo* spelled with a *K* distinguishes that part of West Central Africa inhabited by the *BaKongo* who all speak local dialects of *KiKongo* and directly or indirectly trace their common history back to the former Kongo Kingdom. People in Mayombe refer to their language (dialect) as *Kiyombe*.

3. '*Nkondi*' in central Kikongo as found in the Laman material; sources from Mayombe consistently give '*khonde*' which corresponds to the Kiyombe dialect. My orthography of Kiyombe terms follows contemporary Yombe conventions - being a product of Catholic missionary teachings.

4. The otherness of the African worshipper is extra underlined by his pose, which is more characteristic of Islam than of western

Christian piety (see Stanley 1885: 128).

5. This unique documentation is now preserved in the National Archives in Stockholm.

6. The term 'Mayombe' as used by the Congolese today denotes a forested area stretching out from Lukula north of Boma well into Congo-Brazzaville. East of Lukula is called 'Kakongo,' reminiscent of the small nineteenth-century Kakongo 'kingdom.'

7. Missionaries of the 'Congregation of the Immaculate Heart of Mary' or 'CICM' better known as 'Missionaries of *Scheut*', a place in Anderlecht in the vicinity of Brussels.

8. *Missiën in China en Congo*, November 1902. All objects on the table were most likely collected in the immediate neighbourhood of the mission of Kangu.

9. Letter from Director of *Direction de l'Industrie et du Commerce*, Mr. V. Ernst to Provincial Superior of CICM at Kangu, Boma, 8-05-1911; Central Archives of CICM, Rome, Fol. O.II.a.11.3.

10. The collection arrived in Tervuren on 4-07-1919 after being stored during the First World War in the depots of the British Museum, see copies of letters by Mr. Fuchs, General Governor at Boma, to Mr. Renkin, Minister of the Colonies, in archives Royal Museum for Central Africa (RMCA), Tervuren, section of Ethnography, *D.E.* 380. The objects were registered and given ID-numbers beginning with 224*xx*, and their origin, the Scheut mission of Kangu in Mayombe, was never retrieved.

11. RMCA, section Ethnography, *D.E.* 380.

12. Central archives CICM, Rome, Fol. Z.III.d.5.19. Aloïs Tembo is today still remembered as one of the first converts of the village of Kiyombo Kangu. He died young at the age of perhaps 22. His 'History of Kangu' was published in the Kiyombe mission journal *Tsungi Mona* in 1924 and translated by L. Bittremieux in the journal *Congo* (1924).

13. Central archives CICM, Rome, Fol. Z.III.7.a.

14. The museum was mentioned by Scohy (1952: 84-89) and in *Congo Belge et Ruanda-Urundi: Guide du Voyageur* (Bruxelles 1958: 367).

15. Aloïs Tembo from Kangu, '*Bakisi ba Mayombe*,' 1913; Central archives CICM, Rome, Fol. Z.III.d.5.19.

16. See the work of Z. Volavka, R. Lehuard and M. L. Felix.

17. Paul Mpanzu from Kavuzi, 1-12-1934; replies to a questionnaire about witchcraft, archives CICM, Kangu, D.R.C., Fol. IV.1.82.

18. People nowadays still remember some of these ateliers that prospered in the north of Mayombe, and they may well mean the 'Chiloango River workshop' discussed by Bassani (1977).

19. A. Masevo, '*Biuvu bi vutula kudi Tata* Jules,' 1940s; Archives CICM, Kangu (D.R.C.).

20. '*Bilongo bi Nkisi Mambuku Mongo*,' anonymous manuscript, probably 1930s; archives CICM, Kangu (D.R.C.), Fol. IV.1.82. *Ntiaba khuni*, meaning 'cutting firewood,' as an ingredient for *minkisi* was described also by Kionga, one of Laman's collaborators (translated in MacGaffey 1988: 196).

21. Nsemi Isaki from Kingoyi (translated in MacGaffey 1988: 199).

22. One example is *nkisi Makuani* from the Aloïs Tembo collection, wearing a bowlers hat; see RMCA Tervuren, nr. 22482.

23. Gerard Lubamba from Kizu (Mayombe), Nov. 1933; Archives CICM, Kangu (D.R.C.), Fol. IV.1.82.

24. Tembo, '*Bakisi ba Mayombe*.' *Nkisi Kingu Masunda* is nr. 61 in Tembo's list.

25. Armand Phongi from Kavuzi (Mayombe), 1934; Archives CICM, Kangu (D.R.C.), Fol. III.2.726. Armand Phongi was a teacher and the chief catechist at the mission of Vaku in Mayombe (east of Kangu). In 1934 he wrote a 40 pages account of *minkisi* for Father Armand Schermers (cicm). Later he became a local judge in the *Secteur* of Mbavu, Tseke Mbanza Territory and an ally of the Scheut missionaries in the struggle against local rises of Kimbanguism.

26. François Ngoma from Tsinga Kala (Mayombe), 1930s; Archives CICM, Kangu (D.R.C.), Fol. IV.1.83.

27. Constant Mayema from Nzobe (Mayombe), 1930s; Archives CICM, Kangu (D.R.C.), Fol. IV.1.83.

28. Vincent Malonda from Luvu (Mayombe), 1933; Archives CICM, Kangu (D.R.C.), Fol. IV.1.82.

29. Armand Phongi from Kavuzi (Mayombe), 1934; Archives CICM, Kangu (D.R.C.), Fol. III.2.726.

30. Armand Phongi, *Ibid.*

31. Arnold Ridyard was a chief engineer on the Elder Dempster Shipping Line and collected for the Liverpool Museum between 1895 and 1916 around 6500 natural history and ethnography objects from the coastal regions of West and Central Africa. I am indebted to Louise Tythacott for information on the Ridyard collection. See correspondence in the Manchester Museum, quoted by MacGaffey (1993: 42).

32. In April 1945, for example, a woman from Kangu who was healed of epilepsy donated her *nkisi* Mambuku Mongo, together with a chicken, some tobacco, a mat and a bit of money, to the mission; anonymous notes, Archives CICM, Kangu (D.R.C.).

33. 'Collection de Fétiches du Mayombe,' typescript probably by F. Rombouts (cicm), ca. 1960; F. Bontinck Library, Kinshasa. I am indebted to F. Bontinck for a copy of this document.

34. Journal of the mission of Kangu, 28-10-1915; Central archives CICM, Rome, Fol. O.II.d.3.2.5.

35. Notes by L. Van den Bergh; Archives CICM, Kangu, D.R.C., Fol. III.724.

36. 'Fetisjen in Mayombe,' typescript probably by L. Van den Bergh, 1950s; Archives CICM, Kangu, D.R.C., Fol. III.725.

37. 'Collection de fétiches du Mayombe,' ca. 1960.

Bibliography

BASSANI, E. 1977. Kongo Nail Fetishes from the Chiloango River Area. *African Arts*, **10**, 3, 36-40.

BITTREMIEUX, L. 1910. Drie Mayombsche Bezweringen. *Onze Kongo*, **1**, 285-290.

BITTREMIEUX, L. 1913. De Mayombsche Regenboog. *Onze Kongo*, **4**, 83-112.

BITTREMIEUX, L. 1930. Een Heidensche Godsdienst: de Sekte der Basantus. *Congo*, **1**, 1, 44-54.

BONTINCK, F. 1979. Boma Sous les Tshinus. *Zaïre-Afrique*, **135**, 295-314.

DE HAULLEVILLE, A. 1910. Le Musée du Congo Belge à Tervueren. *La Revue Congolaise*, **1**, 2, 206-225.

DUPRÉ, M-C. 1975. Le Système des Forces *Nkisi* Chez les Kongo d'après le Troisième Volume de K. Laman. *Africa*, **45**, 1, 12-28.

GILMONT. 1899. Le Mayombé. *Congo Belge*, **2**, 186.

GREEN, M. 1997. Witchcraft Suppression Practices and Movements: Public Politics and the Logic of Purification. *Comparative Studies in Society and History*, **39**, 2, 319-45.

JANZEN, J. M. 1972. Laman's Kongo Ethnography: Observations on Sources, Methodology, and Theory. *Africa*, **42**, 4, 316-328.

JANZEN, J. and MacGaffey, W. 1974a. *An Anthology of Kongo Religion: Primary Texts from Lower Zaïre.* Lawrence: University of Kansas Press.

JANZEN, J. and MacGaffey, W. 1974b. *Nkisi* Figures of the BaKongo. *African Arts*, 7, 3, 87-89.

MACGAFFEY, W. 1987. Lulendo: the Recovery of a Kongo *Nkisi. Ethnos*, **52**, 3-4, 339-349.

MACGAFFEY, W. 1988. Complexity, Astonishment and Power: The Visual Vocabulary of Kongo *Minkisi. Journal of Southern African Studies*, **14**, 2, 188-203.

MACGAFFEY, W. 1990. The Personhood of Ritual Objects: Kongo *Minkisi. Etnofoor*, **3**, 1, 45-61.

MACGAFFEY, W. 1991. *Art and Healing of the Bakongo Commented by Themselves.* Stockholm: Folkens Museum Etnografiska.

MACGAFFEY, W. 1993. The Eyes of Understanding: Kongo *Minkisi.* In MacGaffey, W. and Harris, M. (eds), *Astonishment & Power*, 21-103. Washington and London: Smithsonian Institution Press, National Museum of African Art.

MACGAFFEY, W. 1994. African Objects and the Idea of Fetish. *Res*, **25**, 123-31.

MAES, J. 1935. Fetischen of Tooverbeelden uit Kongo. In Anon., *Annales du Musée du Congo Belge - Ethnographie*, Série VI, Tome II, Fasc. I.

OLBRECHTS, F. 1946. *Plastiek van Kongo.* Gent: Standaard-Boekhandel.

SCHILDKROUT, E. and KEIM, C. 1998. Objects and Agendas: Re-collecting the Congo. In Schildkrout, E. and Keim, C. (eds), *The Scramble for Art in Central Africa*, 1-36. Cambridge: Cambridge University Press.

SCOHY, A. 1952. *Etapes au Soleil.* Bruxelles: Editions du chat qui pêche.

STANLEY, H. 1885. *Cinq Années au Congo, 1879-1884.* Bruxelles: Institut National de Géographie.

STRUYF, I. 1910. De Godsdienst bij de Bakongo's, VI. Animisme. *Onze Kongo*, **1**, 357-72.

THORNTON, J. 1983. *The Kingdom of Kongo: Civil War and Transition, 1641-1718.* Madison: University of Wisconsin Press.

VAN LEUVEN, W. 1903. De Godsdienst bij de Congolezen. *Missiën in China en Congo*, **15**, 9, 193-99.

'Imina Sangan' or 'Masques à la Mode':

Contemporary

Masquerade in the Dogon Region

Polly Richards

The tradition of masks never changes. It is like the Hogon that remains always in one place'
(Young man's interpretation of Dama songtext 1996).

The Dogon masks currently displayed in the African Worlds Gallery form a collection that is curiously homogeneous. Examples of wooden *sirige* and *sim* masks display a rigid red, black and white uniformity, and in an adjacent case two examples of *waru* (antelope) masks share in their generic form; cuboid heads dissected in two, with long rectangular trenches into which square eyeholes are set.[1] The accompanying video evokes a mythic past and perpetuates a vision of an authentic Africa, at odds with the rapidly evolving world that is more familiar to us.

Behind the scenes of the museum however a recently commissioned collection of masks await fumigation, revealing qualities at odds with the ones on display. Here a *kanaga* mask (fig.1) is surmounted by the same double cross superstructure of the *Sim* mask but its characteristically stark black and white superstructure is in this instance covered with a mass of blue graffiti. Furthermore the 'modern' collection contains a *na* (ox) mask that bears a close resemblance to a real animal in both sculpted and painted form. A fibre *pulloyana* (fulani woman) mask is dyed in a vivid green, its crest and tresses decorated with lottery tickets, and strips of re-cycled sardine cans; and another fibre mask *imina policier* (policeman mask) incorporates a peaked cap into its woven form. Complete with khaki uniform, fake gun and holster this mask could be nothing other than a 20th century phenomenon. So what kind of 'authenticity' could possibly have given rise to this?

Polly Richards

Figure 1: Kanaga mask showing the name and village of the owner and the date of the Dama performance in which it was used. Horniman Museum Collection.

(Photograph: Horniman Museum 1999)

Ever since the 1930s when they were first brought to the attention of the western world through the studies of the French anthropologist, Marcel Griaule and his team, the Dogon have attained widespread attention for what has been presented as their highly developed philosophy and their poetic sensitivity to their world. The masks for which the Dogon are famous have been said to represent the public face of such esoteric views. In the words of Griaule's key informant Ogotemelli: 'For the society of the masks are a picture of the whole world, for all men, all activities, all crafts, all ages, all foreigners, all animals can be represented in masks or woven into hoods.' (Griaule 1965: 189)

Griaule's benchmark study *Masques dogons* (1938) provided a seemingly thorough ethnographic account of the mask society, and of the numerous masquerades extant at that time. However sixty years on, with the annual exodus, and return, of young men to cities seeking work, with the influx of tourism, and most importantly with the penetration of Christianity and Islam, and the political changes consequent upon the colonial and post-colonial government, Griaule's major work no longer provides an accurate account of the current state of the mask complex. In this paper – also the subject of my own ongoing PhD research – I intend to outline the external factors shaping masquerade and to demonstrate their impact on performance practice and evolving mask forms.

The area identified as Dogon country spans roughly 50,000 square kilometres of southeast Mali extending into the north-western corner of Burkina Faso with a population of approximately 400,000.[2] Archaeological evidence (Bedaux 1972). suggests that by the 15th century the Dogon were established along the Bandiagara cliffs, a dramatic escarpment stretching for some 200 kilometres throughout the region. Even though Dogon is a Voltaic language, oral history recounts their migration from the Manding heartland, the traditional centre of the Mali empire, to displace a population of small 'red men' living in the cliffs whom they called Tellem (Dieterlen 1941).[3]

From the 15th century onwards this area was exposed to extremes of political upheaval and violent warfare. The Dogon periodically engaged in battles with Mossi, Peul, Bambara, Tuareg, and Toucouleur; all islamized groups sharing this realm. During this time the Bandiagara cliffs repeatedly provided an impenetrable shelter to retreat to. In 1893 the French entered the region, but their arrival was met with similar resistance. Peace with the Dogon was not established until 1920 in the village of Tabi when the French emerged victorious from a final bloody battle (Arnaud 1922).

The physical difficulty of travelling between villages, combined with the constant threat from outsiders, had the effect of paralysing communication for long periods. This may have promoted some of the differences in ritual practice from one village to the next, still much in evidence today. It may also account for the huge range of dialects that exist throughout the region. Today however, in contrast to the romanticised paradigm of isolation maintained by the tourist industry, the Dogon villages exist in a state of constant interaction with their proximal and distant neighbours, both Dogon and non-Dogon.

In the 20th century, the Dogon tradition of masquerade was perceived by scholars as providing an open system of historic accumulation and change. Griaule was aware that the *Awa* (mask society), existed in a state of flux, crucial to its own survival.[4] In his concluding remarks to *Masques dogons* he writes: 'We have seen that the *Awa* was a factor for the conservation and evolution of a large part of the Dogon people. Thus we must expect to discover that anything that can influence it will act directly on that society's institutions.' (Griaule 1938: 815) So what factors have impacted on Dogon society since the 1940s and what has been the response to such changes?

In the latter part of the 20th century, changes in religion, governmental institutions, climate, and tourism have all contributed to the accelerating mutation of Dogon society, and while all such factors interconnect and are therefore difficult to separate, it is worth spending a moment outlining the various aspects at play. However at this stage it is important to add the perhaps obvious point that no human process of replication can ever be exact. Through repetition over time, incremental changes are bound to occur that articulate with changing discourse and social practice.

The spread of Islam throughout the region was generally hampered by continued poor relations of the Dogon with neighbouring islamized ethnic groups. One notable exception is Pignari, to the west of the plateau, which, jammed between the two ancient Muslim capitals of Cheiku Amadu and Tijani, adopted Islam in the 19th century. (Brasseur 1968: 376). Nonetheless, the late 20th century saw a rapid diffusion of Islamic faith notably amongst the young. Factors contributing to this have been identified as the increase in the commercial activities of the Dogon with their islamized neighbours, the temporary migration of the young to urban zones and the settlement in villages towards the Seno plain (Jolly 1995: 82). Christianity was introduced in 1930 with the first Protestant mission in Sanga. The first Catholic mission was established in 1949 at Sege and from that point Catholicism was actively promoted through the establishment of schools, community clinics and through the distribution of aid (Jolly 1995: 84).

In the villages at the heart of Dogon country, particularly in the *toro* and *dono* speaking zones situated along the escarpment, those practising the traditional religion are identified locally as being in the majority. They distinguish themselves – in French as 'animiste', but in Dogon as 'sacrificers' (*buroburo*) – from Christians and Muslims or 'those who pray' Some acknowledge the destructive impact of new religions on 'traditional' culture; in the words of one lamenting villager: 'with the new religions everything is changing'. But while all can identify their religious affiliation, distinctions are often less clear-cut. Religious practice is often seen to operate on multiple levels; people taking from each that which best suits their immediate individual and familial needs, and the adoption of one form of religious practice does not necessarily incur the cessation of another.

With the establishment of colonial rule in Mali, the Dogon region saw the imposition of four administrative regions and the regular imposition of monetary taxes. With Mali's independence in 1962 a period of growth saw the building of schools and roads, facilitating the import and export of goods (in particular onions) to the expanding commercial centre of Mopti.

Over the second half of the 20th century there has been a drying out of the area accompanied by deforestation. The effects of climatic change are being exacerbated by ecological pressure from the local population, making farming less and less productive. This in turn has lead to the annual mass exodus from villages of young people seeking more fertile land in settlements towards the Seno plains, or in search of urban employment, in centres as far as Ghana and Côte d'Ivoire. Whilst such trips are often intended to be temporary, it may be years before youths return; necessity and family honour demanding that they don't come back empty handed.

The arrival of European visitors to the area followed on quickly from the establishment of French colonial rule. As early as 1938, Griaule noted with disdain that with the presence of tourists, and the dancing of masks as 'a courtesy rendered to visitors of note' (1938: 817), a pattern had already established itself for the performance of masquerade as a 'secular activity'. Ironically as the work of Griaule and his team gained widespread acclaim, so the numbers of tourists arriving in the area increased; and today the model promoted by tour operators presents a view of tradition that is conspicuously 'griaulist', placing as Lane points out, particular emphasis on 'the exegesis of Dogon society through a detailed understanding of their mythology. When this is combined in travel brochures with colourful descriptions of the scenery of the Bandiagara escarpment, an image of a mysterious exotic and remote society can be skilfully created. Visitors arrive in the Sanga region with expectations based on this imagery.' (1988: 66).

Before examining the effects of these changes, it is worth understanding how the notion of 'change' is configured within the context of tradition and the masquerade tradition in particular.

I began this paper with an interpretation by a local youth of one of the first songs of the entrance of masks (*wara segeru*) to the village of *Diamini Na* as part of a *Dama* ceremony.[5] In 1996 I witnessed how the masks paraded in descending order of age of each person, led by a group of elders who sang the following lines over and over again: 'the mask elder is dead, the hogon never moves from his place, clap hands for the hogon, the hogon is strong like the hyena, one must applaud the masks. The *wara segeru* is old'. Later a local youth from Banani clutched my tape-recorder to his ear, translated each line and then lent his own interpretation: 'The song is like a proverb... the tradition of masks never changes. It is like the *Hogon* that remains always in one place.'[6]

Such an example clearly demonstrates a local concept of tradition in which practice is legitimated by past precedent and works on the assumption that it has been going on since time immemorial. 'What it does is give to any desired change (or resistance to innovation) the sanction of precedent, social continuity and natural law as expressed in history.' (Hobsbawm 1983: 2).

Exploring this notion further, Van Beek proposes that the whole pattern of change for the Dogon fits comfortably within an existing culture of assimilation. 'The Dogon do have a way of fitting new elements into their existing cultural patterns: new etiological tales are joined with the traditional myths, new divination techniques supplement old ones new material objects are joined with artisanal techniques and new relations with outsiders are incorporated into existing social networks... Then the new elements become 'traditional' meaning they are quickly considered as *tèm*, 'found', and the difference between the recent innovation and the old legacy gets blurred.' (Van Beek 1991: 73) In this context adaptation and innovation may frequently occur, but are rarely acknowledged as such.

The mask society today concerns itself with a broader range of masquerade practice than that detailed in *Masques dogons.* Formerly masks would appear in connection with funerary rites (following burial), in Dama ceremonies for important elders, and in additional rites including the protection of fruit crops and corrective rites referred to as *puro,*curbing the behaviour of women. Since the establishment of colonial rule however, the scope of mask performance has expanded to accommodate visiting dignitaries and tourists flocking to the region.

Existing literature to date has tended to divide masquerade practice into two clearly defined categories. Firstly, that which fulfils the original purpose (such as funerary and Dama rituals), and secondly that in which the original practice has been adapted to cater for a 'foreign' audience. In existing texts, terms such as 'traditional' and 'adapted', 'indigenous' and 'tourist', 'sacred' and 'secular', 'ritual' and 'non-ritual', have been frequently applied. But for Dogon people all masked dances are referred to as *imina go* (mask dance) and there are no such distinctions in any overt verbalised form.[7] Tradition is open to adaptation, a quality that in reality guarantees its survival; all mask performers are indigenous, and dances commanded by tourists often attract an indigenous audience; and ritual inevitably pervades all masquerade performance as do rules to which the dancers must adhere. Most importantly however all such performances occur within the remit of the mask society, as a single category of mask practice. Whilst no clear terms exist in the Dogon language to distinguish between the variant contexts for masquerade, some of the differences evident in practice are remarked upon locally and will be referred to in due course.

Formerly, all men with the exception of smiths, leatherworkers and griots, were obliged to join the masks.[8] In practice, 'joining the masks' means that, once circumcised, young men would make a payment of food, usually a set amount of cereal or grain to the elders at the head of the village, in order to gain the right to approach and dance masks, and to have masks dance at their funeral. Today entrance amongst the masks is left to individuals. Among those who have converted to Christianity and Islam, many continue to make payments as a sign of respect for the elders, indicating their commitment to village life. Many continue to take part in masked dances, others just join the crowd of spectators attending mask performances.

The funerary ritual that follows the death and burial of an elder may often occur several years later when the necessary foodstuffs and millet beer have been accrued for participants and visitors. Masks with fibre and wooden headpieces will dance on the roof of the house of the deceased and in the public place as part of a sequence of rites that usually includes singing, gun-salutes, dancing, and beer drinking, and serves to commemorate the life and achievements of the elder (fig. 2). Subsequent to this, for important elders, and in some villages only on the death of the *hogon*, a Dama ritual will be observed marking the end of the time of mourning and the completion of a cycle of rites transferring the deceased from the world of the living to

younun (the world of the dead). The specific nature of the ritual varies from village to village, lasting from several weeks up to several months for a really big Dama. It is marked by a period of preparation and practice of mask dances, culminating in the ritual entry of the masks from the bush to the village where they perform. At the heart of the Dama ritual, the deceased men are transferred to a certain status amongst ancestors, through sacrifice to the mask altar. Whilst this important ritual occurs in private and often at night, it is in the public display of masquerade, and the abundant provision of beer and foodstuffs that accompanies it, that the wealth and status of the deceased members and their families is asserted.

The more or less recent changes in the use of masks, e.g. in celebratory festivals accompanying the inauguration of schools or roads, or in masquerades for tourists, have been best accounted for to date by Imperato (1971) and Lane (1988). Such performances are differentiated by local people from Dama and funerary rituals by three key factors: the location of the dance, the make-up of the audience, and the aesthetic appearance of the mask.

In terms of location, performances for Dama and funerary rituals will usually occur within the public place (*tay*). Dances for tourists and visiting dignitaries however will occur in a clearing on the edge of the village or (in the case of official openings) close to the new school, road, or clinic being celebrated. As one villager explained: 'To dance on the public place would be a bad omen since it is usually something done for the dead'.

The quality of performance and of audience participation is quite different when the majority of the audience is local. In a Dama, the audience both anticipates and responds to masks with which they are familiar. When the *Kanaga* and *Sirige* masks dance in solo, people chorus 'ééé...' (yesss) and chatter in loud appreciation to encourage individuals that perform particularly well. Masks that are perceived as difficult to dance such as the *tingetange* (stilt-walker) are rewarded with money in praise of their skill. They may also be encouraged by elders who call out in *Sigi-so* the secret language of the mask society. Those that are less proficient will be criticised on the spot; a mask elder may slap the ground with a stick at the feet of a mask dancer who has got out of time with the accompanying drumbeat, to command him to start his movement again. Such performances are highly competitive, and heated discussions to agree upon the best mask dancer continue long after the event.

In addition to the more spectacular performances satirical masks have emerged. For instance, a policeman mask (*imina policier*) gives out paper tickets with fines for bad behaviour and receives real money from delighted individuals. Similarly an audience member sneaks up on a healer mask (*imina dyodyonune*) to steal his carefully arranged possessions and a game of hide and seek ensues, the audience roaring with laughter. Such acts are often silent. Some masks however interact with the audience with dialogue spoken in character. 'You are in need of a love potion for your girlfriend, give me 100cfa' said the healer mask as he handed over a pile of stones to the unwilling audience member who proceeded to enter into a mock disagreement.

In villages such as Sanga – where some of Griaule's research was based – in peak season, dances requested by tourists may occur up to three times daily. Such performances, not surprisingly, no longer attract the attention of villagers, who have become used to the daily cycle of events. Dances may be as short as fifteen minutes, whilst by comparison, in the context of a Dama, dances may last for several hours. In the tourist dance only a couple of masks will perform a solo and there is an emphasis on the more acrobatic masks, such as the *kanaga* (fig. 3) and *sirige* that flip their headpieces to the ground. In this the satirical masks, that demand audience recognition and participation, are notably absent. Whilst a few roving children may attend, the performance seldom gathers the climactic momentum that occurs when the local audience is present. However in certain villages away from Sanga, where a regular pattern of dancing for tourists may not yet have developed, the occurrence of a mask performance requested by tourists may still be enough of a novelty for villagers to

Figure 3: Kanaga masks dancing at the 1996 Dama at Bongo. (Photograph: Polly Richards).

attend and enjoy. On such an occasion, and particularly in the presence of visiting dignitaries, a large crowd may gather and the event is noted locally to take on the character of a Dama performance. For big events – such as the opening of the clinic I witnessed in Tireli in 1996 – people from several villages may attend and participate, bringing with them their own masks, as part of a programme of festivities including dancing and wrestling, enjoyed by both men and women. The visiting dignitaries are almost peripheral to these celebrations which will often continue long into the night, after their departure. As in the Dama, performances in this context provide an opportunity for a comparison of skills and a demonstration of difference amongst villages.

In the light of contemporary influences, the position of women in relation to masks would appear to be undergoing an accelerated process of democratisation. The context of performances for outsiders, has provided a new arena for watching masquerade in which the rules and sanctions normally imposed on women during the Dama period, are not in force. Where previously women would retire to a distant rooftop or rock they now appear to have the increased confidence to creep to the side of the performance space where they are likely to be ignored. Women who are chased away by the *waru* (antelope) mask react as if it was a game and laugh as they move on. Once such changes are sanctioned in the context of masquerade for outsiders, they become harder to insist upon subsequently.

For example, at a Dama celebrated in Ireli in 1999, women who were asked to move away from the dance arena, made their objections clear to the elders. In addition, mask-making has in many villages now entered the familial domain, in which masks under the threat of theft from roaming art-thieves are now stored within the man's hut and made within the confines of the village. Previously the making of masks occurred outside of the village, in an area exclusive to the mask society. In the light of such changes, rites such as *puro* that sanction the beating of women by masks, have become less and less acceptable, to both perpetrators and victims, and are said to occur with less frequency.

Tourist dances are often requested at short notice and many of the masks that will have been made and worn for local use, will be re-used for the tourist performance; but there are exceptions to this. Markedly absent from performances for tourists and visiting dignitaries are the *saku* bark masks and *sanukouroy* leaf *masks* that require lengthier preparation and with which (seldom seen in publications and promotional material) tourists are less familiar.[9] Some individuals choose also to omit specific masks and certain accessories, such as magical charms worn for protection, on the grounds that they will spoil, or bring harm to others if worn for tourist performances.

Visually the aesthetic appearance of masks for tourists were as noted locally: 'a poor comparison to the real Dama' for which masks are brightly painted and fibres crisply cut. Formerly the making of masks was restricted to the Dama period and reparation of the masks outside of this period was forbidden. Whilst in many villages there has been a gradual relaxation of such rules governing mask production, there is still less incentive to beautify masks for the tourist audience who, it is felt, 'don't know the difference'. So, ironically enough, tourist dances are seen from within as 'old-fashioned', by contrast to the 'new' aesthetic that pervades the Dama; as one individual exclaimed: 'Of course, would a bride wear old clothes to her wedding?!'

Western literature has been brief and vague concerning the changes in the formal qualities of the masks over the last century. Griaule noticed an increasing 'abstraction' in sculpted form; Imperato by contrast observed an 'increased naturalism', and Doquet most recently proclaimed that the 'masks have known no radical change' (Doquet 1997: 504). In my experience a comparison of masks documented and collected by Griaule with masks extant today reveals that the development of mask styles has occurred in diverse directions, aspects of which have been commented on locally.

In some cases, changes have been incremental; the details of existing forms, as observed by Griaule having altered gradually, over time, as the same form is copied again and again. For example *samana* masks of Sanga, were seen to have more elongated heads, than examples observed by Griaule in the same village. In similar fashion the conical mouth of the *kanaga* mask of the same village is now curved upwards, its tip touching the nasal section. Such changes, though barely perceptible to the unaccustomed eye, were remarked upon by local people to whom I showed photos of pieces in Griaule's collection.

For other wooden and fibre mask forms, a more clearly perceptible invention of detail could be identified. I recall, for example, the addition of fibre crests and fake magical medicine to the *adagaye* (robber) masks of Banani, and the insertion of grain-store shaped eye holes into the *satimbe* mask by the smith of Bormon. In cases where the artist was present, the innovative addition to the earlier form was usually acknowledged. Where the artist was not present, and the change had perhaps occurred less recently, there was a tendency for informants to deny change, saying that the mask form was the same as it had always been. Such new details, when they occur and are accepted, are quickly absorbed by those that use the masks into a notion of what is typical and soon it becomes a means by which the mask itself is identified.

Where newly invented masks were concerned, I could not necessarily prove that masks not listed by Griaule were in fact new. Legitimisation of any innovation was either on the basis of past precedent, or else denied outright: 'It is not a new invention...' said an informant of a *banyon* (devil) mask observed at *Yanda*, '...but is based on a mask that was described by elders to have once existed'. Similarly of a cat mask observed at Ireli, somebody said: 'it has always existed', and of a donkey mask performed at a Dama in the village of Banani: 'he invented it to make money from tourists' (fig. 4).

Figure 4: A cat mask at the 1999 Dama of Ireli. Possibly one of the newly invented masks of the late 20th century.
(Photograph: Polly Richards).

Whilst a simplification of form could be observed in certain examples of the *djon* (hare) mask, Griaule's observation of an overall schematisation of form is untenable. In contrast, Imperato's observation of an increasing naturalism of form, was recognised by certain locals, and was found to be accurate with regard to specific examples such as the *satimbe* (sister of the masks), *na* (ox), and *dege* & *omono* (black & white monkey masks) (see fig. 5 & 6). Contemporary versions of these masks, though still existing in varying degrees of schematisation, were acknowledged and preferred for looking 'more like the real thing'. With regard to wooden headpieces people agreed on an overall improvement in carving skills, attributed directly to the economic incentive to make masks for sale. Significantly, the aforementioned masks, and particularly the *satimbe* tend today to be the work of the smith or specialist. Thus within a context where it is in the interest of all men to learn to carve well, the skills of the smith have changed accordingly, and his services therefore continue to be required.

Polly Richards

Figure 5: Satimbe mask. Collection: Musée de l'Homme, Paris. One of many masks collected by Marcel Griaule in the early 1930s.
(Photograph: Musée de L'Homme).

Figure 6: Satimbe mask, Banani. Typical for contemporary satimbe masks is that the body and face of the figure are less schematised and more clearly defined than the earlier example collected by Griaule (fig.5). The head of the figure is ornamented with plaited hair and jewellry. The right hand holds a carved spoon, referring the ritual spoon held by the yasige (female mask initiate). Also, the artist added the innovatory detail of grain-store shaped eyeholes.
(Photograph: Polly Richards, 1996).

In the present-day production of masks for tourists, mask carvers have shown a certain aspiration to meet the western craving for the 'authentic'. In some villages sculptors referred to their own copies of European publications to replicate earlier mask forms and types no longer extant in the region. While for the Dogon masks are valued for their newness and bright colours and 'the patina of long usage so prized by the Europeans has no appeal' (Van Beek 1988: 64), they have developed their own techniques for 'aging' artifacts to be sold.

One of the biggest impacts on the visual appearance of the masks has been the increase in new products now available in the Dogon marketplace; materials which have been imaginatively recycled and incorporated. The crest of a *pulloyana* (fulani mask) is, for instance, bedecked with pill packets and recycled mono-sodium glutamate wrappers, its tresses sparkling with cut-up strips of sardine cans in a manner imitative of the ornate

Figure 7: Pulloyana (Fulani or Peul woman) mask headpiece worn at the 1994 Dama of Idyeli. It is decorated with pill and mono-sodium glutamate packets and cut-up strips of sardine cans. (Photograph: Polly Richards).

Figure 8: A kanaga mask at the 1999 Dama of Ireli. The number '2' painted on the front marks the rank of the dancer as decided by his peers. (Photograph: Polly Richards 1999).

hairstyles of the Fulani women today (fig. 7). In another recent trend, some mask-makers have replaced the former plaited head-covering attached to wooden masks with a piece of sacking. Dyed and with a fibre fringe attached to each end, it fulfils the same function as its plaited precedent.

Where colour is concerned Griaule first noticed the use of imported inks for the preparation of mask fibres but it is difficult to know how widespread this was at the time. Today ink imported from Saudi Arabia, enamel paint, battery charcoal, washing blue (a bleaching agent) and coloured chalks are combined with indigenous colour preparations and contribute to a wealth of colour combinations that now adorn the headpieces and mask fibres. Where their use is concerned, for some masks anything goes. Individuals may be knowledgeable of earlier red, black and white colour combinations prepared with local pigments but possess the freedom to move beyond this. In other cases, for example where the preparation of the *imina na* ('great mask') altar is concerned, the indigenous preparation of pigment, mixed in this case with the blood of animal sacrifice, is maintained.

Masked performance today provides an arena for individual excellence not previously sanctioned in Dogon society. As noted by Van Beek: 'a tendency to lessen the anonymity of the masks has emerged in it...' (Van Beek 1991b: 70). However, there are questions about the nature of this anonymity and about the status of the mask itself; issues that still need resolving. We cannot make the assumption that the mask previously effaced the wearer's identity 'therein and thereby re-defining it as something other' (Picton 1989: 188). 'Secrecy' regarding the wearers identity may be continuing to be essentially 'a manner of talking...construed as part of the apparatus of dramatic distance' (ibid.: 193) between masquerader and audience when in actuality the performers everyday esteem is heightened by the quality of performance.

In performances today, the mask itself provides an opportunity for prestige display and individuals have incorporated accessories newly acquired in local markets and urban centres further afield, into the mask attire. Dancers with financial means adorn themselves with strands of amber, agate, plastic beads and metal wrist watches. Fibre mask skirts and chest-pieces are accessorised with leather studded belts and nylon money-belts; beneath which (alongside the traditional indigo) are now worn shorts, trainers and even freshly pressed t-shirts and vests. In some villages the opportunity for 'prestige display' is reflected further in the mask headpiece itself. For some the *pulloyana* (Fulani woman) mask provides a more literal occasion for the display of riches – mirrors, earrings and coins are added to a mass of cowry shells decorating the headpiece. Likewise a *Satimbe* mask statuette dons a pair of mirrored sunglasses, it's neck draped in bands of necklaces; enhancing the appearance of the mask and simultaneously displaying the status of the masquerader. In some villages the *kanaga* mask shows the name of the wearer and the name of his village written on both sides of the mask.[10] In other cases the tip of the mask may also be painted with a number (1,2 or 3) declaring the rank of the dancer in relation to his contemporaries (fig. 8). From a mask in which the wearer's identity was formerly effaced, the wearer's identity is now visibly promoted.

The incorporation of exotic materials and foreign-style attire is a continuation of the existing tradition of beautification of the mask, and provokes no objection among local 'consumers'. However in tourist performances, in villages such as Sanga, western-style dress (with the exception of shoes) is significantly absent from the masks attire. Here Imperato (1971) noted the constant adaptation of masked performances to suit tourist requirements but in recent years, modifications have taken on a self-consciously traditionalist slant that is worth examining.

In Sanga in 1996 a masked performance could be commanded for about £50.00, a sum that was divided up by the organiser at the *Bureau de guides*, between himself, the dancers and the musicians. Elders who accompanied the masks and those in the orchestra of drums and singers, would only be paid if dressed in 'traditional' outfit – indigo robes, trousers and straw hats. Youths were required to be bare-chested. Clothed on the bottom half in baggy indigo trousers, they were forbidden from wearing western style T-shirts and shorts beneath their fibre mask costumes.

In January 1996 I observed a performance which was being filmed by a visiting television company. At the beginning, the organiser of the mask dance announced to the audience that they would be witnessing 'a vision of an authentic Africa'. The dance lasted approximately 20 minutes and was a much shortened version of a dance observed for a Dama. The dancers entered and encircled the site several times in single file. Only the *kanaga, sirige* and the *tingetange* mask danced individually, the rest would dance as a group to a varying assortment of drum rhythms. Compared to the dance observed by Imperato – where the order of entrance of masks resembled that of the Dama performance – the order of entrance and subsequent dancing had been changed so that the *satimbe* mask was at the front of the line, in order, it was later explained to me, 'to signify the first woman to have discovered the masks'.

Apparently, organisers respond to the demands of tourists for overt explanation of everything they see. In 1996 the dance ended with a line-up of the masks for a photo cum explanation session (fig. 9) , in which the organiser promised 'to reveal the symbolism of each mask in turn'. Of the *kanaga* it was said that it '...represents the antelope. It symbolises the vitality of man and the creation of the world. The upper axis represents the sky, the lower, the earth and the vertical plane is the axis that unites the two' The *sirige* plank mask, it was explained '...represents the Guinna house of the first ancestors. It symbolises the metamorphosis of the first ancestor into the snake'.

While some public explanations were acceptable by many locals, other were not. A young man in Banani told me: 'The *sirige* mask bows its head down forwards and backwards as a homage to the deceased. The guides of Sanga say that when the *sirige* circles his head round the crowd it indicates that the world is round and flat, but they [the guides] have invented this.'

Doquet raised the question as to the possible impact that the acting out by locals of this 'traditional model' for tourists might incur on their own masquerade practice, and asks: 'will not the mask itself be affected by this game?' (Doquet 1997: 494). In recent years villages have indeed constantly readjusted their position in relation to their own rituals in order to cater for tourist demand.

Formerly, only youths who had participated in a Dama were permitted to dance in performances for tourists. However the increasingly poor crop yields, delaying the celebration of these rites, and the resulting exodus of young men in search of work, has reduced the numbers of dancers able to participate. In some villages, accommodation to this is apparent. To the fury of the other villagers, in Ireli

Figure 9: Tourists line up in Sanga for a photo-call with the masks.
(Photograph: Polly Richards, 1996).

in 1994 four out of eight wards brought forward the date of their Dama – previously celebrated at a regular interval of 50 years. The reason for this was so that new members could enter amongst the masks and learn the skills of mask performance, in order to be able to dance when tourists and visiting dignitaries requested it. Likewise in Tireli the *Imina Berkoi* (chief of mask altar) gave permission for young men (who had been circumcised), to dance masks at tourist dances, with the proviso that an extra payment be made to the mask society when the moment of the Dama finally came. In contrast, in Komokan at the arrival of their Dama in 1999, in angry response to the low numbers of youths making payments to 'join the masks', elders forbade those who had not paid from either making, dancing or selling masks. This resulted in the albeit belated payments of many men, anxious neither to displease the elders nor to lose the opportunity for this valuable additional source of income. The anger demonstrated by 'traditionalists' at such moments however is usually short-lived. Ultimately a compromise is achieved and the pattern of the continuing 'tradition' shifts accordingly.

Within the context of masquerade, innovation is an act of daring on the part of the masquerader and its acceptance depends directly on the response of its immediate audience. It is either accepted and absorbed, or rejected out of hand for not conforming to established boundaries of the tradition. Such responses are not always the conflicting views of young and old. In Banani a youth expressed his accord with the actions of an elder who had wiped off the multi-coloured paint on his friends *kanaga* mask, a style which in the distant village of Idyeli Yéré another elder had been previously seen to praise.

Nonetheless, 'traditionalists' do seem to assert a greater deal of influence in some villages more than others. In Sanga aspects of the 'traditional' approach manifest in tourist performances appear to have carried over into their own performance domain; and changes identified to have occurred in more remote villages have in Sanga remained in check. *Kanaga* masks sometimes have numbers painted on them, but are devoid of any writing; their head-coverings continue to be plaited in contrast to the newer trend of using imported sack-cloth. The range of more than fifty different mask types recorded as being in use by Griaule, has been reduced to a core of twenty or so different types, of which one of the few more recent inventions – a mask representing a tourist using a camera[11] – has already fallen into disuse. Most noticeably, where the mask fibres are concerned, while imported inks are used, a rigid tri-coloured code of black, red, and yellow in single hues (and seldom green) has been maintained, where villagers elsewhere prefer a multi-hued jamboree of colours. In addition, Sanga maintains rules that are not applicable elsewhere. The preparation of masks is forbidden for anything other than a large Dama, and an effort is made to stress the anonymity of masqueraders.

In many villages the celebration of Dama and funerary rituals have been noted locally to occur with less frequency than in the past. Elders have blamed this directly on poor crop yields rendering it impossible for families to accrue the foodstuffs essential for their undertaking.[12] However in villages where the majority of the inhabitants are either Christian or Muslim, the adoption of these religions has been held responsible locally for the demise of the mask society and the subsequent disappearance of related rituals at which masks appear. Some scholars have emphasised this view. Imperato (1971: 28) states: 'In the view of Muslims and Christians, these dances have neither meaning nor purpose and are logically discarded along with the communal activities once associated with their performance'. However in some villages, the mask is proving to be less than predictable and aspects of older rites may still be maintained. As an example of this, in a ward of the village of Guimini, whilst the dancing of masks at funerary ritual have been abandoned, the mask society continues to operate and performances of *sanukouroy* and *saku* masks are undertaken annually by Christian and Muslim adherents, serving as one man said 'to keep women at a distance'. Clearly in the light of changes in religion the complexities of continued mask practice still require further exploration.

In this paper I have highlighted the changes in Dogon mask production and masquerading in the latter half of the 20th century and demonstrated the constant process of adaptation that occurs within the apparent constraints of these traditions. But what can be said of the general reaction to such developments ?

Some changes are met with positively: 'Before.. for women and children, if you weren't initiated, you would be afraid of the masks. But now with the new developments everything has become public...without fear'. But for others the past is viewed with nostalgia and regret: 'When we were young we held onto our customs with two hands... today the young don't undertake Dogon customs and at the same time they haven't arrived at an understanding of the customs of white people... they are half white and half Dogon'. For some the ultimate disappearance of traditions in the future seems inevitable, 'consequence of all this: sure and certain deterioration of our practices and customs. What will surely happen is the death of our culture, the symbol of Dogon unity' (Head of Sanga Campement interviewed by Niangaly (1982: 64)).

The masks displayed at the Horniman suggest a static tradition, far removed from the 21st century reality of the Dogon region. Whatever changes have been effected by national politics, world religions, tourism and climatic change, the range of masquerade practice in the Dogon continues to be expanding. Newly invented masks are performed for local audiences in contrast to the self-consciously 'traditional' performances for tourists. The skills of mask makers are enlarged by the comparative wealth of new and imported materials and the production of masks for sale. Many young men returning from cities during the dry season, who have perhaps never acquired the skill of carving and are less knowledgeable as to local tradition and ceremonial practice are nonetheless enthusiastically renovating faded masks, in terms of 'urban novelty'. Moreover, masks continue to be performed by youths with skill and pride whatever their religious persuasion.

Scholars have been quick to predict a future when masquerade is only performed for visiting dignitaries and tourists. But is it not also possible that Dogon masquerade unhitched from its ritual context, and with the progression of Christianity and Islam, may continue to thrive? If we look to the examples of pantomime in Europe, and Caribbean carnival in England, there are numerous precedents for masking forms now separated from their religious origins. In the Dogon case, in adapting masquerade for changing audiences, as I have illustrated here, the unhitching process of masquerade performance from the ritual content of the mask has already begun. With every school, road, hotel and clinic that is built; masquerade is part of a regular programme of events that people from neighbouring villages flock to attend, participate in, and inevitably comment upon, thus impacting upon its continued evolution. And in the light of the obvious commitment, enjoyment and pride in a tradition that has evolved over time to be a marker of Dogon identity within and beyond the Dogon region, one cannot predict the extinction of the mask just yet, if at all.

Acknowledgments

Fieldwork has been undertaken in 1994, 1996, 1998, and 1999 covering a total of eight months to date and has been made possible with funding from the University of London Central Research Fund, S.O.A.S. Scholarships Committee, and the Friends of the Horniman Museum. I am also indebted to my friends and colleagues in the field. including Wagaserou Douyon, Etienne & Jeanne Guindo, Dagalu Girou, and Apomi Saye for their invaluable assistance, advice and support.

Notes

1. All Dogon words in this paper are in the *toro-so* dialect. *Toro-so* and *dono-so* (so = word) are two among thirty-two dialects recorded by Calame-Griaule (1956). The Fulani language is often employed by Dogon speaking different dialects.

2. This figure is provided by Jolly (1995). A population of 850,000 can be calculated from the 1998 census (*Direction Nationale de la Statistique et de l'Informatique*, Mali, 1990), a total of the four 'Dogon' administrative regions (Bandiagara, Bankass, Kouro, and Douentza).

3. *Tellem* translates as 'we have found them' (Bedaux 1972: 155).

4. The word *awa* translates as 'mask' in *Sigi-so*, the secret language of the masks. It is used in Sanga to refer to the society of masks but this is not a use that I have found in villages elsewhere.

5. *Dama* means 'forbidden'. The *Dama* marks the end of certain prohibitions related to a persons death that affect the entire community (Griaule 1938: 343).

6. In the past the *hogon,* the ritual chief of the village (and usually the eldest man) would be installed in a designated dwelling from which he would never move.

7. The word *imina* (mask) refers to the mask as a whole, including the wooden or fibre headpiece, the fibre costume *and* the performance. It may also be used to refer to a man who has made his payment to enter 'amongst the masks' even if he is not physically 'masked'.

8. The society of masks is a society of men. Like many African masking traditions the exclusion of women, with the exception of select female initiates known as *yasige*, is justified by myth in which a woman finds the first mask, puts it to misuse to scare men, and is then found out and has the mask taken away from her.

9. *Sanukouroy* leaf masks – identified by Griaule as being only an amusement for young boys – form an important early stage of the boys' entrance amongst masks in villages to the south-west of the escarpment where they perform in the annual rites at the onset of the rainy season.

10. The writing of the wearer's name on the *kanaga* mask is first mentioned by Van Beek in his published work of 1991.

11. The tourist mask, photographed by Imperato in 1970, is a re-invention of the earlier *anasara yana* (european madam mask) that appeared during the colonial period. The policeman mask (first observed by Dieterlen in 1974) is the only new mask to have emerged in Sanga since 1940.

12. Some elders have acknowledged the strain that the provision of foodstuffs for such rituals places upon their family and have requested not to have their death commemorated in public funerary rituals.

Bibliography

ARNAUD, R. 1922. Le Dernier Épisode de la Conquête du Soudan Français (l'affaire de Tabi), *Renseignements Coloniaux* (Supplement of the *Bulletin du Comité de l'Afrique Française et du Comité du Maroc)*, **32**, 8.

BEDAUX, R. 1972. Tellem Reconnaissance Archeologique d'une Culture de l'Ouest Africain au Moyen-age: Recherches Architechtoniques. *Journal de la Société des Africanistes*, **42**, 103-185.

BEEK, W. VAN 1988. Functions of Sculpture in Dogon Religion. *African Arts*, **21**, 4.

BEEK, W. VAN 1991b. Enter the Bush: a Dogon Mask Festival. In Vogel, S. (ed), *Africa Explores 20th Century African Art.*

BRASSEUR, G 1968. *Les Établissements Humains au Mali.* Dakar.

CALAME-GRIAULE, G. 1956. *The Dogon Dialects, Africa.* **26**, 62-71.

DOQUET, A. 1997. *Les Masques Dogons Sous le Regard de l'Autre: Fixité et Changement dans une Societé Ethnographiée.* (doctoral thesis). University of Bordeau II.

DIETERLEN, G. 1941. *Les Âmes des Dogon.* Paris: Institut d'Ethnologie.

GRIAULE, M, 1938. *Masques Dogons.* Paris: Institut d'Ethnologie.

GRIAULE, M, 1965 (1948). *Conversations with Ogotomelli.* London: Oxford University Press.

HOBSBAWM, E. 1983. *The Invention of Tradition.* Cambridge: Cambridge University Press.

IMPERATO, P. 1971. Contemporary Adapted Dances of the Dogon. *African Arts*, **5**, 1, 28-33 & 68-72.

JOLLY, E. 1995. *La Bière de Mil dans la Société Dogon* (Doctoral thesis). Paris X Nanterre.

LANE, P. 1988. Tourism and Social Change Among the Dogon. *African Arts*, **21**, 4, 66-69.

NIANGALY, A. 1982. *L'impact du Tourisme sur la Culture Dogon.* Bamako.

PICTON, J. 1989. What's in a Mask? *African Languages and Cultures* **3**, 2, 181-202.

Tania Costa Tribe

Candomblé Shrine in
the African Worlds
gallery at the
Horniman Museum.
(Photograph: Horniman
Museum, Heini Schneebeli).

Candomblé Shrines

Tania Costa Tribe

Candomblé structure

The term 'Candomblé' designates certain Brazilian religions with marked West African roots, and denotes both the large body of beliefs and ritual practices brought to Brazil by African slaves and the physical localities where their deities are enshrined and their ceremonies are held (Omari 1994: 135). Many different African groups, including the Bantu (from Angola and Congo), Jeje (Benin), Yoruba and Hausa (Nigeria), contributed to the formation of these religions. The contribution of the large contingents of Bantus that the Portuguese had brought to Brazil since the early days of colonisation in the sixteenth century can be seen in the very word 'Candomblé', which according to Yeda Pessoa de Castro probably derives from the Bantu term *kà-n-dómb-él-é*, meaning the act of praying, deriving from the verb *kulomba* (*kubomba*), to praise, to pray, to invoke. Thus 'Candomblé' comes to mean ritual, praise, prayer, invocation or ritual place (Castro 1981: 60).[1]

Fragmented by war and slavery, the many African ethnic groups that arrived in Brazil did not simply undergo a straightforward transposition of their mother cultures to their new surroundings. Rather it was a rapid, multifaceted process whereby many cultural variables came into sudden contact, generating a profound rearrangement of the slaves' ethnic and cultural memory. Despite the wide variety of religious traditions that had arrived in the country it was the practices of the Yoruba that became dominant, because from the eighteenth century until the final shipment in 1851 this group made up the largest contingent of imported slaves. The rich and complex cosmology of the Yoruba and their rigidly defined social hierarchy provided a general framework within which most of the other transposed ethnic groups reconstituted their own beliefs and practices, sometimes adding certain Amerindian and European elements in the process. From this reformulation arose what are now called the *Nações de Candomblé*, the Candomblé Nations, generally identifiable according to which African language they still use.[2] These diverse types share a similar cult dynamics, expressed in their ritual clothes, attributes and ceremonies. But each of them also maintains its own lexicon, naming its deities differently, employing different chants and offerings of sacred plants and animals, and generally maintaining forms of religious lore which specifically link the group to its own African cultural memory (Voeks 1997: 54).

Although there is some evidence of organised African-Brazilian religion dating back to the mid-1700s, one particular candomblé house (*terreiro*), known in the Yoruba language as Ilê Iyá Nassô[3] and in Portuguese as Casa Branca, is considered the mother of all Bahian, and by extension all Brazilian, candomblés. Situated in the Engenho Velho district of the city of Salvador, the Ilê Iyá Nassô was, according to tradition, founded around 1830 or even earlier by three African women, Iyá Nassô, Iyá Detá and Iyá Kalá, becoming the first Yoruba ritual centre to be publicly acknowledged in Brazil (Cacciatore 1988: 144). Later leadership disputes resulted in the establishment of two other important candomblé houses in Salvador, the Ilê Iyá Omin Axé Iyá Massê, situated in Alto do Gantois, and the Axé Opô Afonjá, in São Gonçalo do Retiro, both of which also rigidly maintained the ritual practices and cosmological views of the Yoruba (Voeks 1997: 52).

In the Brazilian conceptual framework of Yoruba origin, the universe is at the same time sacred and concrete: *aiê* is the physical world, the earth, material life; *orun* is everything else, the supernatural world which also surrounds and permeates the earth. There is constant interaction between these two dimensions through the condensation and distribution of *axé*, the life force which animates all things throughout both the material and the extra-material dimensions and is a central concept in Candomblé (Augras 1983: 55-57). Candomblé members (known in Portuguese as *filhos de santo*, meaning candomblé sons or daughters) acknowledge the existence of a supreme God, whose name in Yoruba is Olorum, who is perceived as distant and unapproachable by humans. Beings known as *orixás* (or 'saints') function as the earthly presence of Olorum, embodying natural forces, economic activities, war and mythical ancestors, and being associated with all aspects of everyday human life.

The number of *orixás* that have survived in Brazil varies. There seem now to be about sixteen major ones, plus several others found only in a few *terreiros*. There are cases when an *orixá* is unexpectedly 'rediscovered' in a certain *terreiro*. There are, moreover, forms or types (*qualidades*) of the *orixás*, whose names are not freely spoken so that *axé* is not dispersed,[4] but who do exist and are ritually treated like all the others. In Rio de Janeiro, the pantheon of *orixás* appears to have been further reduced, except in the few candomblés founded by important Bahian religious leaders (Augras 1983: 58-59). The *orixás* – also called *voduns* in the Jeje candomblés and *inkices* in those of Bantu origin – have equivalent names in those languages.

Each person is considered to be linked to a specific *orixá* through his or her head (*ori*). Through the ritual known in Portuguese as *assentar o santo* ('seating the saint') the vital energy belonging to the *orixá*, the *axé*, is 'fixed' in the *ori* of the son or daughter, impregnating also the entire *terreiro*. The person's individuality is situated not just in the head itself (*ori inu*): it exists also as a spiritual double, located in the extended dimension of the world (*orun*). Each aspect of an individual's personality – like every living or natural thing – exists at the same time on the spiritual and the material planes. When a person is born the *eledá* – a collective vital force of a generic nature – activates this link, which is then made manifest in the form of an individual's *dono da cabeça* ('lord of the head', or *orixá*). By being the site for this junction of the individual and the collective, the head (*ori*) is the point of intersection where the sacred forces are gathered, through which the person can develop fully (Augras 1983: 61). All those *filhos de santo* linked to a certain *orixá* share the same body of abstract concepts relating to that *orixá*, which is symbolically expressed by the use of certain prescribed colours, food restrictions, particular emblems, herbs, the right days for worship and annual festivals (Santos 1976: 35).

Known in Portuguese as *mãe* or *pai-de-santo* (candomblé mother or father) and in Yoruba respectively as *ialorixá* or *babalorixá*, the leader of the *terreiro* represents the principal line of communication between the material world of humans and the spiritual world of the *orixás*. Usually dominated by women in candomblés of Yoruba origin, the *terreiro* hierarchy is dominated by men in the Angola and Jeje nations. But in all cases the *ialorixá*'s or *babalorixá*'s authority is absolute, as they are the 'living repositories' of the sacred knowledge and the principal educators of initiates, responsible for maintaining respect, carrying out ritual obligations and protecting the secrets of the candomblé (Voeks 1997: 63, 65). According to tradition, the first Bahian *ialorixá* Iyá Nassô was a daughter of the *orixá* Xangô, and had been in charge of this *orixá*'s cult in the king's palace in the city of Oyó (Nigeria) before setting up her *terreiro* in Salvador (Beniste 1997: 327). Embodying concepts of kingship, and perceived as a legislator and state-builder, Xangô would have endowed Iyá Nassô's personality with the qualities of knowledge and leadership required for her role in the structuring a religious centre, no doubt under adverse conditions.

After periods of initiation that last from one to three months and may include a further period of seclusion of up to a year (Lody 1995: 203), certain members of the candomblé known as *iaôs* – individuals who have been specially chosen by the *orixás* through divination – become able to incarnate their own personal *orixás* during special sessions of ritual drumming, dancing and possession trance (Voeks 1997: 65). During their initiation, which involves complex rites, the *iaôs* learn the ritual behaviour which is associated with their particular *orixá*, as well as the dynamics of the candomblé as a whole (Cacciatore 1988: 148). As Mãe Stella de Oxóssi, head of the traditional Bahian candomblé Ilê Axé Opô Afonjá and one of today's most respected candomblé leaders, explains:

> *In addition to the usual duties of candomblé members, iaôs are subject to many other, more complex ones. They have to know everything about terreiro life: the cycle of feast days, obligations of the older members, bori, the coming-out of the iaô after initiation, funerary rituals. They must participate as much as possible in different obligations, so they can learn. They must learn to dance, sing, respond in the chants, behave with dignity, consideration and sympathy. [...] It is essential for them to carry out the humblest tasks, such as cleaning, kitchen work or the ecological upkeep of the garden, stopping people dropping rubbish. And they have to learn to dress suitably, to look smart without affectation.*[5]

Whatever the nature of his or her individual *orixá*, the initiate is part of the totality of the *terreiro*, tied by the initiation process and the sharing of a common *axé* to the leadership of that *terreiro*, particularly the *mãe* or *pai-de-santo* (Santos 1976: 36). These ties of symbolic kinship are extended so that the new son or daughter becomes also brother or sister to all other members of the candomblé community (Ortiz 1978: 188). This family-like aspect of the candomblé is extremely important, as it gives social cohesion to the whole group despite the inevitable internal conflicts and power struggles that may ensue.

Another cohesive element is the rigidly hierarchical structure which dominates the candomblé, as Mãe Stella makes clear: 'Hierarchy is everything: beginning, middle and end. Without it you have chaos...'[6]; and 'A novice is always a novice in religion: you have to start with the ABC. Hierarchy and discipline have to be maintained. Respect for the Agba [the elderly, the wise] is the essence of Yoruba culture; the bowing, ritual greetings, etc.'.[7] This hierarchy includes such functions as *mãe-pequena* (literally 'little mother'), second-in-command in the *terreiro*; the *ekédis*, helpers for the *filhas de santo* in trance; the *ogãs*, respected male members of the candomblé who contribute financially and politically to the *terreiro*; the *axogun*, in charge of animal sacrifices; and the *mão-de-ofá*, the *terreiro* leaf specialist (Voeks 1997: 65).

The ritual space of the Candomblé

Robert Voeks has pointed out that candomblé *terreiros* vary enormously in their physical appearance, reflecting the wide social and economic distance between a select few aristocratic *terreiros* and the far greater number of more modest houses. While the former can claim direct descent from the recognised houses established during slavery, and consequently receive the attention of the media and are generously endowed by famous performers, government officials and intellectuals, the much humbler establishments are frequented by washer-women, domestics, street hawkers and rubbish collectors (Voeks 1997: 67). Despite these differences, all *terreiros* share basic features of spatial arrangement and decoration to meet the strict requirements of the cult.

Essentially, all *terreiros* are divided into two main areas with distinct characteristics and functions: an 'urban' space, comprising the public and private buildings, and a 'virgin' space, which includes trees and a water source, equivalent to the African forest (Santos 1976: 33). This 'forest' area, which can occupy almost two thirds of the total space, provides trees and plants grown specially to supply essential ingredients for ritual and healing use, since Brazilian candomblés function as centres of healing where African medical and magical traditions were able to take root. But the 'forest' is seen as sacred and dangerous and tends to be avoided by most of the inhabitants of the *terreiro*. Only the priests of Ossaim, patron *orixá* of vegetation, and those of the hunting *orixás* – Ogun e Oxóssi – normally perform the rites that must take place there (Santos 1976: 34).

Within the 'urban' space are situated the shrines known as *peji* or, in more traditional houses, *ilê-orixá*, where the sacred materials belonging to each *orixá* are ritually placed as an *assento* (or *assentamento*) by the *filhos de santo*, as will be discussed in greater detail in the next section. The 'urban' space of the *terreiro* also contains an area called *ilê-axé*, comprising the buildings where the collective ritual activities of the *terreiro* take place under the guidance of its leaders and with the participation of its entire religious community. It includes the *barracão* (public hall), *roncó* (initiation room), kitchen and sometimes a divination room. Some *assentos* belonging to *orixás* who do not require to be kept in the open (like Oxalá, Oxum, etc.) may be kept in indoor shrines in this area. The *ilê-axé* may also include permanent or temporary accommodation for some of the *filhos de santo* and their families, and a waiting room for clients and visitors (Santos 1976: 33-34).

The *barracão* is the area where all public ceremonies are conducted. It is generally a rectangular room or hall, sometimes with a straw roof and a main door leading to the *roncó*. The floor is of earth or concrete, and the walls may be painted or papered with symbols of the *orixás*. Paper decorations may hang from the ceiling. There are chairs for the head of the *terreiro* and important guests, and benches for the audience. The *barracão* also includes an area reserved for the three special drums (*atabaques*) which are ritually beaten to accompany the dancing – the *xiré* – a circle performed by the *filhos de santo* in honour of the *orixás* around a central post. Sometimes called *ariaxé*, this post is not necessarily a structural element in the architecture and does not always reach up to the roof, but it is the focal point in the *barracão*. After being duly initiated, the three drums summon the *orixás*, who manifest themselves through their sons and daughters in trance by means of codified dance movements, gestures, facial expressions, the colours of their ritual clothing and the emblematic objects they display.

The strict hierarchical organisation which is the hallmark of the candomblé is clearly manifested in the areas reserved in the *barracão* for the different groups that make up the religious community, from the *ialorixás* and longest serving *filhos de santo* to the occasional visitors. According to Mãe Stella, 'The *barracão* for the ritual ceremonies is the sacred space where we are privileged to praise the *orixás* manifested in their sons and daughters. Having bathed and dressed, the *Olorixá* on entering the *barracão* pays respects to the door in honour of the ancestors, the drums, the *ialorixá, iyá-kékeré, agba* and other *oloyé*, and then takes his or her place according to the hierarchy. Those without seven years' status sit on mats, *egbon* on stools or benches, *oloyé* on chairs'.[8] This hierarchy is also expressed in the organisation of the *xiré* itself, where the positioning of the dancers in the circle is determined by each person's seniority, established in terms of the number of years since their initiation and the level and complexity of the initiation rituals they have undergone.

The *roncó* is a strictly private area, intended for the seclusion and initiation of novices. The most secret candomblé rituals are performed there, such as when a new *filho de santo* is gradually prepared to enter the state of trance necessary for his or her particular *orixá* to appear. All rites of passage at all levels of initiation focus on the cult of the head. For instance, before offering a sacrifice to the gods all the participants must make an offering to their own head (Augras 1983: 62). In the roncó, initiates prepare their *assentos* for their personal *orixás*, lords of their heads, in which the sacred forces will be fixed. For the rest of their lives the *filhos de santo* must constantly renew the links between their heads and the forces of the *orixás*; the role of the votive foods they offer to the *orixás* is one of mediation between the sacred and the profane (Ortiz 1978: 188).

In the kitchen these special foods are ritually prepared to be offered to the *orixás*, who need the *axé* they contain in order to maintain their dynamic force. The majority of these votive dishes are of African origin, some having survived unchanged while others have been modified in Brazil. Some foodstuffs are prepared with the meat of animals which have been ritually sacrificed, others with fish, prawns, vegetables, flour, etc. Many are highly seasoned with onions, salt (except Oxalá's), herbs, etc., and some contain honey. Most of the savoury foods are made with or fried in *dendê* (palm-nut) oil. For some *orixás* only sweet oil or honey will do. All food offerings are beautifully arranged and presented according to the ritual specifications associated with each *orixá*. They are changed every week on the set day prescribed for each *orixá*, when the vessels and the *peji* are cleaned. On this occasion the old foodstuffs are ritually disposed of in particular places. During certain ceremonies, some of the *orixás'* foods are shared among those present, and nothing may be left over (Cacciatore 1988: 90-91).

The *terreiro* functions as a living being who must receive regular sacrificial offerings. The focal points of the *barracão* – on the floor, under the central post and on the ridge of the roof above the *ariaxé* – must be 'fed'. During the annual ritual known as Águas de Oxalá (Oxalá's Waters), it is said that 'the whole house eats, from the floor to the roof,' as the *ogãs* sacrifice animals not just by the post but also on the roof of the *barracão* itself. Seen as a sacralized whole, the spatial dimension of the *terreiro* is considered an extension of the *axé* emanating from its patron *orixás* (Silva 1995: 174). Like the individual's head (*ori*), the *terreiro* may be related to more than one *orixá*, creating a kind of complex symbolic narrative known as *enredo de santo* (loosely translated as 'candomblé story' or 'plot') which combines elements and characteristics of all the *orixás* involved (Silva 1995: 175).

The most sacred of spaces in the *terreiro* is the private space of the *roncó*, where the *axé* is manipulated in order 'to give birth to' or revitalise the *orixás*, and the *pejis*, where the *assentos* for the *orixás* are kept. These are the places where the *axé* is deposited, and consequently only those who have been fully initiated have the right of access or are allowed to manipulate the sacred elements (Silva 1995: 175-6). The 'less' sacred spaces are the rooms and areas to which access is generally free, the most important being, of course, the *barracão* where public ceremonies and sacred drumming take place. When an initiate is allowed to dance closer to the *ariaxé* (the central post where the *axé* relating to the founding *orixá* of the *terreiro* is 'planted'), it reveals the dancer's intimacy with the vital forces of the *terreiro*. Phenomenologically, the closeness to or distance from certain focal points in the *terreiro*, and the right to circulate within certain areas considered to be more charged with *axé*, indicate the position that a person occupies within the candomblé hierarchy, as only those who have experienced several cycles of this ritual structure and have performed its many ritual obligations have the right to enter these sacred spaces reserved for the production and conservation of *axé* (Silva 1995: 154).

The physical space of the *terreiro*, the ritual objects used and the *ori* (head) of the initiates must be constantly revitalised, that is, carry *axé*. The main elements used in rituals conducted for this purpose are sacred leaves and animal blood, poured on all the objects, plants, stones and other symbols and emblems which relate to the *orixás* and the *ori* of their sons and daughters. All places, rooms, recesses, and objects are loci of the *axé* which permeates the whole *terreiro* (Santos 1995: 49).

The establishment of each new reputable candomblé house requires that this ritual fixation of *axé* should take place on the site to be used for the new *terreiro*. All the necessary ritual obligations are determined by means of divination, and they must be scrupulously carried out and maintained, so that the many different loci of *axé* can be effectively created (Beniste 1997: 255). When the land for the new *terreiro* is acquired, the use of divination decides whether the chosen place is adequate and meets the requirements of the *orixá* that will govern that particular candomblé. Undesirable spiritual forces are neutralised by means of sacrificial offerings performed as the land is being cleared and prepared and the *terreiro* buildings constructed (Beniste 1997: 283). Special objects and substances are placed or buried in certain areas to allow the process to take place. Highly respected priests and priestesses 'carry' the *axé* from the candomblé where they were initiated and bury it under the *ariaxé* of the new house in order to set its foundations, in a process called 'planting the *axé*', which effectively establishes a close network of personal and symbolic ties. The spread of the candomblé religion should be understood as an organic process whereby this vital force, which ultimately originated in Africa, creates a living network of close ritual ties among the many *terreiros*.

Within its limited space, the *terreiro* brings together the memory of the regions of Africa where the elements of the candomblé originated. Whereas in their native lands the *orixás* would have been worshiped separately, in distant villages and different regions, the many shrines (*pejis*) in the *terreiro* and the sequence of *orixás* dancing together in the *xiré* indicate the composite nature of the candomblé within a single ritual space (Santos 1976 p34). Yet the physical positioning of the *pejis* and the order of the dancing *orixás* symbolically reconstruct a ritual topography of Africa, the cosmological logic of which is reflected throughout the candomblé.

Shrines

The *pejis* contain the symbols, emblems and ritual food offerings for each *orixá*, and are located within the physical space of the candomblé according to strict rules. Depending on the availability of *terreiro* space, a *peji* may be either a collective shrine dedicated to a group of *orixás* with related characteristics, whose *assentos* can thus be placed together, or an individual shrine for a single *orixá* (Silva 1995: 176). In the first half of the twentieth century the *peji* was a covered table on which images of Catholic saints were placed to avoid police persecution, while the ritual vessels and offerings were hidden underneath. Tables like these may still be found, but often a peji will be a masonry structure containing staging or shelves on which the *assentos* are placed.

Certain *orixás* must have their *pejis* indoors in the *roncó* or even in more private areas only accessible to the most important members of the candomblé. In *terreiros* of mixed origin an *orixá* may have a *peji* in a private area and also an altar in the public *barracão* with images of syncretised Catholic saints (Cacciatore 1988: 209). For some *orixás*, like Xangô, Oxum and Oxalá, the *peji* must be closed. Others, like Ogun, must have open shrines, as they need to be able to wander freely. The cult of *orixás* related to leaves and forests, like Ossaim, Tempo, Iroco e Oxóssi, must be performed in the open air, preferably beside trees or plants. Obaluaê (Omulu), powerful and severe lord of the earth and its diseases, must have his sacred emblems buried in the open air; and the cult of Oxumaré, a long serpent coiled around the earth and represented by the rainbow, frequently focuses on a well (Silva 1995: 177). Exu, the dynamic principle that enables the constant exchange between the many collective and individual aspects of the world (Augras 1983: 62), must have his *assentos* placed in a closed *peji* near the entrance to the *terreiro*. Votive dishes for Ogun too are frequently placed near the entrance to the candomblé so that Ogun will protect it.

Individual candomblé members are allocated their own personal place in the *peji* consecrated to their *orixá* where they can ritually deposit their *assento* and care for the sacred materials of which it is made. These sacred materials are arranged within a special vessel and placed in the *peji* in a ritual designed to 'fix' or harness the *orixá's* vital force. The materials used to make each *assento* are very specific to the *orixá* in question, expressing through their forms, colours, textures and consistency the *orixá's* diverse aspects and establishing the magical nature of his or her dwelling-place within the *terreiro*.

The main component of most individual *assentos* is the *otá*, a sacred stone whose *axé* is 'fixed' in a special ritual ceremony. Each *orixá* has a specific *otá* which will differ in origin, composition, texture or appearance from that of the others. The *otá* represents the body, over which a required mixture of blood will be poured during the ritual offering. It may then be immersed in honey or oil (according to the *orixá*) and placed in a special covered china or earthenware vessel, which may be dressed in the *orixá's* ritual clothes. The *otá* and all the other *axé*-releasing elements are kept in the *peji* together with other symbols of the *orixás*, such as a sword for Ogun, snakes for Oxumaré, a double-headed axe for Xangô, etc. Votive offerings, including beads, emblematic objects, foodstuffs and the *axé* of sacrificed animals, are placed in front of the vessel (Cacciatore 1988: 200).

According to the preferences of each *orixá*, the plates, dishes, bowls, pots and jugs used for the *assentos* may be made of wood, gourds, china or earthenware, and will be plain or coloured. But it is the combination of the vessel and its content which is most specific to the variety of *orixá* and the nature of the *axé* that the *assento* is intended to reach. The mixture of earth plus water can represent fertility, for instance, so an earthenware vessel containing water may symbolise a pregnant womb, as in the water-filled jug of the mother deity Nanā. When placed in the appropriate *peji*, each *assento* is accompanied by a *quartinha,* a particular type of lidded earthenware jug which contains the liquid sacred to the *orixá* and is sometimes 'dressed' in the *orixá's* garments (Santos 1976: 201-203; Cacciatore 1988: 217).

The installations in the *terreiro* and the *assentos* for the *orixás* signify the relationships which have been symbolically formed within that particular candomblé, thus giving shape to the religious and ethnic identity of that religious community. All *assentos* must be ritually consecrated, that is, made carriers of *axé*. As they are all designed for a certain function, expressing different qualities and categories of *axé*, the materials, colours and shapes are chosen so that they can function as emblems or symbols and not just as mere material representations of the sacred. Objects which meet the necessary aesthetic and material requirements but have not been ritually 'prepared' lack *fundamento*, the sacred foundations rooted in the *axé* that circulates in that particular candomblé, and consequently they are mere forms which can elicit aesthetic responses and display craftsmanship or artistic expression. Their sacred character can only be imparted by means of a ritual during which *axé* is stored in them. It is the *axé* present in the objects which enables them to function fully and meaningfully, stimulating the ritual process and activating the entire physical and spiritual dimension of the candomblé (Santos 1976: 37).

Pai Roger's terreiro – a candomblé within the city

In 1997 the Horniman Museum, London, commissioned a complete candomblé shrine dedicated to the three open-air *orixás* – Ogun, Oxóssi and Ossaim – from Roger de Omulu, *pai-de-santo* in charge of a Jeje (Fon) Candomblé situated in the Rio de Janeiro suburb of Jacarepaguá. An intelligent and articulate young candomblé leader, Pai Roger is one of a new breed of *pais-de-santo* who strive, in the words of Vagner da Silva, to reinscribe the sacred within the social space of a modern metropolis, making it co-exist with contemporary rational thinking and the utilitarian secular ethos. Through these modern *pais-de-santo*, some of whom are now making use of radio and television programmes (Silva 1995: 15) and even the internet for religious purposes,[9] the old tribal and rural *orixás* continue to effectively function within the sceptical urban environment of contemporary Brazil (Silva 1995: 32). Many of today's sons of Ogun – the enraged god, lord of iron, inventor of tools and civilising hero (Augras 1983: 104; Santos 1976: 93) – are now steel workers, mechanics, engineers and systems analysts rather than the traditional soldiers, smiths and street fighters of a hundred years ago, thus extending the cluster of 'aspects' normally associated with this *orixá* (Silva 1995: 127).

The hallmark of these contemporary urban *terreiros* is the assimilation of certain new values, such as an attention to hygiene in rituals, providing comfort for the *terreiro* members, and making more 'rational' use of the spaces in the candomblé house. Such concerns were observed, for instance, among the initiates of a São Paulo *terreiro* in 1987 who took care not to dirty the floor with mud during a ritual in honour of the *orixá* Nanã, whose main element is a mixture of earth and water (Silva 1995: 181). An acceptance of the contemporary may also condition the ritual form accepted as 'appropriate' for the cult, altering the religious rules which have organised the ritual use of sacred *terreiro* space. This is the case of certain *pais-de-santo* who are now known to avoid carrying out rituals that require that certain materials be permanently buried in the *terreiro*, as this can be awkward when the community is renting its religious premises (Silva 1995: 181-2).

In discussions with the group collecting material for the Horniman Museum,[10] Pai Roger de Omulu expressed some rather unorthodox views relating to key aspects of candomblé life, revealing his ability to respond to current social values. In particular, he disagreed with traditional notions of gender roles in the candomblé, where women are normally assigned repetitive tasks like cooking and cleaning, being expected to maintain the day to day running of the *terreiro*, whereas men are usually allocated more creative functions, as Pai Roger put it, like atabaque playing. In his views – and in blatant contrast to the passionate call for the upholding of these traditions by Mãe Stella, of the Ilê Axé Opô Afonjá (Santos 1995, *passim*) – the traditional rigid allocation of candomblé tasks without regard for gender equality or individual tastes reflects an undesirable dynamics of power within the candomblé which must be reviewed.

Pai Roger is acutely aware of the need for today's urban candomblés to adapt to the requirements of the modern working week, so that religious duties will not clash with their sons' and daughters' work commitments. He is critical of the requirement for modern candomblé members to maintain certain traditional customs which can today appear anachronistic, like tribal marks and bodily incisions, and is also careful to emphasise that candomblés, although of African origin, are distinctly Brazilian. In this he differs from the rhetorical message put forward by some traditional candomblé *terreiros*, particularly in Bahia, where direct and close links with Africa are considered to be an important factor in establishing claims to purity and religious superiority. This has sometimes led to conflict between the traditional Bahian *terreiros* and the new ones in Rio de Janeiro and São Paulo. These are often regarded by the traditional candomblé hierarchy as devoid of any real *fundamento*, or founding *axé*, and merely inauthentic and commercialised simulations. Criticisms of Bantu *terreiros* are particularly common, even though they may be just as faithful to their origins as those of Yoruba descent (Silva 1995: 73).

Although he began his religious life in a *terreiro* of Yoruba roots, Pai Roger de Omulu finished his training in a Jeje Candomblé, which provided him with the *axé* for founding his own *terreiro*. He is acutely aware of his own line of religious descent, which goes directly back to the famous Bahian Jeje town of Cachoeira: 'We descend from the house founded by Antônio Pinto, who was the first man to be fully initiated within Cachoeira. He was initiated there, and we are linked there too, as he is a son of that *axé*.[11] But he also emphasises the distance that today separates his own candomblé from its roots in Cachoeira: 'These days we've drifted apart. We're part of the family, but we've been drifting apart. They think they have more *fundamento* than we do here in Rio.'

Despite resenting the ideological distancing of his Bahian candomblé relatives, Pai Roger is in no doubt about the strength of the *fundamentos* which identify his own candomblé nation and validate his *terreiro*, creating firm symbolic and ritual markers within the urban space of greater Rio de Janeiro. His discourse shows his total confidence in the significant role he and his community have to play in the religious life of his city. As in so many modern candomblés, contemporary urban values permeate not only the ritual structure of his candomblé but also its material and spatial manifestation, reflecting the prestige given in candomblé to material wealth and financial status (Silva 1995: 169).

As urban *pais-de-santo* ascend the social ladder as a result of a successful religious career or personal wealth, there is a proliferation in the large Brazilian cities of such *terreiros*, specially built and adapted not only to meet their ritual requirements but also to satisfy the new demands of sophistication and comfort which are characteristic of modern urban societies. In these *terreiros* the symbolic needs of the cult are often expressed through the very architectural design of the site. Vagner da Silva mentions the wealthy *terreiro* of Pai Laércio in Itapecerica da Serra, a town in São Paulo state. Known as the 'palace of Oxum', its spacious *barracão* was deliberately built in fashionable Colonial style so Pai Laércio could be reminded of the 'big house from slave times'. Its floor is exquisitely tiled and the walls are covered with decorative emblems relating directly to the needs of the cult, including pictures of the *orixás* and stained glass in the colours of the *terreiro's* main *orixás* – yellow for Oxum and blue for Oxóssi (Silva 1995: 177-181).

Pai Roger's *terreiro* in the suburbs of Rio de Janeiro also displays this preoccupation with taste and comfort. Occupying a long rectangular plot stretching from the road to the foot of the adjacent hill, it incorporates all

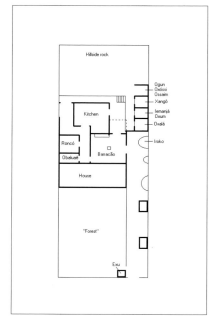

Figure 1: Approximate plan of Pai Roger de Omulu's terreiro in Jacarepaguá, Rio de Janeiro.

Figure 2: Pai Roger's *terreiro* viewed from near the entrance gate, the main area of 'forest' lying to the left in front of the house where Pai Roger and his mother live.
(Photograph: Keith Nicklin and Jill Salmons)

the required features of a candomblé complex, organised around the house that the *pai-de-santo* shares with his mother (fig. 1 & 2). The spacious barracão has a modern floor tiled with decorative marble. A clear concern with aesthetic values is evident in the arrangement of the several pictures of *orixás* hanging on the whitewashed walls. This is reinforced by Pai Roger's manifest interest in the work of artists and craftsmen associated with the candomblé, which emerged several times during our conversations. The central post displays a statue of Obaluaê, the lord of Pai Roger's head and consequently the patron *orixá* for the entire *terreiro* (fig. 3). Obaluaê, or Omulu, is an earth *orixá* and is immensely powerful, since he is the one who both causes and cures disease. There are other visual references to Obaluaê in the decoration. Rather than occupying its normal place in the open air, Obaluaê's shrine is situated inside the building, signifying the fundamental role played by the *orixá* in this candomblé. As is the norm, Obaluaê's shrine also houses the *assentos* for Nanā,

Figure 3: Pai Roger beside the central post, or *ariaxé*, in the *barracão* (public hall) of his *terreiro*. The figure on the *ariaxé* is that of Obaluaê/Omulu, the patron *orixá* of the *terreiro* and lord of Pai Roger's head. (Photograph: Keith Nicklin and Jill Salmons)

Obaluaê's mother, and Oxumaré, the rainbow serpent, his brother. Obaluaê's *peji* is strategically placed next to the *roncó* and the small room used for divination. All these rooms open onto a narrow corridor which links them to both the *barracão* and the large kitchen.

The opposite side of the *barracão* opens onto the long cement path which leads up from the front gate to the wall of rock at the back of the *terreiro*. The 'forest' or garden is situated near the entrance to the candomblé, not far from the *peji* for Exu, somewhat hiding the 'urban' space of the candomblé from passers-by on the road outside and creating a symbolic wilderness which protects the house and its *axé*. A well is located in this lower part of the plot. More trees and plants are interspersed between the path and the *pejis* opposite the *barracão*, the closest one of which to the *barracão* entrance is that of Iroko, surrounded by vegetation. At a higher level behind the main building are closed shrines dedicated to Oxalá, Iansã, Oxum and Iemanjá, and an open *peji* for Ogun, Oxóssi and Ossaim next to a small 'forest' area.

The shrine supplied to the Horniman Museum

There is no apparent tension or conflict between Pai Roger's deep attachment to the *axé* of his *terreiro* and his equally comfortable immersion in the scientific and commercial values of contemporary Rio de Janeiro. His unproblematic approach to this coexistence was clearly present in the way he conducted his agreement with the Horniman Museum. Although he agreed to supply a *peji* in return for a substantial sum of money, he was careful to point out that he would only do so on condition that the *assentos* supplied would not contain the sacred matter that consecrates the emblems of the *orixás*, activating their *axé*. There would be no *otás* and no sacred clay, liquids or leaves inside the containers; rather, the ironware symbols associated with the chosen *orixás* would be 'planted' in papier maché to resemble a ritually prepared *assento*. In other words, no *axé* would be transferred from his *terreiro* to be dispersed abroad.

Instead, Pai Roger concentrated on cultivating the aesthetic aspects of the *assentos* he was to provide, emphasising the need for taste and beauty. He also showed a strong didactic concern, teaching the researchers about the nature of the *orixás* whose *assentos* he finally chose to duplicate – Ogun, Oxóssi and Ossaim – and advising them as to how and why these *assentos* should be displayed. As *orixás* who love the freedom of the outdoors and the forest and who are closely associated with each other in many traditional candomblé activities, Ogun, Oxóssi and Ossaim require their joint *peji* to be built near the 'forest' in the *terreiro* (Augras 1983: 111). Pai Roger explained something of the nature of these *orixás* when showing the *peji* built for them in his own *terreiro* (fig. 4):

> *This is a room that basically contains these 'saints' associated with iron; that is, Ogun, Oxóssi and also Ossaim. Oxóssi is all those [assentos] with the bows and arrows [...] His basic element is the hunt, although the legends have it that he does not kill or cut animals open or rip their heads off, nothing like that. The one who does that is Ogun; Ogun's element is the knife. So Oxóssi hunts for Ogun to kill, for Ogun to cut the animals open for food. And Ossaim – this one here is an Ossaim – he lives together with these 'saints' because they have similar elements, elements like Oxóssi's; he lives in the forest and is the lord of the leaves; he lives to make medicines, ointments for wounds, for internal diseases. They live together because it's the same element.*

Figure 4: Part of the shrine, or *peji*, dedicated to the three *orixás* Ogun, Oxóssi and *Ossaim*, showing several of the *assentos* prepared for them. (Photograph: Keith Nicklin and Jill Salmons)

In any *terreiro*, three basic elements obtained from mineral, plant and animal sources are used in the necessary activation and circulation of *axé*. According to Juana Elbein dos Santos, these elements obey a symbolic logic, which is linked to the meaning of three basic colours: red, black and white. The red element is present in the sacrificial blood of animals and in yellow and orange-coloured substances like palm-nut oil (*dendê*) and honey, as well as metals like copper, brass, bronze and gold. The white element, linked to bodily secretions like semen, milk and saliva, and the sap of trees, is also present in alcohol, white kola nut, cotton, yams and manioc flour, water and the *efun* powder, the white powder used to mark the *iaôs* during initiation. The black element is obtained from the ashes of sacrificed animals and all dark vegetable juices, as green and blue are considered forms of black. Coal and iron too are carriers of black, as is the earth (Santos 1976: 41-2).[12]

The red element is normally associated with female *orixás* like Oxum and Iansã, while white is closely linked to Oxalá, the wise elder. Black, however, marks the essence of the three *orixás* – Ogun, Oxóssi and Ossaim – chosen by Pai Roger for the Museum *peji* (fig. 5). Whether in trees or iron, Ogun's power resides in the element 'black', expressed in the long iron chain he forged, which became the axis of the world (Augras 1983: 108). Ogun is also closely associated with the mystery of the trees and consequently with Ossaim, who is lord of forests and leaves. Ogun's *assento* is 'planted' at the foot of a *cajazeira* tree (*Spondias latea*), surrounded by an evergreen hedge of *peregun* (*Dracaena fragrans*), also known in Brazil as Ogun's sword (Santos 1976: 92). Oxóssi, originally a deity in Ogun's clan, is the *orixá* of hunting and the protector of hunters. He lives in the forest and is linked with Ogun (according to legend they are brothers) and also Ossaim. Master of all wild plants, Ossaim is lord of the leaves, where the *axés* that govern nature are concentrated (Augras 1983: 116). Pai Roger summed up the character of these three deities: 'People ruled by Oxóssi tread carefully, are vain, they like perfumes, and bracelets, and wearing fine cloth. But Ogun prefers to be covered with leaves, he doesn't drink water or wash and is clothed in mud and blood. Ossaim is calmer, more open-minded, thoughtful, well educated; he knows medicine, he has studied, he has a lot of knowledge. *Orixás* can be too playful and can frighten people, but his jokes are quiet ones.'

Figure 5: The three 'assentos' prepared at Pai Roger's *terreiro* for the Horniman Museum (clockwise from the left): for Ogun, Oxóssi and Ossaim. In each case the iron emblem has been 'planted' in papier maché within its earthenware dish, without the use of sacred materials.
(Photograph: Keith Nicklin and Jill Salmons)

Pai Roger explained the choice of components for the *assentos* to be provided by relating them to the nature and personality of his own *filhos de santo*, for whose initiation the *assentos* in his house had been made. The placement of each *assento* within the *peji* in his own *terreiro* followed the same hierarchical structure as governs the candomblé, with Pai Roger's own *assentos* placed prominently on its top shelf. Those related to the more senior *filhos de santo* occupied the top and middle shelves, while the bottom shelf contained the *assentos* prepared for *filhos de santo* who had only recently been initiated. As leader of the house, he was expected to 'seat' the sacred force of all his own *orixás* thus giving symbolic shape to his own *enredo* – the sacred narrative which defined the full complexity of his personality. The *assentos* of each of Pai Roger's other *orixás* were prominently displayed in their corresponding *pejis*, the most important one being that offered to Obaluaê, his dominant *orixá* and the lord of his *terreiro*. Pai Roger was very particular about meeting the demands of the *orixás* and providing them with all their appropriate offerings. The *assento* for his Oxóssi, for instance, included the nest of an ovenbird – a species known in Portuguese as a *joão-de-barro* (literally, 'john-of-clay'), which builds its nest in the shape of a round clay oven with a small entrance – because, in Pai Roger's words, 'clay belongs to Oxóssi', and a nest 'is always something attractive and welcoming'.

Although *axé* was not to leave his house, Pai Roger was careful to prescribe all the correct emblematic

Figure 6: Pai Roger de Omulu in the 'forest' of his *terreiro*.
(Photograph: Keith Nicklin and Jill Salmons)

objects for the Museum to acquire, so that the final replicas should as far as possible represent the true nature of the *orixás* in question. He also constantly reiterated the need for the *assentos* to be displayed within an equally convincing replica of the natural environment preferred by those *orixás*, especially the thick tropical vegetation. All the required objects were to be acquired in the Mercadão de Madureira, a large indoor market in a bustling suburb of Rio de Janeiro which specialises in the sale of African-Brazilian religious articles – statues of and sculpted emblems for the *orixás*, beads in all the required ritual colours, the right types of cloth for ritual dressing, containers for the offerings, *atabaques* (drums), leaves and other materials.

The main emblems normally used for Ogun are miniature reproductions of his favoured iron tools and weapons – knife, sword, hoe, spear, shovel, pick, etc. – in groups of 7, 14 or 21 items, attached to an iron bow; this is known as 'Ogun's implement' (*ferramenta*), and is kept in a clay dish next to the *otá* – in this case a lump of iron ore – in palm-nut oil. Oxóssi's main emblem is the *ofá* or *damatá*, an iron bow and arrow in miniature, likewise kept next to his *otá* (a piece of forest rock) in palm-nut oil (Augras 1983: 108, 111). The principal emblem for Ossaim consists of seven iron rods, symbolising a seven-branched tree, surmounted by an iron bird. The *assentos* made for the Horniman Museum further express the nature of the *orixás* involved by also including a thick iron chain for Ogun, two buffalo horns and a whip for Oxóssi, and four clay dishes for Ossaim.

Since all three *orixás* are normally represented by 'aspects' of the black element, their *assentos* are wrapped in strings of beads – known as *guias* ('guides') – in the ritual colours derived from black: dark blue for Ogun, light blue for Oxóssi and olive green for Ossaim. *Guias* are used in many situations in the candomblé to adorn both persons and objects. This visual text is read and understood by all members of the candomblé, and codifies the symbolic and social life of the *terreiro*. Learning to identify the types of beads and their religious and hierarchic functions is part of the process of initiation that takes place in the *roncó*, which begins with the beads being washed in water and leaves sacred to the *orixá* in question. The beads are also washed – imparted with *axé* – during sacrifices and other rituals, so that they can share in the communal *axé* circulating through the *terreiro*, involving its people, its objects, and its built-up and virgin spaces (Lody 1995: 202-3). Beads are worn by the members to indicate the ethical and cultural commitment that the human being makes towards the *orixá*, the *terreiro* and the candomblé Nation, situating the individual clearly within the candomblé community (Lody 1995: 205). They are one of the few physical signs by which the Jeje candomblé Nation can be identified, as Pai Roger explained: 'All the *orixás* here wear a *brajá*, which is a *guia* of Becém, the king of our Nation.' The Nagô equivalent of Becém is Oxumaré, the rainbow serpent.

Assentos also require the right types of leaves and vegetation. In general terms, plants function within the candomblé as magical protective filters at doorways and gates, shielding people and their affairs (Lody 1995: 186-7). They relate closely to the architectural spaces of the *terreiro* and play their part in the regular rituals. Some are closely associated with particular *orixás*, such as Ogun who is the son of the palm; newly sprouted palm fronds are another major emblem of his, as important as the iron axe with which he hacks a path through the forest (Santos 1976: 93).

All rituals use the juices of plants and involve the collection, maceration and infusion of the leaves that the oracle indicates. Coins may be placed on the ground as an offering before the leaves are picked, as no one can enter Ossaim's domain without first asking permission. Pai Roger, however, is in his element amidst Ossaim's vegetation (fig. 6), as there is a close link between his personal *orixá*, Omulu/Obaluaê, and the *orixás* of the forests and leaves. Indeed, all the epiphytic plants growing on the branches of large trees belong to Obaluaê (Augras 1983: 117-8; p127-8). Pai Roger also acts as a spiritual healer, who knows how to pick leaves from his own 'forest', knows their origins and uses, and is at home buying medicinal plants in the Mercadão de Madureira.

The candomblé holds natural elements such as mountains, rivers, the sea and forests as sacred, since that is where *axé* is found (Silva 1995: 197). But as part of the modern city, it may come into unavoidable conflict with the realities of modern society, with its relentless destruction of natural habitats. This was revealed, for instance, in Pai Roger's search for the deer antlers needed in the *assentos* offered to Oxóssi, since trading in such objects had been banned under Brazilian law and they had become extremely expensive to acquire.

Just as the values of the modern city have been inscribed in modern candomblés, the values traditionally upheld in the *terreiros* also permeate the spaces of the modern city. Many of the rituals must take place outside the spatial boundaries of the *terreiros*, in open areas believed to harbour the vital forces associated with the *orixás*: by the sea, in the forest, near rivers and waterfalls, as well as in built-up areas and especially at crossroads. As a result, the cultural and symbolic markers made by the candomblé are often seen in and around the city, bringing down the barriers between the profane context of modern life and the candomblé's sacred environment. With the transformations typical of urban industrial societies, as Vagner da Silva has pointed out, the cult of the *orixás* has begun not only to live within the city, because of the growing shortage of 'natural' spaces, but also to interact with other concepts, religious or otherwise, of these spaces. In some cases the candomblé will add new meaning not just to nature but to spaces like streets, cemeteries and crossroads, and 'mythical forces' will become attached to them through the presence of the deities (Silva 1995: 198).

Together with the healing activities associated with the presence of Obaluaê as lord of the *terreiro*, this process of reinserting the sacred into the city is one of the most important functions performed by the *terreiro* of Pai Roger de Omulu. In choosing to supply the Horniman Museum with the *assentos* of those three *orixás* rather than any others, he in fact supplied something of his own symbolic essence even though the assentos contained no sacred matter as such. So, whether consciously or unconsciously, he extended the process of re-sacralisation into the distant urban environment of London.

Notes

1. According to Olga Gudolle Cacciatore (1988: 78), another word of Bantu origin, *candombe*, was possibly a combination of the Kimbundu *ka*, habit or practice, and the Kikongo *ndombe*, black, designating the slave dances performed on the colonial plantations as well as the drums used on those occasions. Probably without any religious meaning, *candombe* may also have come to be associated with the term 'candomblé', in a semantic relationship which indicates the link between certain forms of drumming and dancing and the state of religious possession which is induced during the performance of candomblé ceremonies.

2. The following Candomblé Nations are recognised today: Nação Ketu-Nagô (Yoruba), Nação Jexá or Ijexá (Yoruba), Nação Jeje (Fon), Nação Angola (Bantu), Nação Angola-Congo (Bantu), Nação de Caboclo (Afro-Brazilian). There can also be mixed candomblés, like the popular Jeje-Nagô form (Lody 1995: 43, note 2).

3. Although there is a movement, especially in Bahia, to give words and names taken from the Yoruba their original spellings, the widely used Brazilianised spellings will be used here, in keeping with common practice in Rio de Janeiro.

4. Mãe Suzete, a *ialorixá* from Rio de Janeiro, interviewed by the author in 1989.

5. Translated by the author from Santos (1995: 27).

6. Translated by the author from Santos (1995: 26).

7. Translated by the author from Santos (1995: 28).

8. Translated by the author from Santos (1995: 49).

9. Noted by the author.

10. The group, consisting of Keith Nicklin, Jill Salmons and myself, interviewed Pai Roger at his *terreiro* in August-September 1997.

11. This and subsequent quotations from Pai Roger de Omulu are taken from the 1997 interviews and translated from the Portuguese by the author.

12. See also Augras (1983).

Bibliography

AUGRAS, M. 1983. *O Duplo e a Metamorfose: A Identidade Mítica em Comunidades Nagô*. Petrópolis: Vozes.

BENISTE, J. 1997. *Òrun Àiyé: O Encontro de Dois Mundos: O Sistema de Relacionamento Nagô-Yorubá Entre o Céu e a Terra*. Rio de Janeiro: Bertrand Brasil.

CACCIATORE, O. 1988. *Dicionário de Cultos Afro-Brasileiros*. 3rd ed. Rio de Janeiro: Forense Universitária.

CASTRO, Y. 1981. Língua e Nação de Candomblé. In *África, Revista do Centro de Estudos Africanos da USP*, 4, pp. 57-77.

LODY, R. 1995. *O Povo do Santo: História e Cultura dos Orixás, Voduns, Inquices e Caboclos*. Rio de Janeiro: Pallas.

OMARI, M. 1994. Candomblé: A Socio-Political Examination of African Religion and Art in Brazil. In Blakeley, T., Van Beek, W., and Thomson, D. (eds), *Religion in Africa: Experience and Expression*. pp. 135-159.

ORTIZ, R. 1978. *A Morte Branca do Feiticeiro Negro*. Petrópolis: Vozes.

SANTOS, J. 1976. *Os Nàgô e a Morte: Pàde, Àsèsè e o Culto Égun na Bahia*. Petrópolis: Vozes.

SANTOS, M. S. 1995. *Meu Tempo é Agora*. Curitiba: Projeto CENTRHU.

SILVA, V. 1995. *Orixás da Metrópole*. Petrópolis: Vozes.

VOEKS, R. 1997. *Sacred Leaves of the Candomblé: African Magic, Medicine, and Religion in Brazil*. Austin: University of Texas Press.

Contradictory Images:

Bwaba Leaf Masks

and Fibre Masks with

Carved Heads (Burkina Faso)

Michèle Coquet

The Voltaic and Mande societies of Mali, Burkina Faso, and the northern parts of Ghana and Côte d'Ivoire – and more generally the peoples that inhabit the vast savannah in the bend of the Niger River – have invented an original sculptural tradition, in which masks play an important role, owing to their sheer number and aesthetic quality.

Beyond their differing languages, the peoples of the Mande and Voltaic cultural zones have much in common. Besides the similar climatic and geographical conditions, they have comparable social and political structures. Kingdoms and big chiefdoms belong more to the past than to the present. Now, lineage and clannish forms of organisation prevail. The farming populations in this territory attach foremost importance to the land, not just as 'fields' that are cultivated but also as a layered structure, comprising the ground level, where plants grow, as well as the underground level, where the dead rest. The land is a power which requires a shrine, whose custodian is usually the elder of the lineage that has founded the village. Fields surround the village and additional fields lie further out in the bush where wild animals and supernatural beings roam. Despite the increasing scarcity of virgin land, the contrast between the village and unfarmed land is still present. Mande and Voltaic societies also share mythical themes, such as the idea that earth and sky were separated long ago or that human beings have emerged through gradual metamorphoses. The arts and crafts attest to the fact that these peoples have influenced each other for a long time now and have come to constitute a stylistic and iconographic community. The Bwaba belong to this cultural zone.

Numbering about 450,000, the Bwaba inhabit several nonadjacent regions, spread over an area of

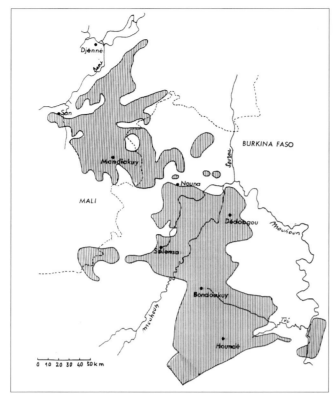

approximately 300 km from north to south, reaching from western Burkina Faso up to the right bank of the Bani River in Mali (map 1). Their dialects differ so much that people of villages lying far apart can hardly, if at all, understand each other. Nonetheless, they feel they speak the same language. The Bwaba use different names to refer to themselves: (in the plural) Bwa, Booba, Bwawa, Bwaba….

Fibre masks with carved heads seem more widespread in the southern areas, where the people call themselves Bwaba. The plural 'Bwaba' and the singular 'Bwanu' are the two terms used in the dialect around Houndé.[1] Bwamu refers to both the language and the area inhabited by the Bwaba. Here, the Bwaba are divided into two farming groups, the Dako and the Kademba (map 2). The term Bwaba, which is used for the whole community, refers in particular to those who work the land, i.e. the majority of the population. But other groups are also part of the Bwaba community: the Fulani herders and lineages of bards and blacksmiths. The latter play a major role in the institutions involving masks. Among blacksmiths one distinguishes several subgroups: those who used to smelt iron ore (*budeba*, singular: *bude*), the blacksmiths in the strict sense of the word (*likiba*, singular: *likinu*), and segments of blacksmith lineages who are now musicians or weavers – elsewhere in the Mande zone, these two occupations are reserved for bards. The smiths call themselves craftsmen (*kaani*, singular: *kaanu*).

Although language and territory do not unify the Bwaba, one cultural element connects all of them: the Doo cult. The masks used in the Doo cult are made of plants — leaves, straw, vine, and bark. Neighbouring ethnic groups, such as the Bobo (where the cult is called Dwo), Bolon and Marka, all of whom make leaf masks, also observe this cult. The masks made of plants manifest Doo's power and presence. They are called *bièni* in general, but each type of leaf mask has its own name. The Bwaba consider the leaf masks to be older than the fibre masks with carved heads. Leaf and fibre masks must be studied together since they coexist — even though only the latter have won a place in museums.

Fibre masks with carved heads were introduced in Bwaba ceremonies at least a century ago. Their origin is known: they have been borrowed from the Winiama (singular: Winie) and Nuna, the Bwaba's eastern neighbours (map 2). Apparently not enough time has passed to erase the social and religious changes wrought by the introduction of fibre masks. Even today, the Bwaba see them as foreign. Studying them is an opportunity to observe how ceremonial items and paraphernalia are imported and adopted.

The Doo cult

The leaf masks are made in a society that assigns an important place to plants, especially trees. Like many Africans who cultivate the land, the Bwaba have a diet based on cereals; and the sauces accompanying the millet meal are usually prepared with varieties of leaves, including those from trees such as the baobab. Trees are used not just for their leaves, fruit and fibres. The wood is used to build houses and make furniture. Tellingly, a tree is planted whenever a homestead is built.

Bwaba myths evince this strong attachment to the world of plants, particularly to wild plants. Gathering leaves, wood and fruit in the bush, is an activity performed by women. Harvesting honey and felling trees are male activities. Both are central to the local economy and figure prominently in the conceptions of human nature. Roaming in the wilderness means rediscovering a mythical time – when the first human beings wandered around the wilderness and ate what they happened to find – the time before farming satisfied nutritional needs. According to the traditions of blacksmiths in the Houndé area, Doo, a leafy creature, and Haa Doo (Woman Doo), his twin sister, were the first children of Dofini (God). Doo and Haa Doo lived during the golden age, before human culture and death existed. From Doo the present world originated – a world where the sky is *above* the earth and where people live in organised communities separated from the wild, the bush.

The time of the year devoted to the Doo cult is situated between the last harvests (tobacco and calabashes) and the beginning of seedtime (millet, fonio, peanuts and corn). During this interval, major collective activities are performed in preparation for the new farming season: clearing the land, cleaning the fields and sowing. 'Doo's time' is delimited by two visits to Doo's earthenware shrine. The first one, marked by the *hen doo nipiè* ceremony, 'open Doo's mouth/lid', takes place normally in March but often nowadays in late February. The ceremony performed during the second visit is called *doo nipiè*, 'Doo's mouth/lid' and takes place in June or in July if the rains are late. During the first ceremony, the pottery is opened and closed during the second ceremony Leaf masks attend the start of the farming season but not the end. The masks with carved heads tend to follow this same ritual calendar.

After opening Doo's earthenware shrine, a rite called *punka loo*, 'push anything harmful out of the village', is performed.[2] Along the way leading from Doo's shrine outside the village to the house where ritual objects are stored, the people wearing leaf masks scrape and brush the walls of granaries and houses as well as their inhabitants with a leafless branch (fig. 1). They brush away the 'dust' and anything harmful that has settled on the community. This rite is normally repeated over several days. Also during Doo's time, leaf masks are brought out to perform various tasks: mending the walls around a well dedicated to Doo, repairing the roof of the smithy, bringing initiates back from the bush, training new age-sets, preparing seedtime, and holding the funeral of Doo priests. In these masked appearances the whole community, men and women alike, participate.

There is an initiation into the Doo cult. The first cycle of initiation involves young people, both male and female, approximately from 13 to 27 years old. In the Houndé area, it is called *fua ba bièhu*, 'cutting the leaf mask', while further north it is called *ho tyènu*, 'the action of eating'. These names refer to two outstanding moments during the ceremony: (a) children cutting the leaves that are to be tied to masqueraders, and (b) children ritually chewing the masks' leaves. During this first initiation cycle, initiands have to fight with the masks, learn to make and recognise various types of costumes, and learn certain dance steps, itineraries and songs. From about the age of 16 up until the beginning of old age, men are supposed to wear the leafy costumes and dance during

Figure 1: Leaf masks during the annual purification ceremony (Houndé), 1993. (Photograph: Michèle Coquet).

Doo's time. The age-set system, itself inseparable from initiation, deeply shapes relations among villagers by creating networks of alliance independent from those between lineages.

Throughout Bwamuland, in the course of Doo's time, leaf masks dance in patterns that differ from village to village (Coquet 1995). During ceremonies, children chew leaves from the masks. The leafy costumes only last one day. Secretly made in the bush by initiates, in early afternoon they make their appearance in the village and dance until night falls, when they are burned at the shrine of Doo. The costume is made with fresh, juicy leaves. Their moistness is a sign of the fertility and nutritional value of plants. The masks come out during Doo's time, a little before nature springs back to life following the first rains. They bear the promise of rebirth.

Blacksmiths who claim to have come from among the Mande peoples living to the west, are said to have brought the Doo cult to the Bwaba of the Houndé area. Regardless of the cult's origins, these blacksmiths usually officiate. The Doo priest (*doo banso*) is nearly always the elder of the smith's lineage. Besides holding this ritual office, the smiths know the etiological tales concerning the cosmogony and the cult and its objects – they are the ones who produce and reproduce these tales. Officially, farmers know nothing about any of this. However, the smith lineage has married into the farming lineage whose ancestors founded the village. The village earth priest, a member of the founder's lineage, assigns portions of the land to newcomers. In order to express this alliance with the smith's headmen, priests of the Doo shrine, the lineage of the earth priests sends a representative to attend the Doo ceremonies. Furthermore, a farmer from the founding lineage sets the date of the opening of the Doo earthenware shrine that signals the beginning of Doo's time. Owing to this close association, the blacksmiths share at least part of their knowledge of myths and ceremonies concerning Doo with their 'hosts'.

Leaf masks compared with fibre masks

Many Bwaba villages do not use fibre masks with carved heads which are more widely found among the Kademba. Among the Dako, farming lineages seldom use fibre masks, but all the blacksmith lineages have them. In both blacksmith and farming lineages, an initiation specific to these masks exists. When initiates come back to the village from the bush camp, the masks come out. These masquerades may also occur on market-days or at the occasion of a lineage head's funeral – moments when leaf masks stay out of sight. In both Dako and Kademba villages in the Houndé area, only blacksmiths may carve the wooden masks. The smiths are recognised to lack the ritual expertise to perform other than their own ceremonies. Further to the east, the wood-carvers allegedly tend to come from neighbouring ethnic groups, the Winiama and the Nuna.

The costume that covers the whole body, is made of dried and dyed Guinean hemp fibre. The dominant brown of the fibres may be set off by a collar and skirt brightly coloured with yellow, red, green or purple industrial dyes (fig. 2). The mask itself is always made out of a single piece of wood. It is either worn like a helmet or else tied to the head; and the person's face is always hidden. In both cases, a long headpiece may reach up above the mask. The designs painted on or carved into the wood's surface are coloured white, black and/or red.

Most of the fibre masks with carved heads are easily recognised as representations of particular wild animals, whereas others combine traits or features from different animals. Only a few types – *e.g.* the long *nwantentè* or the *dambiri* masks (fig. 3 & 4 respectively) – do not represent any specific animal.

These masks, as found among Kademba farming and blacksmith lineages are not indigenous. The animal masks and the masks with vertical headpieces come from the east, from among the Winiama and the Nuna.[3] On morphological grounds, the helmet masks found

Figure 2: Buffalo mask (Boni), 1983. (Photograph: Michèle Coquet).

Figure 3:
Nwantentè
mask (Boni),
1983.
(Photograph:
Michèle Coquet).

Figure 4:
Dambiri mask
(Boni), 1993.
(Photograph:
Michèle Coquet).

among the Dako have been associated with Bobo masks (fig. 5 & 6).[4] It is hard to track down the diffusion of the fibre masks with carved heads among the Bwaba. It is not surprising that the blacksmiths, despite their leading role in the Doo cult, own carved masks. They assert openly that they come from far away – this migration that dates back to mythical times, is common knowledge. Their masks with carved heads are, in actual fact, reserved for ceremonies related to the smithery; and their costumes stand out owing to the natural colour of the fibres, which are never dyed.

However long ago these fibre masks with carved heads may have arrived in Bwamuland, they form a striking contrast with the leaf masks. Made of recently gathered leaves, the latter are destroyed after they have been used for only a few hours. Contrarily, fibre costumes and wooden masks are meant to last. The leaf masks are made by (inexperienced) initiates who braid and knot bark straps on the leafy branches, while the production of fibre masks requires specific skills such as carving, painting and dyeing. The forms of the leaf masks, despite many variations, are less diverse than those of the fibre masks. Finally, the leaf masks are part of a widespread cult whereas the fibre masks are only used in lineage cults.

Fibre masks with carved heads are widespread among the Kademba; and the lineages owning them often compete to possess the most varied mask types. When twenty some of these masks parade in a village, the show impresses everyone. In the past, such spectacular masquerading was sometimes seen as outshining the Doo cult and could lead to fights between villagers who stayed faithful to the leaf masks and those who adopted fibre masks. These foreign masks have been integrated to varying degrees (Voltz 1976: 96-103). Some villages and lineages still categorically refuse to accept them and only make use of leaf masks. In other villages, certain lineages have adopted them as part of their ancestor cults, since they do not want to break with the traditional Doo cult. In this way, using these masks does not endanger the Doo cult's community spirit. Occasionally, the new masks may not be accepted, and their users excluded from the Doo cult. As for those lineages who have broken with tradition, the ceremonial role that used to be played by leaf masks (during annual purification rites or initiation) has been shifted onto the fibre masks. These cult objects were introduced along with the roles and duties related to them in their homeland: dance steps, songs and the intellectual system in which they bore meaning.

In the interpretation made by the Bwaba lineages who have converted to them, the fibre masks are closely associated with the founding of the lineage. They represent and celebrate the local spirits of the wilderness or wild animals who allowed the lineage's ancestors to settle where they did. The fibre masks and cults rival the community's Doo cult and masquerade

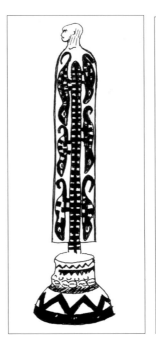

Figure 5: Mask from the village of Kari.

Figure 6: Mask belonging to the Boñana lineage (Houndé).

that celebrate the forces of plant life in the bush. The myths told by the blacksmiths, speak of the the leaf masks as representing humanity's sudden appearance, when the human world emerged out of a universe mostly filled with plants – a mythical world of which the bush (where the leafy creatures, Doo and his twin sister, lived) is all that is left (Coquet 1995). In contrast, the fibre masks with carved heads call to mind stories that are a full part of the human world, as evinced by the material nature of these masks: painted, carved objects, which are the product of human craftsmanship. The fibre masks with carved heads are distinctly human artifacts. Most leaf masks, on the other hand, are made to look like moving bushes; little is done to give shape to the jumble of leaves and branches (fig. 1).

A similar contrast can be seen among the Bobo whose Dwo cult uses both sorts of masks. As among the Bwaba, the leaf masks – manifestations of Dwo – epitomise the power of the wilderness. Unlike the leaf masks who were bestowed upon mythical ancestors, the Bobo fibre masks – manifestations of Dwo at a later date – were revealed to real persons who transmitted knowledge about them to their lineage descendants (Le Moal 1980: 327-336).

Among the Bwaba, even in the case of the fibre masks used in a lineage ancestor cult, this complementarity between leaf and fibre masks is not recognised. The fibre masks bear the indelible mark of their foreign origin. Aside from the lineage masks that are fully part of the blacksmiths' Doo cult, these masks never convey the values attached to the Doo cult. Quite to the contrary, the lineage who owns them may, in extreme situations, claim a special relation to the land, a relationship paying no heed to the rules of precedence whereby, in each village, the lineage of the first occupant's descendants holds the office of earth priest.

Iconographic themes

Iconographically, the fibre masks with carved heads – whether Bwaba, Winiama or Nuna – manifest a relative thematic unity. This unity encompasses, too, some of the leaf masks consecrated to Doo and, more broadly, masks in the entire Mande and Voltaic zones. The mythology sheds light on a common world-view: the world's principal axis connects earth and sky, which used to be one before they were formed. According to several tales, the creation of people, animals and plants by the gods caused the earth and sky to separate. The earth is not only the place where people dwell but also the underworld – a dark, damp place where the sun sets at dusk, where plants germinate, and where deceased ancestors rest before coming back among the living through yet-to-be-born children. The sky is the seat of certain supernatural beings. From it comes light, heat and rainfall, which make life possible.

The fibre masks with carved heads are designed with this fundamental contrast between sky and earth in mind. Periodically manipulating them maintains a continuity between these separate worlds by celebrating the regularity of natural cycles: the daily appearance and disappearance of the sun, the waxing and waning of the moon, the seasonal cycle, and the regular return of the rainy season. Certain Dogon, Bwaba and Winiama masks have a headpiece as long as three or four meters. When dancing, this Bwaba python mask, which resembles the Dogon *sirige* mask, bends over backwards and forwards, from east to west, so that the tip of the headpiece touches the earth (fig. 7). This mimics the sun's course; and the curve it makes joins heaven to earth. The snake as animal of renewal – symbolisation of its periodic slough – is called on to play that role.

There are recurrent animals in this mask-related symbolism: reptiles (python, crocodile, lizard, chameleon, turtle), birds (rooster, hawk, hornbill), horned mammals (buffalo, ram, various antelopes) and other animals (monkey, warthog, aardvark, pangolin anteater). These animals are depicted either in full or in part, showing certain characteristic elements such as the hornbill's jutting beak. They are presented alone or in a group. In

Figure 7: Python mask (Lopui in Pê), 1985. (Photograph: Michèle Coquet).

Figure 8: Rooster mask (Bouéré), 1993. (Photograph: Michèle Coquet).

Figure 9: Mask with hornbill feathers (Boni), 1985. (Photograph: Michèle Coquet).

the latter case, the group's composition usually seems to ensue from a 'logic' based on the separation of heaven and earth. The 'earth' is represented by animals with 'subterranean' habits – most of the reptiles (python, lizard, crocodile, turtle) and a few mammals, especially those that root (pangolin, aardvark, warthog). The 'sky' is represented by the birds (especially the hornbill) and, too, by animals who dwell in between heaven and earth (the chameleon who lives in trees or animals with horns reaching up into the air). Societies in this cultural zone have their own preferences. Kademba farmers, for instance, prefer the buffalo, python, crocodile and antelope. Each blacksmith lineage owns a set of *hombo* masks, which always includes a rooster with an oversized comb that, painted bright red, represents the sun (fig. 8) – however each lineage carves this mask, in particular the cockscomb, in its own special way. Besides the rooster, the *hombo* masks include the buffalo, a 'horse' antelope and the *dambiri*. Like the *nwantentè*, this fourth mask has a vertical headpiece, but the board is carved in an *H*-shape, which is said to represent horns. Furthermore, its forehead always bears a very stylised hornbill, recognisable by its beak. The *dambiri* is partly covered with bright, red and black, seeds from the *Abrus precatorius* tree; they are called the 'rooster's eye'. The main colour of the carved part is the red of the sun and the blacksmith's forge (fig. 4).

Among both the Kademba and Dako, there is a leaf mask with an impressive crest of white hornbill feathers fastened with porcupine quills (fig. 9) but this mask does not represents a specific animal. Though barely visible, the quills suggest, along with the feathers, the fundamental opposition between earth and heaven.

Just as most Mande and Voltaic peoples share the same major iconographic themes, the styles of their objects have much in common. This holds, in particular, for the masks among certain Voltaic peoples. The use of three colours and of geometric decorations, the many animal-shaped masks, a particular way of stylising animals, the wearing of a loose-fitting, dark-coloured fibre costume that covers the whole body, the frequency of masks with a long headpiece, all these characteristics endow the carved masks with a strong family resemblance. Those of the Winiama, Nuna, Marka and Bwaba have, unlike the masks of other peoples, costumes that are often adjusted to the wearer's body. These masks resemble each other so much that it is hard to distinguish a Bwaba buffalo mask from a Winie or Nuna one: the horns form a circle above the animal's head; three surfaces in a triangle form a muzzle; concentric circles always surround the slightly protuberant cone-shaped eyes (fig. 2). Although the Bwaba masks resemble the animals they represent (except, as already pointed out, for the quite original rooster mask), the *nwantentè* mask has evolved away from the original Nuna and Winiama models. The vertical headpiece is longer: 132 cm. among the Kademba as compared with 102 cm. among the Nuna (Voltz 1976: 225) and figurative motifs are used in decoration. Furthermore, the headpiece is cut in a fairly stable, rectangular pattern. On Winiama and Nuna masks of this type, the headpiece may be cut so as to form a line of circles, or it may have human- or animal-shaped, rounded embossments carved on it. Such forms are seldom seen among the Bwaba.

Appropriating the fibre masks

Unlike many animal masks, masks with a vertical headpiece are easily recognised as of Bwaba origin. They provide us with an example of how new forms are adopted from a foreign cult. In this case, modifying the overall form has entailed reworking the decorative motifs. The mask's face usually has a single pair of eyes, unlike many Nuna and Winiama masks. The mask shows checkerboard patterns, broken lines, chevrons, and borders with small triangles. These designs stand out against the white background, and are bigger than those observed on Nuna and Winiama masks. These stylistic characteristics are especially visible on the masks of western Kademba villages. A striking stylistic modification can be observed on masks from Boni and Dossi, two villages where the vertical headpieces show a big cross-shaped design on the front (fig. 3). This motif is the distinctive mark that used to be scarified onto the foreheads of these villagers and of those persons who, though born elsewhere, had a paternal or maternal forebear from there. At closer inspection, we notice that most of the motifs carved and painted on these masks are also used to mark bodies. The broken line, the chevrons and the border of triangles were the basic motifs of body scarification. Most of these designs, the cross being an exception, are not made with a few broad strokes but with a series of small, vertical cuts into the skin.

The similarity between designs on the body and on the masks leads the Bwaba to propose a single interpretation of both. Didiiro, a big blacksmith clan divided into many lineages, has settled among the western Kademba in the Houndé area. The smiths are often asked to carve the masks with vertical headpieces for farming lineages in Boni and Dossi. They know the meaning of the designs which were once used as scarification patterns. This body art was closely associated with the Doo cult and its cosmogony. Among the western Kademba, the introduction by farmers of these vertical headpieces with foreign origins has led not just to changing the size of the headpiece but also to adopting a pre-existing system of signs and transferring it onto another material. Nowadays, this operation can be interpreted as follows. It seems that certain farming lineages have managed to 'dispossess' the smiths of the knowledge (and of the power related to it) of what these designs mean and of how they can be manipulated. The sharing of knowledge in the context of inter-lineage alliances between smiths and farmers in the context of the Doo cult, now seems to be looked upon negatively. The smiths are kept out of the village cults that use these masks. In the aforementioned villages, these cults play the role that the leaf masks used to play in the Doo cult. Whatever the case may be, the Kademba seem to be using more and more masks with vertical headpieces, even though the practice of scarring the body has disappeared.

The iconography of these long masks uses themes specific to the vast Mande and Voltaic cultural zones. The *nwantentè* mask with the long rectangular headpiece would represent a sort of fish (silure) associated throughout this zone with a phase in the development of the foetus. This mask has three parts, from bottom up: a round face, a vertical headpiece and, on top, a crescent, which suggests the fish's tail and the tips of its fins. The widespread crescent motif, though a reminder of the tips of the fins, is mainly taken to be the early first quarter of the moon. The mouth with teeth on the mask's face represents a well, which is understood to be an entrance leading toward the underworld of the deceased. Sticking out from this entrance, a curved piece of wood represents both the male sexual organs and the hornbill's beak. This proboscis may appear several times on the axis running up through the middle of the mask – it can also be seen in an identical form on Nuna and Winiama masks. The Bwaba associate the hornbill, an animal thought to have taken part in the genesis of the world, with the moon. The big eyes formed by concentric circles are those of a night bird, an owl – the same eyes appear on the *dandièhoun* (butterfly) masks, which have a horizontal headpiece (fig. 10). The masks with vertical headpieces bring together the world from before birth to the world of the deceased, they join the sky and the underworld. In this way, the Bwaba masks with vertical or horizontal headpieces evince the continuity in and modification of the forms and styles characteristic of the Mande and Voltaic zones and, too, of the ideas they express.

Lineages adopt certain decorations for their masks from a shared corpus of geometrical, non-figurative designs. The designs chosen to be carved by a craftsman, usually represent objects such as animal tracks, hills, leaves or checkered blankets. Comparable or identical designs represent these objects on things other

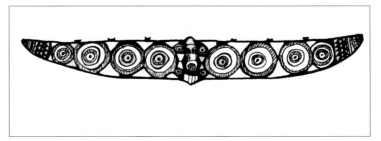

Figure 10: Dandièhoun ('butterfly') mask (after Roy 1987, p273).
(Picture: Michèle Coquet).

than masks — on skin, earthernware or metal. Through interpretation and public exegesis, lineages associate these designs with their history, in particular, with their foundation narrative or the revelation of the first masked beings. In Boni and Dossi, the cross shape has several names and allows several interpretations; among them, the spider's web or the traps set on the paths leading to the place of initiation. These explanations are woven into the stories told by various lineages. Nonetheless, the cross, which used to be a template for body scarification, has a common meaning in both villages: it is a design not of a cross but of two triangles joined at the tip, and recalls the mythical time when the sky still touched the earth. The triangle that represents the earth is a recurrent theme in Bwaba and, more generally, Voltaic iconography. It can be seen in the hills outside Boni and Dossi – where these masks were originally revealed and where, since then, initiation takes place. Non-figurative geometrical designs are often found alongside other, clearly understood motifs, since they represent Mamiwata (a water divinity of Indian origins with a mermaid's body – her cult originated in Nigeria), the chameleon, owl, python, pots, whistles, stars, etc. The geometrical motifs seem restricted to the rather narrow Voltaic corpus of designs used to scarify the body and decorate objects. In contrast, there is more freedom to invent and create figurative designs.

Most of the helmet masks with carved headpieces have figurative designs (fig. 5). Such masks can be found among Dako farmers. The semicircle on top the mask in figure 6,[5] – a mask that belongs to the earth priest's lineage of Houndé – shows the obvious designs of a bullroarer, a snake and a checkered circle. The snake is the python, who named the lineage (*boñana*) and gave it land. The checkered circle represents the opening of the sacred well where the python dwells; a blanket belonging to the earth priest hides this opening from sight. On the helmet itself, we notice the *didiiro* fish with its mouth open; this animal protects the affinally related blacksmith clan of Houndé. Another circle with a point at the center represents the earth shrine (Voltz 1976: 107-108).

Figure 11, drawn by a blacksmith of the Didiiro clan, portrays the front and back of a mask carved by a craftsman from the clan.[6] The designs refer to the story of the mask being revealed to a future diviner. In Bwamuland, becoming a diviner entails, among other ordeals, spending time in the bush, where supernatural

Figure 11: Mask from
the village of Didio
(front and back).
(Picture: Michèle Coquet).

Figure 12: Mask from
the village of Didio.
(Picture: Michèle Coquet).

beings appear to the applicant. They always ask him to have objects made that will be needed for divination. The figurative motifs on the mask suggest this meeting. It does not allude to what happened during the meeting but refers to the places where it took place and to the objects that the supernatural being asked to have made. On the lower obverse side, a broken line suggests the range of hills where the revelation took place. Just above are strings of cowry shells, as used for divination. On top of the cowry shells, from left to right, are designs of the pot holding the shells; a necklace with a spherical pendant showing a cross that represents the rays of the sun; a rectangular amulet; a circle filled with wavy lines representing a termite-mound; and, finally, a staff carved by a diviner. In the next layer we see the first quarter of the moon surrounded by stars, a reminder of the period of the month that is propitious for divination. The following row portrays, from left to right, a key, two whistles and a hatchet. The headpiece's upper part has a belt decorated with cowry shells and containing protective 'medicine'. The circles at the very top represent the eyes of an owl. This motif also appears on the backside of the mask, as does the belt with amulets and shells. In the center, a design represents the entrance to the underworld, the hill where the future diviner meet the supernatural being. This entrance is shut by a door, which is represented in the bottom row by the two zigzags – the key on the other side of the mask opens this door. There is an eclipse of the moon in the center of the entrance. The shells around the arched entrance suggest the special shirt worn by the diviner whenever he visits the world under the hills.

The 'logic' underlying these figurative motifs is, to an extent, shared by the abstract, geometric designs that, for example, indicate the place of revelation (a zigzagging road, a ridge line, a mound, an entrance to the underworld) or refer to a lunar calendar (the crescent, the stars, or the checkered motif representing the alternation of days with/without a moon). However, introducing figurative motifs 'bootstraps' the meaning of an image, irrespective of the use of language. The Didio mask lists nearly all the objects owned by the diviner. Likewise, the mask belonging to the Boñana lineage visibly indicates both the marital alliance with Didiiro, the smith lineage, and the mythical being (a snake) thanks to whom the lineage settled in the Houndé area and acquired the office of earth priest.

By comparing figures 11 and 12, drawn by different people but representing the same mask, we notice

Figure 13:
Dambiri masks.
(Picture: Michèle Coquet).

slight differences in the motifs: the reverse side of the mask in figure 1 does not contain the key and the hills. On the small rectangle sticking out at the end of the headpiece, we notice a motif representing an amulet instead of cowry shells. As these illustrations show, a degree of freedom in designing and interpreting exists within the limitations set for transcribing information about how a spirit revealed the masks.

Decoration as fascination

What is impressive about the mask parade is not so much their size or general form as the large surfaces covered with coloured designs. The foregoing examples help us understand how both those who have carved and painted the masks and those who look at them perceive them. The designs on the *dambiri* masks (figure 13) show that the surfaces of masks are ideally suited for combining motifs in potentially endless patterns.[7] Through these drawings by young blacksmiths from the Didiiro clan, who had already begun learning how to make masks, we can sense the pleasure of designing. But this art is not intended merely for decoration. It stands out. During ceremonies, the masks with vertical headpieces and, to a lesser extent, the animal-shaped masks present designs that only a few persons are able to interpret, as also used to be the case, not so long ago, of body scars. The effect of these designs on those who see them is all the greater insofar as the latter only understand them as signs of the alliance with spirits and of the power and prosperity of the lineage that owns them. Like most Mande and Voltaic societies, the Bwaba widely use carved or drawn designs in their visual environment. These designs are understood as 'physical presences' that, with an astonishing visual impact during the ceremony, convey a knowledge that is not widely shared or not very accessible – in brief, that is hidden. The impact of designs reaches far beyond village ceremonies, since it fuels the trade in masks. Copies, as big as the originals or in miniature, are sold to tourists and to government employees working in the local area, who hang them on their wall for decoration. Copies of the masks with long headpieces are among the 'exotic' objects most appreciated by French decorators. Even the drawings we saw, made by young Didiiro smiths, demonstrate that the carved masks attract more attention than the fibre costumes.

In the struggle between those who remain faithful to the Doo cult's leaf masks and those who have adopted the fibre masks with carved heads, other factors come into play than those already mentioned. Although safeguarding a religious community's values certainly carries weight, wanting to use new artistic forms that are felt to be completely different is a factor that should not be overlooked. When making leaf masks, attention is focused on using a material calling for gestures and a perception of forms so that what counts is not the knowledge of how to use the material but the power to express, without altering them, the force and vitality of plant life. To do this, initiates hang leaves on the costume so that, whenever the wearer runs, the leaves move and rustle. By combining various types of leaves, they modify the silhouette, since, like a garment, the folds of the leaves change. They also modify the visual impact of the leaves, since the latter, always fresh, reflect light differently depending on the species used. By making leaf masks, initiates recreate the original plant world. By putting on the *nwantentè* mask, the headpiece displays designs that, though understood by very few people, subsist as pure, bright visual presences. In reality, these two aesthetics are felt to be contradictory.

Translated from French by Noal Mellott (CNRS, Paris)

Notes

1. All Bwamu names will henceforth be given in Houndé dialect.

2. The Bobo observe an identical rite.

3. In the literature, these masks are sometimes said to be of 'Nunuma' origin. Nunuma, however, is a word coined by the Winiama to refer to their northern Nuna neighbours. For photographs of masks from the Voltaic zone, see Roy (1987).

4. Michel Voltz (1976), the only author who has attempted a stylistic study of these masks, made this comparison on the basis of the helmet shape and the fact that, among the Dako, this mask may be anthropomorphic. I believe that associating Dako with Bobo masks is probably going too far, taking into account the fact that certain Mossi masks also have these characteristics.

5. Figures 1 and 2 are drawings made from photographs published by Voltz (1976: ill. 74, 75 and 26).

6. This mask is said to be in Didio, a village near Boni. It is also probably related to the story about the founding of the lineage, but I do not possess any proof of this.

7. Especially in a context where the surfaces of walls, natural shelters, textiles, etc., are seldom decorated in this way.

Bibliography

CAPRON, J. 1957. Quelques Notes sur la Société du Do chez les Populations Bwa du Cercle de San. *Journal des Africanistes*, **27**, 1, 81-129.

CAPRON, J. 1973. Communautés Villageoises Bwa, Mali-Haute-Volta. *Mémoire de l'Institut d'Ethnologie* IX Paris: Institut d'Ethnologie, Musée de l'Homme **1**, 1.

COQUET, M. 1993. Les Savanes de l'Afrique de l'Ouest: Les Masques Sculptés. In *Le grand atlas de l'art* Paris: Encyclopaedia Universalis **2**, 448-449.

COQUET, M. 1995. Des Dieux Sans Visage: de la Morphologie des Masques de Feuilles Bwaba (Burkina Faso). In de Heusch, Luc (ed), *Objets-Signes d'Afrique,* 21-35.

CREMER, J. 1927. Les Bobo (la Mentalité Mystique). *Matériaux d'Ethnographie et de Linguistique soudanaises* 4. Paris: Paul Geuthner.

LE MOAL, G. 1978. Rites de Purification et d'Expiation. In *Systèmes de Signes. Textes Réunis en Hommage à Germaine Dieterlen,* 349-357.

LE MOAL, G. 1980. Les Bobo. Nature et Fonction des Masques. *Travaux et Documents de l'ORSTOM* **121**. Paris: ORSTOM.

ROY, C. 1987. *Art of the Upper Volta Rivers*. Meudon: Alain et Françoise Chaffin.

RASILLY, B. 1965. Bwa Laada: Coutumes et Croyances Bwa. *Bulletin de l'Institut Français d'Afrique noire,* série B, **27**, 1/2, 99-154.

VOLTZ, M. 1976. *Le Langage des Masques Chez les Bwaba et les Gurunsi de Haute-Volta,* **1**. Ouagadougou: Université de Ouagadougou.

Masks and Styles: Yoruba Masquerade in a Regional Perspective

10

William Rea

One of the most vital elements of Yoruba visual culture is masquerade. Masks are performed in most of the towns in south-western Nigeria that lay claim to an identity defined by the people as Yoruba. The popularity of masquerading amongst the Yoruba public is still evident despite the prevalence of other forms of popular culture, such as video and television. Masquerading also maintains its presence despite admonishments from various Christian groups, particularly those of a more Pentecostal persuasion. It is clear that to many of the participants in masquerade festivals across the south-west, whether as performers or as audiences, the continuation of masquerading is intimately bound up with ideas about identity and meaning.

Masquerade in Yorophone south-western Nigeria has also been the subject of numerous academic papers. As with Yoruba art in general, more is probably known and written about Yoruba masquerade than any other masquerade form in Africa. The sheer productivity of Yoruba artists (performers, weavers, woodcarvers), not to mention the social formations that have ensured masquerade a continued popularity into the twenty-first century, has meant that there is plenty to write about. There are however, a number of problems in the literature on Yoruba masks and masquerading. Problems that might distract from wider considerations about masquerade practice in south-western Nigeria. One of the more significant of these is that the literature on masquerading tends to define specific areas of types of mask practice, ignoring the fact that different mask practices may be co-existent.[1]

There is a prevailing view of Yoruba cultural diversity in masquerade which labels certain regions as 'home' to certain types of masquerade style. In this view the centralised Yoruba produce Egungun, those of the south-

Map 1: The Kingdom of Ìkòlé and its neighbours in Ekiti

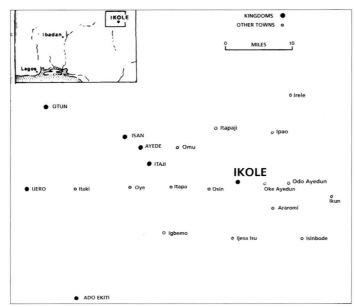

west make Gelede and in the north east it is Epa that is the predominant mask form. As an understatement of the diversity of Yoruba masking practices, this is unfortunate. What is more problematic, however, is the way in which this labelling (packaging) creates a view of bounded ethnic identity related to cultural practice which does not allow for the diversity that in fact prevails. The idea of specific cultural 'areas' of mask practice serves to further reify a concept of 'Yoruba Culture' which is itself an 'invention' of the later nineteenth century, although the roots of this invention may lie further back in time (Obayemi 1981; Peel 1989). Thus although there are differences, all these mask forms are supposedly part of a bounded Yoruba identity. As research proceeds this 'art-history' of the Yoruba is being challenged, but as I left for Nigeria in 1990 I still expected to find Epa masks in Ekiti rather than the Egigun that were being actively performed in the town of Ikole where I worked. Consequent to the problem in the art-historical literature is the idea that it is mask 'styles' that define the boundaries. In fact style is often the material manifestation of a whole series of other mediations; style is the vehicle of meaning but not meaning itself. Undoubtedly part of the recognised meanings that are incorporated in masquerade practice and performance is a sense of identity; often of individuals, certainly of towns, but rarely of entire regions.

Rather, I argue, a view that incorporates a comparative perspective allows the analysis of Yoruba masking to move beyond formal categorisations that mark out different areas of practice. This approach works not so much toward an understanding of different stylistic practice marking distinct boundaries, but rather toward discerning continuities that in turn might allow better understanding of the ontological status underpinning masquerade in the south-western region of Nigeria. In order to demonstrate this variation in the following sections, I will give an account of two different masquerade performances (Epa and Egigun) found within the same geographical Yoruba region. Each offer alternative interpretations of meaning, cult practice, individual and local identity, both within their own performances and as against each other. Yet, I conjecture that art-historical categorisation on the basis of formal styles disguises an underlying ontology that may encompass a much wider region than that simply labelled Yoruba.[2]

Masks and identities in Ekiti

There are a number of historical and cultural reasons why the Ekiti region of Nigeria regards itself as autonomous from other Yoruba districts. A distinct landscape, dialect and social organisation have all served to produce a stated Ekiti identity within the city states in which the majority of people in Ekiti lived. It was the *Ekiti Parapo* (Ekiti 'gathering'), however, formed in the late nineteenth century to defend the area from Oyo intrusion, that saw the emergence of a distinct identity. In 1996 the political identity of the region was recognised by the federal government when Ekiti was awarded its own state government.

Within Ekiti, masking practice is extremely diverse and the boundaries of a particular mask style seemingly arbitrary (Poyner 1987: 56). Rather than suggesting that there is an Ekiti style of masquerade, different mask styles are much more likely to belong to particular towns, groups of people or even families. It is not uncommon to find two or three different masking complexes co-existent within the same town, although only very rarely would they be performed together. The general name for 'mask' in Ekiti as in other Yoruba regions is *egun*. However under the rubric Egun are a number of entirely differing mask styles. While working in a small area of northern Ekiti, around the town of Ikole Ekiti, I witnessed performances of masks that were known as Egigun, Epa, Alasase, Egburu, and Ore. Within categories there were definite differences in form and names – thus in some places Epa is one thing and Egburu another, in others the Egburu masquerade is an Epa.

In order to address this overlapping of different masquerade forms I want to focus briefly on the performances of two types of masquerades in the Ikole local government region. This is a region of roughly thirty square miles, and yet contains within it a variety of different masquerade styles. Ikole town was once the centre of what Obayemi (1976) has described as a mini empire and it seems clear that the villages that are now incorporated into or surround the central town were once a part of an Ikole led confederation. The Oba of Ikole (the Elekole) describes himself as *primus inter pares* in relation to the other villages.

The mask styles that I address here are Egigun and Epa. Both types of masquerade are performed in the Ikole district, as well as across Ekiti. In museum collections of Yoruba art it is the Epa-type headpiece mask that is the better known of these two masquerade types. In Ekiti, however, the type of masquerade that is most frequently performed and in some form seems to have an increasing popularity is Egigun. In some towns in Ekiti the spectacular appearance of the Epa type mask is in decline; in part because many of the masks have been stolen and not replaced by local carvers and patrons and in part because there is less interest in the cults associated with these masks. In other places however, these masks are the centre piece of annual civic celebrations.

Egigun in Ikole

The masquerade that occupies most attention in Ikole is known as Egigun. As with its better known counterpart in central Yoruba districts, Egungun, this is a masquerade form that relates to the return of ancestral beings from *orun* (heaven). In theory the various forms of this masquerade appear bi-annually, but in practice certain types will perform annually at the largest of the town's festivals, celebrating Ogun, the god of iron and war.

Within Ikole there is an acknowledgement that the masks of Egigun are similar to the Egungun masquerades that are more familiar in the literature on Yoruba masking.[3] It appears that they occupy a similar 'cosmological' space in relation to ancestral powers. They are *ara orun* (people of heaven) as seems to be the case with Egungun, although no Egigun is ever described as an identified ancestor. In turn this raises the question of how the relationship between performer and spirit is conceptualised. As with Egungun there is no simple answer and the emphasis often differs between the different types of performed masquerade but as a general rule Egigun masquerades conform to Picton's (1991) categorisation of Egungun as masks where the costume is not simply a dramatic device hiding the performer but also invokes a spiritual presence. The conflation between performer and presence is regarded as complete.

As such the comparability, or difference, of the two types (Egungun and Egigun) might seem to rest upon stylistic differences. Within Ikole this is acknowledged. One of the statements that people made to explain the difference between Egigun and Egungun was that Egungun were dressed in cloth, but that in Ekiti they made their own with palm leaves. This is patently true, all the masks that perform under the rubric Egigun use either palm leaves or raffia in their costume. The style of mask that is accredited with being the original Egigun, a mask known as Owi in Ikole, is made entirely of split raffia palms, whereas all other types of masks use a combination of cloth and palm leaves.

There are a number of different styles of mask used in Egigun masquerading, but a broad division, made by the performers, is between senior masks known as Eku and a series of other often more junior masquerades, the prevalent form of these being known as Agbe. Within the category Eku there are three main masks: Aborogi, Egun're, and Ede. (See figs. 1, 2, and 3).

Figure 1: This is the mask of the Aborogi masquerade performed by chief Oloka. It depicts the face of a beautiful woman. Ikole Ekiti, 1990. (Photograph: William Rea).

Figure 2: The Egun're masquerades of Ikole. The upper head covering is of white cloth, while hidden below the etu robe is a red underwrapper. Ikole Ekiti, 1991. (Photograph: William Rea).

Figure 3: Ede, a mask that carries the feathers of the birds of the forest in its headpiece. Ikole Ekiti, 1991. (Photograph: William Rea).

Each of these masks performs separately and it is widely known that they should not meet while performing. Egun're is a masquerade constructed primarily from cloth, although it carries a small 'bundle' of medicinal substance on its head. Three colours of cloth are used: the head covering is white, the main body is covered by a blue *agbada* (large gown) of the type known as *etu* (lit: guinea fowl pattern), which in turn covers an underskirt that is made from red cloth. Aborogi is a mask that represents the mother of the masquerades, and appears in a wooden mask that completely covers the head. The mask is carved as a 'beautiful' woman, and a number of diagnostic features are found in this 'set' of masquerades. They are always carved with a women's hairstyle and feature the mouth with teeth showing, especially with a gap-toothed 'smile'. Other features of the carving vary, but in general show aspects of perceived beauty, such as small scarifications or earrings. Again the main body of the masquerade is covered by an *etu* robe. Ede is a masquerade of some magnificence, its main feature being a headpiece said to be constructed from the feathers of 'all the birds of the forest'. The body is clothed as the other two.

Although iconographically different, the performance of each of the Eku masquerades is closely related. They appear in town, either individually or in pairs, accompanied by musicians Their main performance area is through the interstitial spaces of the town; alleyways and the connecting paths between compounds. Their movement is slow, stately even, and they are known for singing and giving out blessings as they move.

In contrast the masquerade that is predominantly performed by young men is known as Agbe (see fig. 4 and 5). The emphasis in performances of this masquerade is on the dramatic and competitive. The style of the mask is quite basic: a woollen hat pulled over the head disguises the face, and

Figure 4: A typical scene of Agbe masquerades dominating the centre of Ikole during the Ogun festival. Ikole Ekiti, 1990.
(Photograph: William Rea).

Figure 5: Epa mask, Horniman Museum, London.
(Photograph: Horniman Museum, Heini Schneebeli).

the costume is of an *agbada* tunic and women's wrapper, over which is placed a skirt of *mariwo* palm-leaves. Elaboration within this frame however is diverse. Masks are personalised, often with names, but also with distinctive iconographical devices such as small wood carvings attached to the headpiece, horns, beaded dreadlocks. Names often refer to the power of the masquerade, yet this is not necessarily a metaphysical power, it is quite appropriate for masks to be called 'Ninja', 'Niger' or even 'Rasta' – each of these names conveying young men's notions of importance and powerful experience.

Epa

In contrast to the fluidity established in the masquerade styles of *egigun* the masks that have become known as Epa within the West, display a solidity of structure, a solidity that refers not only to the carving but also to their performances. Epa are amongst the most distinctive masks in West Africa, being the largest single-piece wooden masks in the region (see fig. 6). Although made from one piece of wood, the mask is in general separated into two sections. The lower section is an oval 'pot-shaped' covering of the head, often carved with a janus face. The wearer looks out of the mask through an enlarged slit like mouth. The upper superstructure,

Figure 6: One of the Ikun Epa masks (ologbo) appearing from the bush and making its entrance to the market place. 1990, Ikun. (Photograph: William Rea).

which sometimes rests upon a round platform, is usually a sculpture of quite impressive dimensions. Ojo (1978) and Abejide (1984) have noted that the themes portrayed in the sculpted parts of the masks generally fall into three categories: the warrior on horse-back, the female figure surrounded by children, and various animal themes, usually representing animals of the bush, in particularly those that are associated with symbols of royalty or power. Within these themes the styles of representation on the superstructure vary considerably, and within the frame of creativity set up by the Epa-type corpus there is a wide range of differing styles. What is also apparent however is that often those masks that are acknowledged to hold most metaphysical power have little or no iconographical elaboration beyond that part of the mask that covers the head.

Less distinguishable however is the place that they have in Yoruba masquerade practice. Not only is there no single name characterising the masks of this type, there would also appear to be little in common in the various uses that these masks are put to. Ojo (1978) is entirely correct when he states that these masks should not be referred to as 'Epa' but rather as 'Epa-type masks', because the contexts in which masks that are generally known as Epa differ widely. Although there is a cult known as Epa, and Epa-type masks are used in the performances of Epa, the use of this mask type is not confined to performances associated with one particular deity.[4] In the Ikole region alone there are masks of this type that are used in festivals known as Egburu, Olua, Elefon and Ojuna as well as Epa. There is also a wide variation in the names for the deity that these festivals honour. Thus the deity Egburu is Imole in one town but described by some people as Epa in another, Olua is described as Orisa as is Ojuna.[5] Epa is Orisa in some places and Imole in others. In Ikole, Elefon is performed without reference to any mask, but a large mask is carried in other places. This pattern of variation is found throughout the Ekiti region, and it would seem that although the forms of the Epa-type mask is fairly consistent throughout the region , their contexts of use within various cults and the meanings imputed to them, vary considerably.[6]

The festivals associated with Epa-type masks differ considerably from place to place as well. The appearance of Epa-type masks in festival contexts varies from a single mask being carried through one village quarter, through to festivals in which the appearance of the masks are greeted by thousands of people. The cults associated with these masks may encompass only one family or be the major focus of a town's ritual calendar.

The Egburu festival in the village of Ikun provides one example of the context in which Epa-type masquerades are used. In relation to the general literature on Epa this festival appears to be fairly paradigmatic of the type of festivals associated with these masks, yet given what I have mentioned above, it cannot be taken as a standard.

The reason that they have Egburu in Ikun is given in mythic form. Once Egburu and Elefon co-existed in the neighbouring village of Ilasa, and the villages would take it in turns to perform the festival. During one festival the Egburu mask refused to return to Ilasa with the Elefon mask. Ifa was sent for and he gave the reason that the Egburu mask had eaten locust bean soup and liked it so much that he stayed in Ikun.[7]

The festival is run in July every second year and celebrates Egburu, a figure that is described variously as an Imole, as an ancestor to the town and as a great warrior. The town gathers for the festival in front of the market place. The senior figures of the town are seated facing the market place and at a right angle to the

Figure 7: Each mask departs from the dance arena to dance around the town accompanied by female followers.
(Photograph: William Rea).

Figure 8: The mask known as Egburu sitting in front of the shrine house and receiving petitions from women.
(Photograph: William Rea).

painted cult house and a large grassy mound about seven feet high, known as *esin* (a generic name for shrine). The festival begins when one of the *aworo* (priests) runs to the mound and blows a loud note on a horn. This is followed immediately by the entrance of a young boy covered in a white sheet accompanied by another priest. The boy is locked into the shrine house where he remains throughout the day.

Once this is accomplished Epa masks appear from the bush surrounding the town (fig. 6). They each appear separately, and are accompanied by children and proceeded by one man beating a slit gong. The first mask to appear is known as Aredegbe which portrays a man on horse back and comes from the quarter of the town (*adugbo*) known as Iju. This mask is followed by Ologbo (a mask depicting a monkey) from the same quarter, Orosho (a superstructure depicting a female head) from Ilafe quarter and Olomoyoyo a female figure surrounded by children from Ijeru. The final mask is Egburu from Ilafe. This mask has no superstructure, instead there are numerous porcupine quills attached to a large headpiece with bulging eyes. They each file into the shrine house from whence they emerge without the children.

Once in the market place each mask turns to the mound, salutes it by stamping three times on the ground and then leaves the centre of the town to mark out the Adugbo from whence it came. They reassemble in the middle of the town, where each mask dances with the women of its quarter (fig. 7). After dancing for about an hour, Egburu, as senior mask sits in front of the shrine house and listens to the petitions of the town, particularly those of women, said to be primarily petitions for children (fig. 8). Finally each mask returns to the bush.

This is a necessarily truncated description, but it allows for a more general analysis of the Epa-type masks. The action in the festivals within which Epa-type masquerades are used tend to be more prescribed than those associated with the Egigun masquerade. In general there are far fewer masks and each of these masks – but particularly the senior mask – appears to be imbued with the metaphysical presence of a single deity. In part this might be one of the reasons why there is confusion over the naming of these masquerades. 'Epa' refers to a deity, whether Imole or Orisa, while the masks of this type are used to represent other, similar single-named, deities. Hence, Epa-type mask are cult paraphernalia used by certain lineages that subscribe to particular (usually ancestral) cults. In part the very impressive nature of Epa-type masks has perhaps concealed to external commentators the fact that these masks are 'simply' ritual paraphernalia attached to diverse local cults and not a cult in its own right.

If this is the case, it leads to the question as to why these cults have masks associated with them rather than 'static' statuary. In part an interpretation is offered by comparing the practice of costuming of Epa-type masquerades and those of Egigun. Carriers of the Epa-type masks make little attempt to conceal themselves, whereas in those performances associated with Egigun the conflation between performer and costume is complete. I suggest, following Picton, that in part this is to do with alternative conceptions of the way in which metaphysical power is realised by the two masquerade types. In Egigun the conflation suggests that the entire ensemble is regarded as being imbued with metaphysical power, whereas in the other it is the mask that stands as the focus of the *sacra*. This might be borne out by the idea that Epa-type masks are usually described as Imole, whereas Egigun masks are only ever Egigun.

Style and comparison in Yoruba masquerade practice

Schapiro's (1953: 287) definition, that style is 'the constant form in the art of a group or an individual', can have no resonance at the level of formal analysis in an area where diversity overwhelms single categorisation.

In recent years a model of style as communication has received much attention (Preziosi 1989: 147). Wiessner's (1990: 107) definition of style as, 'non-verbal communication through doing something in a certain way, that communicates information about relative identity', follows the more recent definitions that regard style as information exchange. Such a definition raises two fundamental problems in dealing with the artefactual record: the problem of meaning and the use of artefacts in establishing an identity.

There is an association between style and meaning (content). Although this association is essentially arbitrary, it is at the same time perceived as being apt.[8] This does not mean that I believe that style cannot, once established, have meaning in itself. Style has meaning *as style*, which might generate a set of meaningful discriminations. I agree that style is the vehicle for meaning, but it is perhaps a step too far to suggest that style is the 'embodiment of the emotional dispositions and habits of thought common to a whole culture' (1953: 305).

In part the situation where style is regarded as a signifier of ethnicity may have more to do with Western preoccupations with a clearly demarcated and bounded art history. Continuing the linguistic analogy this preoccupation might be contrasted with the argument found in Gates's (1988) signifying monkey. Styles of linguistic rhetoric do not necessarily refer to an originary signified, rather 'style draws upon and plays with a chain of signifiers and not on some supposedly transcendent signified.' (Gates 1988: 52). In many ways the model of style that Gates presents provides a more fluid understanding of the way in which stylistic boundaries are developed by Yoruba masquerade practice. Instead of seeing an easy one-to-one equivalence between signified cult and signifying mask, or indeed between masquerade (masks and performances) and bounded ethnic identity, we need perhaps to regard the kaleidoscope of masquerade in southern Nigeria as a set of overlapping practices, the forms of which have more to do with local circumstances than with any ethnic fixity. Coherence of a particular style seems to apply more at the level of cosmological continuity rather than in formal or stylistic terms.

That a style is regarded as apt is important and presupposes the activity of historical habituation (Sontag 1965: 18). Institutional, individual, geographic, and technological factors upon which, or within which, history 'operates', may all be reasons for the variation of styles. What is explicitly not meant here is the linkage of particular style as form, to any particular definition of ethnic group or identity. That there might be a case for links between a 'people' and material production after a careful consideration of other material, about the masquerades as well as about the constitution of Ekiti society, is certainly true. But as Kasfir (1984: 163-193) and Picton have made clear, to define one particular group of people by one artistic style is more likely to be misleading than constructive.

If the relationship of masquerade style to ethnicity is more a product of anthropologists or art historians conspiring with the reification of ethnic entities (Van Binsbergen 1985) is it possible to offer an anthropology or an art-history that allows for a comparative stance? This is the same question that Fardon (1987) asks in his investigation of Chamba ethnogenesis. His answer implies a regional approach toward analytic categories, rather than units of people. In regard to masquerade in south-western Nigeria this approach may be useful. I am limited by space, but in very general terms there seem to be a number of similarities between the various different masquerades in the south-western region

The area from the middle Benue to south-western Nigeria is as Picton shows (1991: 34-50) an area of striking cultural diversity that overlays a number of fascinating continuities.[9] Underlying the identities of different groups (i.e. as people currently 'know themselves') are a number of general patterns. Picton points out that there are similarities in material technologies, such as iron smelting, as well as in cosmologies. Continuities are found in three particular areas: in relation to (a) divination complexes, (b) Ogun or related deities of iron, and (c) in relation to the world of the dead, ancestors and women, that is, in relation to masquerading. As John Picton (1991: 90n) notes: 'there is an eschatological tradition that suggests a common heritage of ideas, deeply structured in the culture history of the area. Thus the Idoma language has *kwu* (to die), *okwu* (corpse), and *Ekwu* (masquerader). In Yoruba the corresponding terms are *ku* (to die), *oku* (corpse) and *Egun, Egigun, Egungun* masked figure. Ebira have *oku* (corpse) and the *Eku* masquerade.

There is undoubtedly a concern in both Epa and Egigun with ancestral presence. Although the way in which that presence is worked out varies in terms of its metaphysical aspect, mask performances are often about protecting the boundaries of the towns where the masquerade takes place. But protection from what? It is clear that this presence is also related to an explicit concern with children, more particularly with the birth and well-being of the child. In turn this is related to concerns over witchcraft, which is of course something well documented in Gelede performances but also figures prominently in other performances throughout the region.[10] I suggest that underlying a general ontology of masquerading in the south-western region there would appear to be specific concern with the protection of, as well as the bringing forth, of that most precious element of social life, the child.

A general art-history of the south-western region remains to be written, but regional comparison, not so much of forms but rather of practices, might offer an approach to a Yoruba art history that allows a more subtle and historical reading of the way in which material culture and the identity of particular groups has in the past been established.

Notes

1. As Kasfir (1984 and 1985) notes for the Igala.

2. In this article I define cosmology as that set of beliefs in a spritual and or metaphysical presence. By ontology and ontological status I mean that sense of 'being in the world', that underpins the belief in masquerades or at least seems to be a shared set of beliefs (see Miller, 1994 and Rea 1994). The two are connected yet in this article I am arguing that cosmology be regraded as a sub-set of ontology.

3. See for example the work of Henry Drewal.

4 . However this might be defined.

5 . The most obvious and well known example of this being the appearance of Epa-type masquerades at Ire for the Orisa Ogun. At Ire Ogun is regarded as being the tutelary deity of the whole town, Ire being Ogun's home town. Ogun is of course part of the recognised 'canon' of Yoruba Orisa, yet in Ekiti some doubt was expressed as to whether Ogun was Orisa or Imole or simply iron. In some way in Ekiti Ogun acts as an ancestral deity and not as a part of a formalised pantheon of deities. (see Peel 1997: 277).

6. A more detailed working out of the distribution of names and powers can be found in Abegide (1984) and Rea (1989).

7. See Abegide (1984) for a similar version of this myth.

8. See also Sontag (1965: 32-33).

9. See also Kasfir (1985).

10. See Rea (1994) for a wider discussion.

Bibliography

ABEGIDE, E. 1980. *The Epa Masquerades of Ekiti.* Unpublished M.A. thesis. Ibadan: University of Ibadan.

DREWAL, H. 1978. The Arts of Egungun Among the Yoruba Peoples. *African Arts,* **11**, 3, 18-19.

FARDON, R. 1987. Chamba Ethnogenesis. In Ladislav, H. (ed), *Comparative Anthropology,* 168 -188

GATES, H. 1988. *The Signifying Monkey.* Oxford: Oxford University Press.

HODDER, I. 1978. *The Spatial Organisation of Culture.* Pittsburgh: University of Pittsburgh Press.

HODDER, I. 1990. Style as Historical Quality. In Conkey M. and Hastorf C. (eds), *The Uses of Style in Archaeology,* pp. 44-51.

KASFIR, S. 1984. One Tribe, One Style? Paradigms in the Historiography of African Art. *History in Africa* **11**, 1, 163-193.

KASFIR, S. 1985. Art in History, History in Art: the Idoma Ancestral Masquerade as Historical Evidence. *Working Papers* **103**. Boston: African Studies Center.

LAYTON, R. 1990. *The Anthropology of Art.* Cambridge: Cambridge University Press.

MILLER, D. 1994. Style and Ontology. In Friedman (ed), *Consumption and Identity.* Chun

MILLER, D. 1976. The Yoruba and Edo-Speaking Peoples and their Neighbours before 1600. In Ade, J. Ajayi and Crowder, M. (eds), *History of West Africa*, 1, 196-263.

AJAYI and CROWDER, M. 1981. *The Political Culture of the Ekiti and the Challange of the Historiography of the Yoruba.* Paper Presented at the University of Ilorin, Department of History, Staff and Post-Graduate Seminar.

OJO, J. 1978. The Symbolism and Significance of the Epa-type Headpiece. *Man (N.S.)* **13**, 3, 455-470.

PICTON, J. 1988. Some Ebira Reflections on the Energies of Women. *African Languages and Cultures* **1**, 1, 61-76.

PICTON, J. 1989. On Placing Masquerades in Ebira. *African Languages and Cultures* **2**,1, 73-92.

PICTON, J. 1990. What's in a Mask?. *African Languages and Cultures* **2**, 2, 181-202.

PICTON, J. 1991. On Artefact and identity at the Niger Bemue Confluence. *African Arts*, **24**, 3. 34-49.

POYNER, R. 1978. The Egungun of Owo. *African Arts* **11**, 3, 65-76.

REA, W. 1994. No Event, No History: the Masquerades of Ikole Ekiti. Unpublished PhD thesis, University of East Anglia.

SCHAPIRO, M. 1953. Style. In Kroeber, A. (ed), *Anthropology Today*, 287-312.

SONTAG, S. 1965. *Against Interpretation.* London: Eyre and Spottiswoode.

VAN BINSBERGEN, W. 1985. *Explorations in African Religion.* Leiden.

WIESSNER, P. 1990. Is There a Unity to Style? In Conkey, M. and Hastorf C. (eds), *The Uses of Style in Archaeology*, 105-112.

Two Masks From the Yoruba-Speaking Region of Nigeria

11

John Picton

This essay is concerned with two masks in the collections of the Horniman Museum.[1] Both masks are now conventionally identified as Yoruba, and each is typical of its kind.[2] The first is a helmet with its superstructure characteristic of the north-eastern Yoruba-speaking region, a mask form with no one name though generally identified in the literature as 'Epa-type' (fig. 1). The museum has one of these, though it has several examples of the second, a south-western Gelede mask worn at the forehead, as if a hat or cap rather than a helmet (fig. 2). Each provides us with a different answer to the question: what is the artifact identified as? Each thereby constitutes a fragment of a conceptual order, a theoretical framework, specific to the social practices which they each entail and presuppose. It is however worth noting that the Epa-type mask is the subject only of one authoritative paper (Ojo 1978), whereas Gelede has two major books about it (Drewal & Drewal 1983, Lawal 1996; and see also Drewal 1992) as well as several papers. For this reason, this essay gives more attention to Epa than to Gelede. In addition, these masks also allow us to enter specific fields of sculptural work; and it is with these that I begin and conclude.

A sculptor of Opin

The work of the Epa-type helmet mask surmounted by its figure sculpture can be attributed with some certainty to the hand of Fashiku, the Alaye (the village head) of Ikerin.[3] Examples of his work have been published by the late Father Kevin Carroll (Carroll 1967, facing p53, plate 129) and in fact I was with him when the attribution to Fashiku was given (Picton 1994b: 47 fig. 4). Moreover, the attributions to him of work in the villages around Ikerin when I surveyed the Igbomina, Opin, Yagba, and northern Ekiti region in 1964-65 were consistent with the characteristics of work that I purchased from Fashiku himself for the Lagos Museum. There are particular features in the schematisation of the human head and face in his three-

John Picton

Figure 1: Epa type mask carved by Fahiku of the Opin village of Ikerin (Kwara State, Nigeria), probably in the 1930s-40s for a northern Ekiti patron. The central figure shows a woman supplicant with offerings for a deity.
(Photograph: Horniman Museum, Heini Scheebeli).

Figure 2: Gelede mask, probably from Ketu (Benin Republic), surmounted by a turtle, two crocodiles, a snake and, at the back, a lizard. This imagery may have complex proverbial connotations.
(Photograph: Horniman Museum, Heini Schneebeli).

dimensional work which, once seen, are immediately recognisable. The attribution to Fashiku of two-dimensional work, however, such as door panels (see Picton 1994b: 52, fig. 11) or the relief carving around the large drums for the Ogboni association, is a little more problematic because of the relatively small scale of the imagery, though here too we can be reasonably certain.

Ikerin is a village within the Opin group on the northern edge of the Ekiti kingdoms. People in Opin recognised their culture as in many ways like Ekiti, and in the 19th century there was an Opin contingent within the Ekiti Parapo; but nevertheless they regarded themselves as possessing a distinct historical and social identity. [4] One example of this distinctiveness was a form of kingship, not dependent upon a royal lineage but rotating between the constituent villages of Opin, with no central 'palace' and without any claim of descent from Ife. Indeed the mythic accounts of the institution of the Olopin title derived it from Old Oyo. Perhaps this is hardly surprising given that Opin was in fact an eastern outpost of the Oyo Empire until its fall in the face of the Fulani Jihad. Then, in the 1850s, through the military campaign led by Ali Balogun Gambari (Ali the Hausa general) Opin was brought into the recently established Emirate of Ilorin (see map 1).[5]

Opin was originally composed of twelve villages within an area no more than five miles to the north and east of Osi. I found evidence for the work of more than twenty sculptors active in Opin villages in the period since the 1850s, although I was able to establish individual hands for only about half of these. Six of these sculptors were still alive in the 1960s, though largely inactive. Nevertheless, travelling through the Ekiti, Opin,

172

Yagba and Igbomina areas it was evident that these villages, or at any rate three or four of them, had constituted a prolific centre for sculptural work in wood in a period of about one hundred or so years from the conquest by Ilorin. Either a would-be patron travelled to a sculptor's home village; or, as we know in the case of those whose work is the more widely distributed, some sculptors were in the habit of travelling in search of work. They would settle for a while, away from home, in order to encourage commissions.

I was also able to identify three sculptures that provided a hint of this tradition as an inheritance from before that time (see Picton 1994a: 9, fig.1.2; 1994b: 55, fig. 18); and the work of one sculptor, Rotimi Alaari of Ikerin, whose working life

Map 1:
The location of relevant Yoruba-speaking communities in the 20th century, and the southern boundary of the Ilorin emirate. The empire of old Oyo comprised the territory of the Ilorin emirate together with the savanna region from the middle Niger to the coast at Porto Novo.
(Original artwork by Doig Simmonds).

has its beginning prior to the Ilorin conquest (see Picton 1994b: 53, figs. 12-14). Yet Opin was no more than a group of villages on the remote edge of one empire or another. Although its sculpture was found throughout an area within a radius of some thirty miles, none of these locations could be regarded as anything other than, at best, a small provincial town of no particular significance beyond its immediate locality. The sculptors of Opin were not, in other words, serving an imperial court or the temples of national deities. This florescence is astonishing yet inexplicable according to any of the usual criteria; and, curiously, the British Empire in fact gave more attention to it than either of its predecessors. The work of Areogun of Osi-Ilorin, for example, featured in the 1925 British Empire exhibition in London (see Fagg and Plass 1964: 103), but he received no commission from the Emir of Ilorin; and there is no evidence in the mythic and oral accounts of Old Oyo for the imperial patronage of sculptors further afield than the immediate vicinity of the capital itself (see Abimbola 1994).

A tradition and its neo-traditionality

By the 1960s, identifying the original twelve villages was no longer straightforward: the Osi administrative district included villages such as Obo-Aiyegunle, Etan and the Idofin villages, communities that were not Opin at all; while some Opin communities had declined in numbers, combined, then grown and split in ways that did not represent the former combination, others had moved, and others had divided to form a new settlement close to the main road built under colonial rule along the southern edge of Opin.[6] Ikerin was composed of four formerly separate villages, hence its name (*erin* = four): following the devastation of the conquest by Ilorin, they had come together under the leadership of one of them, Iyaye, whose leader, the Alaye, became the head of the new community. The then current holder of this title, Fashiku, an old man by the 1960s, was one of three sculptors still just about active: there was one in each of Isare and Isolo. George Bandele, the son of Areogun had recently returned to Osi-Ilorin after a period of work with Father Carroll, but was not then at work.[7] Another Osi sculptor, Rotimi, had given up on taking the title of Agbana. In Ikerin, Yusuf Amuda had also given up, though in his case it was for lack of work. Indeed, Fashiku's main source of patronage by the time of my research was provided by the traders from Ibadan who fuelled the appetites of the art-hungry expatriate faculty members of Ibadan University. Fashiku thus continued to work, often still producing sculpture on the scale of the Epa-type helmet in the Horniman Museum, but for an entirely external demand. The Horniman mask, however, in my view must have been carved some time well before Fashiku's very late work for the Ibadan traders of the 1960s.[8]

Some time after my research in Opin and Ekiti was concluded Bandele returned to sculptural work at the behest of the Ibadan traders, even to the extent of taking apprentices, one of whom, Shegun Faleye, now works independently in the studio facilities established by the textile artist Nike Olaniyi in Oshogbo (see Picton 1997: 26, 28).[9] That Fashiku was still at work as a sculptor was, however, unusual within the Opin tradition. It was expected, as Rotimi the Agbana of Osi had found, that on taking a chiefly title a man would give up work of this sort: he was, after all, now in the position in which patronage was expected of him. It no longer befitted his status to continue to receive the patronage of others. It may well be that Fashiku had returned to sculpture, as we know Bandele was to do, at the behest of the traders (who would, of course, then encourage the sculpture to rot a little thereby creating an illusion of age for the unsuspecting).[10]

That this was a tradition in decline was, in the mid 1960s, an inescapable conclusion; and yet it has survived through the initial patronage of the late Father Kevin Carroll of the Society of African Missions. Some fifteen years prior to my research, Carroll had come across Bandele working as a sawyer, and had put him to work carving for the Catholic churches that were springing up throughout Ekiti and elsewhere in the Yoruba-speaking region (Carroll 1967).[11] At first, the reception of the work of Bandele and his apprentices, most notably Lamidi Fakeye, was mixed: some liked it, while others saw it as a return to what they had left behind in becoming Christians. However, by the 1960s Lamidi Fakeye had established his own studio in Ibadan, with apprentices drawn from his own family. With the growth of an urban middle class in the context of the development of post-colonial cultural identities in Nigeria, the scope of available patronage for what has become known as the Neo-Traditional movement has widened sufficiently to suggest that it may enjoy a relatively secure future.[12] In 1990, for example, Fashiku's grandson, Lawrence, was running a thriving studio with apprentices and plenty of work in progress in Ife. More recently, Patrick Day, a graduate student of the University of London School of Oriental and African Studies, in his research into public art in Ibadan, has documented the work of some thirty sculptors active in that one city during the past forty years, including three members of the Fakeye family currently working in the Neo-Traditional style. Moreover, shortly before he died, Father Kevin Carroll himself estimated that some twenty-five sculptors were now in full-time work as a result of his initial patronage, in some cases as University teachers, in various parts of Nigeria.

Sculpture as imonle in Opin and Ekiti

Although by the 1960s Islam and Christianity were the dominant religions of the area, they were not wholly to blame for the decline in adherence to local tradition in the arts. First of all, this would misconstrue the relationship between sculptural work and other forms of social practice. Religion was only one source of patronage for sculptors, and certainly not the most demanding; for this was an area in which the houses of the well-to-do were embellished with door panels carved in relief, and veranda posts carved in the round. Secondly, however, the changing technologies of house building had gradually made the work of the sculptor irrelevant.[13] Thirdly, with new opportunities in education, motor mechanics and migrant labour, the pool of potential sculptors was diminished in any case. Fourthly, the advent of party politics had proved to be at least as damaging as Islam and Christianity. For disputes that would once have been settled could now become channelled into open conflict; and if the members of the cult of a deity were to divide along party lines, the annual festivities could not be performed. In Osi, for example, the festival of the local tutelary deity, Baba Osi (literally 'Father of Osi') had lapsed because the village was unable to unite within the authority of a single village head. The problem was that by 1964 there were two village heads, each supported by one or other of the two local parties. The Olosi appointed within local tradition supported the Action Group, and he had in theory been deposed by the provincial government in Ilorin which had tried to replace him with a village head of its own party, the Northern Peoples Congress.[14] This, in effect, split the community in half, and no-one could agree which of the two Olosi should perform the essential ritual duties of the village head in the festival of the local deity. Baba Osi was thereby rendered unperformable.

Nevertheless, in Opin, and in the parts of Ekiti with which I was familiar, it was evident that there was a local theory in which sacrifice directed to a material object, whether an artifact or not, had the authority to bring an *imonle* – also spelled *imanle*[15] – into existence. From Ife eastwards the generic concepts were *imonle* and *ebora*. The word *orisha* signified only one deity (or group of related deities), the deity known in central and western Yoruba as Obatala or Orishanla, the 'big Orisha'.[16] *Ebora* were associated with rocks, trees, rivers, and so forth, whereas *Imonle* were located in material objects within the social world. Thus, to carve an image and sacrifice to it was to bring an *imonle* into existence; and this theory matters for Fashiku's helmet mask, for it is certainly part of how he would have understood the purpose and significance of his work. On the other hand, given that the liturgies of mask use vary considerably in name, order, and intention from one community to another wherever Epa-type masks are used, and given also the manner in which a sculptor's work might be distributed, we cannot know when and how this particular mask would have been performed or what it would have been called. Insofar as there does appear to be a measure of continuity through Opin and many parts of Ekiti, it is described in the reality of the artifact as *imonle*, i.e. as a presence established in its receipt of sacrifice, rather than in some rather more comprehensive cult complex.[17]

Carroll (1967: 65, fig. 50) illustrates a mask in Oye-Ekiti called Ogun, the deity associated with iron, a heroic figure in Ekiti, whose annual feast in June/July included the offering of newly-harvested yam (fig. 3). The helmet, to which sacrifice had been offered, is surmounted by a warrior. Carroll also describes another, at nearby Egosi:

Figure 3: A Helmet mask called Ogun, the god of iron, at Oye-Ekiti, c. 1950, with fresh sacrificial matter over its face.
(Photograph: Father Kevin Carroll).

Then the mask came out ... the head [i.e. the helmet] glistening with fresh blood; it came out slowly and then ran suddenly ... until it was arrested and controlled by the young men in charge of it. Then the people took up the refrain for this mask ... 'princess of Ieshi'. The fierce mask was surmounted by the gentle figures of a woman and child ... they called on the spirit of the mask ... 'Princess of Ieshi ... give me a fine child ..'. Whatever its superstructure, each mask has the fierce face of the imole [sic] masks of this area, and the scarlet blood on the face contrasted with the yellow-green mantle of young palm fronds which covered the body of the carrier ...(Carroll 1967: 67).

As it appeared, coated with fresh sacrificial blood (the dog is the animal usually 'eaten' by *Ogun*, its head severed in a single cut) it was now an object of cult, receiving the prayers of its supplicants, most obviously women seeking healing for their lack of children. J. R. O. Ojo (1978), writing about the appearance of helmet masks in and around Ido-Ekiti, makes much the same point about the healing efficacy of these helmet masks.

The masks described by Carroll in Oye and Egosi were mostly single-faced with dog-like ears and known as *elefon*, the local generic term for this formal configuration; while the helmet itself in receipt of sacrifice was *imonle*. The term *epa* was used in Oye and Egosi for the janus-faced helmets found elsewhere in Ekiti, but this usage was by no means consistent. In the Ijero kingdom, I noted several kinds of masks appearing during the 1964 Ogun festival; and, while these included the helmet Epa-type, masks made of bark and fresh palm fronds were far more frequently in evidence. Sometime in the early 1970s I watched a BBC television programme about the festival of Ogun at Ire-Ekiti, the place where the deity finally disappeared from the world; and here the two key images were an 'Epa-type' mask that paraded through the village, and a leopard made of palm fronds in a forest grove. However, there were no regular appearances of helmet masks in the cycle of feasts and performances in the villages of Opin. Rather, they appeared as part of the post-burial rites of a particular group of titled men. In Opin there were two distinct types of Opin chiefly title: the first were the titles vested in the constituent lineages of a village, while the second type comprised those titles granted to particular individuals on the basis of their personal wealth and other achievements; and it was only for the post-burial rites of this latter group that the helmet masks appeared. Moreover, although Opin people were aware of the Ekiti term *epa*, in Opin they were known generically as *aguru*. There was a cult of *epa* in Osi-Ilorin but however often I spoke with its priest, the *aworo epa*, my enquiries were so completely frustrated by his unwillingness to impart any information that I have no idea what it was about or whether or not there was any relationship between it and the appearance of Aguru masks.

According to George Bandele, the performance of Aguru masks was the responsibility of one of the age grades leading from youth to elder; and the performers wearing the masks were required to jump up on to the top of a mound consistently described as the best part of 90 cm high (six feet). This is hard to imagine, but everyone that I spoke to insisted on this; and at Osi-Ilorin the mound was still there, beside the market, unused and washed by the rains through some forty years by the time I saw it (fig. 4). For it had not be used since the road from Ilorin to Kabba was first built through the middle of Osi in the early 1920s; and yet I could get no explanation for their disuse: they had simply stopped doing it.[18] Andrew Apter tells me, however,

Figure 4: The mound beside Osi-Ilorin market place in 1965 on to which, until the 1920s, helmet-masked performers used to jump as part of the post-burial celebrations of men whose chiefly status was acquired through personal achievement rather than by lineage.
(Photograph: John Picton).

that in Ishan-Ekiti he has seen Epa helmet-mask performers running and jumping up a mound of the height as seen in Osi-Ilorin, whereas Dennis Williams and William Rea reporting from Obo Aiyegunle and Ikole-Ekiti, respectively, found that it was not part of Epa performance.

Epa-type masks are invariably surmounted by sculpted imagery, and in Opin there were five principal figurative schemes: the leopard pouncing on an antelope, the dog usually with a hare in its mouth, the ram, the warrior, and the mother with children. There were others including the supplicant woman, Eshu (the trickster deity), the priest, the diviner, the doctor, and the palm-wine tapper; but those five provided the essential core of *aguru* imagery; and they always jumped in order led by the leopard. This set of forms was sometimes found beyond Opin, especially in adjacent northern Igbomina communities where the performances were either every year or every other year, but further south the range of imagery was different although one would usually expect to find the mother with children and the warrior.[19]

It is also worth noting that in my experience of the north-eastern Yoruba-speaking communities in which Epa-type masks were found, whatever the energies associated with and conjured into the helmet masks through sacrifice, supplication and performance, at other times they were simply inert artifacts. Whether belonging to the community and kept in a communal shelter, or owned individually and kept at home, they were not deliberately hidden away: there was no secrecy attached to them. They might be kept up in the rafters of a house, in which case they were awkward to get out, but that was all. They could be brought out within the sight of anyone, including women; and indeed women were responsible for painting them ready for performance.[20]

It is, I hope, clear that what I have tried to do so far is to place the Horniman Museum Epa-type mask within a configuration of visual and performance practices, a configuration still inadequately documented in each of its diverse manifestations. This must not be taken, and it is certainly not so intended, as a critique of existing published and unpublished research. Rather, it is a measure of the diverse nature of practice beyond the order and control of the major cults of central and western Yoruba. Throughout the area within which helmet masks are found we can of course list the elements of that wide-ranging configuration, the forms, names, rites, celebrations, performance practices and so forth. We also know something of the particularities of some of the helmet-mask-using communities within this area. We are also reasonably certain that the Horniman helmet mask is an *imonle*, and we have managed to attribute it to a particular sculptor. On the other hand, although we also know something of how Fashiku himself would have expected it to have been used within Opin, it seems probable that throughout the greater part of Fashiku's working life Aguru masks were no longer performed in Opin. This suggests that it was almost certainly not commissioned by an Opin patron. Rather, it must have been carved for use within one or other of the many northern Ekiti or eastern Igbomina contexts of helmet-mask use, such as those in which I documented Fashiku's work (though not this precise example, as I recall). In the absence of specific field collection data, therefore, it is more-or-less impossible for the moment to attribute further context or significance to this mask beyond the obvious facts that sculptures of mothers and children are commonplace throughout the area within which Opin sculpture was in demand, and that the mask helmet in receipt of blood sacrifice was an *imonle*.

What's in a mask?

Any discussion of the idea of the mask in general must take account of local terms and conceptual orders, if it is to have any intellectual and comparative validity. Even the word 'mask' cannot be taken for granted; or rather, we cannot simply assume that in any given language in Africa there is a more-or-less comparable word notwithstanding the presence of material artifacts that seem to fit the English word 'mask'. This is a complex affair, of course, to which I and others have referred elsewhere (see Picton 1988, 1990, 1996). The helmet mask, when it is worn in performance, necessarily conceals the face of its performer, although his arms and legs are visible. By effacing his identity it serves as a dramatic device, placing distance between performer and audience. As I have suggested, the precise configuration of the elements of north-east Yoruba visual and performance practice in regard to the helmet mask was specific to a given location. On the other hand, the theory of sculpture as *imonle* was commonplace; and here secrecy was irrelevant. The energy of the mask was literally embodied in its material being through sacrifice and supplication. This contrasts markedly with the Egungun masquerades of the Oyo kingdom where the mask with its costume and other accoutrements conceals the performer so completely that no part of him is seen (Drewal & Drewal 1978), thereby concealing an ancestral presence that cannot, must not indeed, be seen. The Ekiti and Opin helmet mask as *imonle* reveals all there is: what you see is what you get, so to speak. The Oyo Egungun conceals that which is too dangerous to see.

Each of them provides the dramatic distance essential to performance, but to quite different ends; and in this respect each again contrasts with the Gelede masquerades of south-western Yoruba. The Gelede association is found within communities located, roughly speaking, to the west of an imaginary line from Lagos to Ketu, i.e. the cultural groups that include Awori, Egbado (and including the Egbado ward of Abeokuta), Anago, Ahori, Ketu, Ishabe, and some of the western border towns of Oyo. It is not my purpose to summarise the existing literature (in particular Lawal 1996, Drewal & Drewal 1983): its thorough-going substance is too well known to require further comment here. The performances comprise a night celebration in which masked performers known as *efe* sing to the community assembled for that purpose, usually in the market place, while in the following afternoon paired *gelede* masked performers dance; and in any given locality *efe* masks are either larger and more elaborate than *gelede*, or they are simply different, and always more restricted in subject matter. Performances are staged to give pleasure to the mothers of the community. In practice, this indicates the senior women, yet the very phrase 'our mothers' is ambivalent; for this is an environment of the imagination in which women as mothers possess the capacity to create life, and as witches to destroy life. This does not mean that all women are witches, even if, in this imaginary, all witches are women.[21]

In giving pleasure to 'our mothers' Gelede performers of necessity draw close to those very same 'mothers,' and thus to an energy source, indeed, of the greatest danger because of its unpredictability and moral ambivalence. 'Our mothers' possess an *ashe* superior even to that of the *orisha*.[22] The mask is worn by the performer resting at his forehead, his face veiled by the cloth hanging from it. One explanation of the mask, its costume and accoutrements (Drewal & Drewal 1983: 17), is that the performer wears them following a precedent set by Orunmila, the deity who animates the Ifa divination system, when instructed to visit *ilu eleye*, 'the town of the owners of birds'.[23] This is interpreted as a secret forest grove where the witches meet; and witches fly as birds in the night and eat people. As the mask would protect Orunmila, so too it protects its present-day performer from the *ashe* of 'our mothers'. The mask serves, rather in the manner of a welding visor, as a guard against the energies that lie without. Yet through his entertainment the performer also enjoys the protection of the mothers. Asiwaju (1975), in his invaluable account of the historical implications of Efe songs, tells us about a man who went blind having seduced the wife of an Efe performer. The mask, in other words, effects the protection of the wearer from witchcraft, while at the same time it signifies his protection by the witches.

The question of what is hidden, as in Egungun, or revealed, as in the helmet-as-*imonle*, is here irrelevant. Each of these mask types, including Gelede, is entailed in the mediation of an *ashe* that may be manifested in physical strength but is not located therein.[24] Each of these mask types is engaged in the processes of signification, referral and explanation: each entails a 'gathering together' of ideas-and practices, and of people (performers, priests, sculptors, musicians, audience ...); and yet, while each effects a dramatic distance between performer and audience, each also manifests a relationship, essential to masquerade, between performer, mask, and masked identity that is radically different, one from the others (again, see Picton 1990, 1996).

As to the sculptural superstructure and embellishment of Gelede masks, it is evident from the published literature and from the masks I have seen in Nigeria, as in European and American museums, that there seems to be no end to inventiveness (figs. 5 & 6). Market women, masqueraders, motor-cars, Muslims: the list goes on – everything from Christ on the cross[25] to the most flagrant displays of sexual proclivity, as if the whole world is there jostling for attention as configured within a western Yoruba frame of reference (see Drewal & Drewal 1983, Lawal 1996, Nicklin *et al.* 1991); and that is the point. For whatever the underpinning presuppositions of Gelede, an entertainment is provided which has the possibility of several dimensions of signification and interpretation. The traces and referrals are more complex, even, than the catalogue of sculptural forms. It is as if the concerns articulated in performance and those articulated in sculpture do not (have to) explain each other. Rather, sculpture and performance each but differently construct and explain the worlds to which they refer.

Figure 5. A pair of Gelede masks, Lagos 1967, commemorating Chief Taiwo, a prominent late 19th-century merchant, who is shown here at the centre of an extraordinary collection of serpents, paddles, wheels, imaginary figures and mirrors. Each is assembled of several parts, and carved c. 1900 probably at Otta to the north of Lagos, the principal source of Gelede masks in Lagos.
(Photograph: John Picton).

Figure 6. The core of a Gelede mask (as shown in figure 5), and probably carved in Otta. Its attachments are missing, and without these it is impossible to determine its purpose, though commemoration of prominent deceased person is likely.
(Photograph: Horniman Museum).

A little history and geography

It is now worth taking a last look at the helmet masks of Ekiti and Opin (etc), for Carroll (1967: 67) described a contrast between the 'fierce' face of the helmet and the 'gentle' figure sculpture above. Indeed, in his conversations with Bandele (Carroll 1964, published in Picton 1994a: 31) he had already drawn out a formal distinction between *igi* and *ikoko*, i.e. between 'tree,' in the sense of the (piece of) wood used in sculpture, and 'pot' respectively, i.e. between the figure sculpture and the helmet.[26] In other words, here too there is a disjunction; but not between performance and sculpture as in Gelede, where the contrast within the sculpture of the mask is perhaps best described as conceptual rather than formal, the mask itself drawing its implications from its rationale in performance, while the figure sculptures above are alike in style though smaller in scale, obviously (fig. 7). For the Epa-type mask, the contrast is both formal and conceptual, between the relative naturalism of the superstructure and the schematised face of the helmet, the face of the *imonle* to which sacrifice is made, the sacrifice that, indeed, conjures into the human social world an identity of helmet-and-*imonle* to permit supplication (as well as athletic display). As to the repertoire of warriors, mothers, leopards, dogs, rams, and so forth, carved upon the helmet, it is of course a more limited range of imagery than Gelede. On the other hand, it was an imagery widely available to being seen in all the other sculptural contexts of the Yoruba north-east, especially the doors and veranda posts of palaces, temples and well-to-do houses. Leaving aside the three animal species, for which, as noted above, a detailed analysis must yet be worked through, here too we are presented with alternative means of constructing, engaging with and explaining the world to which the mask cults and their imagery refer. The cult of an *imonle* and its sculptural

Figure 7: Right,
Gelede mask carved
with party-coloured
tufts of hair. Left:
Gelede mask
surmounted by two
horse's heads.
(Photographs: Horniman
Museum).

Figure 7: Right, Gelede mask carved with party-coloured tufts of hair. Left: Gelede mask surmounted by two horse's heads. (Photographs: Horniman Museum).

ornament do not (have to) explain each other; but if each is an explanation of the world to which they refer, why then should the imagery of the Epa-type mask be so much more restricted in scope than Gelede?

There is, of course, no clear answer to this question; but it is evident that the north-eastern parts of what has now become the Yoruba-speaking region were on the remote marches of the empires of Old Oyo and Edo (Benin) until the early 19th century when the Fulani Jihad initiated the collapse of Oyo, and the disruptions and imperialism that succeeded it. The Gelede-masking region in the south-west, in contrast, had long been within the imperial control of Oyo at the southern end of a trading network linking the Atlantic coast at Porto Novo to the middle Niger, and thence to Islam and the trans-Saharan trade routes. At the coast, of course, people would have long been familiar with the brutal horrors and the rich pickings to be gained from trans-Atlantic slavery; and sometimes that familiarity was more direct than anyone would have wished. It is after all no surprise that the Brazilian word for Yoruba is Nago, given that the Yoruba peoples in the immediate hinterland of Porto Novo included Anago. Moreover, this part of coastal West Africa had become known as the Slave Coast. It was from here that until well into the 19th century, slaves were taken across the Atlantic. This gave the African cultures of Brazil and Cuba an immediately recognisable south-west Yoruba appearance. It was also on this coast, from Badagri to Lagos, that modern Christian missionary activity (Pole 1999: 33-34; Ajayi 1965) and European colonial rule had their 19th-century beginnings; and it was here too that the liberated repatriate communities returned, the Sierra Leoneans (including Muslims and Protestant Christians) and the Brazilians (Muslims, Catholic Christians, *orisha* devotees).

If there were so many more characters jostling for attention in art in the hinterland of Porto Novo than amongst the distant rocky outcrops of Ekiti, perhaps it was, in part, because of the inevitable disruptions initiated by the decline and fall of the Oyo empire in that coastal port and its immediate hinterland. After all, with the demise of Oyo, coastal access to an inter-continental world was not somehow closed down. Rather, the jostling for attention was magnified by newly-arrived concerns and characters; and for a time people were still being sold into slavery.

Now, it is not my intention to close this essay with some kind of trite 'as-in-life-so-in-art' truism, but to suggest that in the very discontinuities of performance and sculpture, of covert intention and public entertainment, we might recognise the specific realities and conditions of an emerging local modernity, not in a 'western' sense (as if 'we' invented it), but as wrought in the uncertainties of that decline and fall and of the impositions of new colonial orders, including of course the disjunctions of political authority, of economic demand, and of religious identity. This was also all part of the ferment of cultural and intellectual activity that drew forth the modern sense of Yoruba identity, of course; for the new orders imposed from without necessitated an answer to the questions: who are we? what should we wear? which gods do we serve? which is our language? our history?[27] At the same time, there were others for whom these uncertainties would be the very conditions that fire the flames of envy, of jealousy, of paranoia, the fantasies that are at the root of what we call 'witchcraft' (see also Lawal 1996: 273-282). In that case, while sculpture and performance can be seen as differently constructing and explaining the world to which they refer, perhaps the very profusion of sculptural form in the context of performances that are intended to please 'our mothers' is also itself an unwitting function of a concern with the unpredictability of things (a concern that includes an explanation of affliction in terms of some women as birds in the night, flying to meetings at the crossroads to eat their kinspeople), almost a visual paranoia perhaps.

For many people in a country like Nigeria, masquerade is as much part of the modern world as school education. Masked performances persist and in many cases thrive. In 1964 I visited the small northern Ekiti town of Odo Owa, the home of Bamgboye, one of the last great masters of the sculptural traditions of the region. I knew from Carroll's photographs that there were a great many helmet masks to be seen; but it was too late. The Ibadan dealers had successfully persuaded the young men whose responsibility it had been to perform these masks that as modern youth they no longer wanted to do so. Forty masks had been loaded on to a lorry just the previous week. Many of them ended up in the Lagos museum, identified through my access to Carroll's photographs, but without further documentation. It was a tragedy for the study of this art, and, more especially, an impoverishment of the cultural life of Odo Owa; but I do not think it would happen today (notwithstanding the armed robberies of museums and the illegal excavations of archaeological sites). There is greater awareness now of cultural identity and of the possibilities of its accommodation within the expectations of Islam and Christianity, and within a modern education informed by local intellectual interest in the traditions inherited from the past; and in this context masquerade now has proven survival value.

Architectural sculpture is another matter. New building technologies rendered this art substantially irrelevant, and the persistence of the Ekiti and Opin tradition via Neo-Traditionality has proved possible since the 1950s only because of new forms of patronage and a developing subject matter. However, while this art survives almost as a parody of itself, it should not be considered as a tradition devoid of innovation prior to this time. Areogun of Osi-Ilorin documented the District Officer on his bicycle (Picton 1994a: 26); and in about 1915 Olowe of Ise-Ekiti records in his art the first travelling commissioner of the colonial period, Major Reeve Tucker travelling in his hammock in 1899 to meet the king of the nearby town of Ikere-Ekiti (Walker 1998: 36-49). The visit of a European was a rare thing in turn-of-the-century Ekiti, whereas Europeans of various shapes and sizes were long since commonplace in the ports of what had once been the 'Slave Coast'.

While resisting the temptation to impute causality, in contrast to a functional inter-relatedness of things, perhaps it is hardly surprising that in Opin and Ekiti the strength of the art rested in the exploration of a relatively small number of themes, most obviously the mother with children, and the warrior, often on horseback (see Ojo 1978 for authoritative accounts of this imagery). Perhaps this somehow also explains the architectonic development of this tradition during the period from the demise of Oyo to the years just before independence, and its latter-day middle-class domestication within Neo-Traditionality. At any rate, in a 19th-century context of intermittent local warfare, the depredations of Oyo and Ilorin cavalry were known about and provided subject matter for sculptors. However, cavalry posed little threat to the south of Opin, given the rocky terrain of so much of Ekiti. In any case, the changes wrought by the developing imperial concerns of Oyo and Ilorin (and Ibadan), were all within a broadly local cultural remit, unlike the coastal south-west, where the Atlantic coastal trade had been around for some 400 years, and where colonial government and missionary Christianity had been active for a good half century before the first travelling commissioner was carried through Ekiti in his hammock.

Notes

1. The research on which this paper is based was done as an employee of the Federal Government of Nigeria, in what was then its Department of Antiquities. I offer my thanks to the government and people of Nigeria for the opportunity to live and work in their country, I celebrate the memory of William and Bernard Fagg, Kenneth Murray, Father Kevin Carroll, George Bandele, and Philip Allison, and I offer my thanks to Professor Ekpo Eyo, who succeeded Murray and B. Fagg as Director of Antiquities, and to Chief Olu Toriola, then of Ife Museum, who was my field assistant in facilitating this part of my work.

2. For the purposes of this essay Yoruba ethnicity is taken for granted. However it should not be forgotten that a modern Yoruba identity was developed in the period from about 1850 to 1950 in the context of the need to contest colonial rule – see Moraes Farias & Barber (1990), Peel (1989), Picton (1994a, 1995a & b, etc.). I sort of return to this problematic at the close of this essay. For recent surveys of the field of Yoruba visual arts see Abiodun, Drewal & Pemberton (1991, 1994), Drewal, and Pemberton & Abiodun (1989).

3. Alaye = *o ni* [which denoted ownership of] *iaye*, one of the constituent communities that came together c 1950 to form the present village of Ikerin [*erin* = four].

4. Ekiti Parapo is the combined military force that came together in the late 19th century to contest Ibadan imperialism.

5. It is for this reason that Osi, the Opin village chosen with the establishment of colonial rule as the district administrative centre, has always been known as Osi-Ilorin to distinguish it from Osi-Ekiti, a quite different community within Ekiti to the south. Given the failure of some writiers to understand these local subtleties of identity and sentiment, however, the literature is often peppered with confusion on this point. Sometimes this is the result of inept copy-editing.

6. See Picton (1994b: 47, fig. 2); most of the sculptors mentioned here are illustrated in Picton (1994a & b).

7. Bandele and I spent a good deal of time together in late 1964 - early 1965, travelling around in search of his father's work. Wherever we went, he had only to say that he was Areogun's son for people to greet him with great enthusiasm. I could have had no better testimony to the value placed upon Areogun's artistry.

8. Unlike a similar piece in Liverpool Museum which almost certainly is a work of the mid 1960s.

9. After a period of leave in the UK in 1965 I probably would have returned to continue my research in Opin and Ekiti, but my then head of department (Kenneth Murray, who had been brought out of retirement to cover the 'inter-regnum' between

Bernard Fagg and Ekpo Eyo) asked me to move to Ebira and the Niger-Benue confluence region.

10. I did not think of this at the time, and now the questions cannot be asked since neither Fashiku nor Bandele are still alive.

11. See also Carroll (1964) for his account of a conversation with Bandele about technique and critical judgement.

12. See Carroll (1967: 103) for Fakeye's account of the inception of this transformation; and he has, of course, since published his autobiography.

13. Its latter-day resurgence within the rubrics of Neo-Traditionality in a major urban centre such as Ibadan is therefore all the more significant.

14. The Action Group had been founded by Chief Awolowo some 15 years previously to channel Yoruba opposition to colonial rule.

15. A similar but nevertheless entirely different word means 'Muslim'; see Abraham (1958: 307)

16. Ayede, the Ekiti kingdom carved out only in the 19th century and overtly influenced by central Yoruba ritual culture, was a partial exception in this regard; see Apter (1992).

17. The helmet mask, whatever else it might be, is certainly an object of cult, but that cult may well be individual to that particular mask, in contrast to the array of paraphernalia and ritual of Ifa divination (Abiodun 1975), or associated with the Oyo thunder deity. Shango was rare, as it happens, and some times proscribed, even, in Ekiti and Opin.

18. I was also told that at that last performance 'a European' had come from Zungeru, the one-time capital of the northern provinces of Nigeria, to take photographs. These remain unlocated so far.

19. The significance of this set of forms remains unexplored. Ojo's 1978 paper was concerned with this research in Ido-Ekiti where the leopard, the dog and the ram were not among the *dramatis personae*. Nevertheless his exegesis of the mother and the warrior is unsurpassed by any other published source.

20. The helmets were, as one might expect, not the only type of mask used in Opin. The cult of Baba Osi made use of face masks, also with superstructure, but, as noted, the festival had fallen into disuse for political reasons. I only saw the masks in people's houses.

21. This must not be taken as some kind of pan-African paradigm. The south-western Yoruba attribution of malign potential to women may or may not be consistent elsewhere within the Yoruba-speaking region; and in any case whatever is translated as 'witchcraft' may be attributed to men, and to men and women: it all depends when and where you are in sub-Saharan Africa. There are also complex differences and relationships between the overt (if secret) use of magical ingredients – not usually referred to in the Africanist literature as 'witchcraft' – and, as here, the covert (if imaginary) internalised energies some people have, simply because they do; see also Picton (1988).

22. The concept of *ashe* is at the core of ideas-and-practices in this social environment. It is an energy beyond mere physical strength (*agbara,*) an energy accessed through rite, sacrifice, magical-medicine and spell; see Abiodun (1990, 1994, 1995).

23. See also Lawal (1996: 37-70) who gives all the variant accounts of the origins of these masks.

24. And this not only in the jumping of Aguru and Epa. I have seen Gelede performances in Lagos of the most extraordinary

energy, the masked performer turning cartwheels, for example, and eventually having to be restrained by attendants, as Carroll also described for the 'Princess of Ieshi'.

25. I have seen an example of this in a private collection.

26. The technical term Bandele uses to describe this difference is *ipoju*. He is reported as saying: 'the *ipoju* of the face of the stick [ie the figure sculpture] is different from the *ipoju* of the pot'. *Ipoju* literally denotes visual condition: *ipo* = state, condition + *oju* = eye, face, presence (Abraham 1958: 313, 460-461).

27. See references given in footnote 2.

Bibliography

ABIMBOLA, W. 1994. Lagbayi the Itinerant Wood Carver of Ojowon. In Abiodun, R. Drewal H. and Pemberton, J. III (eds), *The Yoruba Artist*, 137-142. Washington D.C.: Smithsonian Inst.

ABIODUN, R. 1975. Ifa Art Objects: an Interpretation Based on Oral Tradition. In Abimbola W. (ed), *Yoruba Oral Tradition*, Ile-Ife, 421-469. Ile-Ife: University of Ife.

ABIODUN, R. 1990. The Future of African Art Studies: an African Perspective. In *African Art Studies: the State of the Discipline*. National Museum of African Art, 63-86. Washington D.C.: Smithsonian Inst.

ABIODUN, R. 1994. Understanding Yoruba Art and Aesthetics: the Concept of Ase. *African Arts,* **27**, 3, 68-78.

ABIODUN, R. 1995. An African Art History: Promising Theoretical Approaches in Yoruba Art Studies. In Abiodun, R. Drewal H. and Pemberton J. (eds), *The Yoruba Artist* 37-48. Washington D.C.: Smithsonian Inst.

ABIODUN, R., DREWAL, H. and PEMBERTON, J. III (eds), 1991. *Yoruba Art & Aesthetics*. Zurich. Museum Rietberg.

ABIODUN, R., DREWAL, H. and PEMBERTON, J. III (eds), 1994. *The Yoruba Artist*. Washington DC.: Smithsonian Inst.

ABRAHAM, R. 1958. *Dictionary of Modern Yoruba*. London: University of London Press.

AJAYI, J. 1965. *Christian Missions in Nigeria 1841-1891: the Making of a New Elite.* Ibadan: Longman Books.

APTER, A. 1992. *Black Critics and Kings*. Chicago: University of Chicago Press.

ASIWAJU, A. 1975. Efe Poetry as a Source for Western Yoruba History. In Abimbola, W. (ed), *Yoruba Oral Tradition*, 199-266.

CARROLL, K. 1994 (1964). Who Said his Work is Like a Box Reprinted. In Picton, J. 1994a, 29-31. Washington D.C.: Smithsonian Inst.

CARROLL, K. 1967. *Yoruba Religious Carving*. London: Jeffey Chapman.

DREWAL, H. and DREWAL M. 1983. *Gelede: Art and Female Power Among the Yoruba*. Bloomington: Indianna University Press.

DREWAL, H., PEMBERTON, J. III and ABIODUN, R. 1989. *Yoruba: Nine Centuries of African Art and Thought*. New York: Center for African Art.

DREWAL, H. and DREWAL M. (eds), 1978 Special Issue on Egungun, *African Arts*, **11**, 3.

DREWAL, M. 1992. *Yoruba Ritual: Performers, Play, Agency*. Bloomington: Indianna University Press.

FAGG, W. and PLASS, M. 1964. *African Sculpture*. London: Studio Vista.

LAWAL, B. 1996. *The Gelede Spectacle.* Seattle: University of Washington.

MORAES FARIAS, P. de and BARBER K. (eds), 1990. *Self-Assertion and Brokerage: Early Cultural Nationalism in West Africa.* Birmingham: Centre for West African Studies, University of Birmingham.

NICKLIN, K. *et al* 1991 *Yoruba, a Celebration of African Art.* London: Horniman Museum.

OJO, J. 1978. The Symbolism and Significance of Epa-Type Masquerade Headpieces. *Man* **12**,3, 455-470.

PEEL, J. 1989. The Cultural Work of Yoruba Ethnogenesis. In Tonkin, E. *et al* (eds), *History and Ethnicity,*198-215.

PICTON, J. 1988. Some Ebira Reflections on the Energies of Women. *African Languages and Cultures,* **1**, 1, 61-76. London: SOAS.

PICTON, J. 1990. What's in a Mask? *African Language and Culture,* **3**, 2, pp 181-202. London: SOAS.

PICTON, J. 1994a. Art, Identity, and Identification: a Commentary on Yoruba Art Historical Studies. In Abiodun, R. Drewal, H. and Pemberton, J. (eds), *The Yoruba Artist* 1-31. London: SOAS.

PICTON, J. 1994b. Sculptors of Opin. *African Arts,* **27** 3, 46-59.

PICTON, J. 1995a. The Horse and Rider in Yoruba Art: Images of Conquest and Possession. In Pezzoli, G. (ed), *Cavalieri dell'Africa: Storia, Iconografia, Simbolismo.* Milan: Centro Studi Archeologia Afrikan.

PICTON, J. 1995b. Islam, Artifact and Identity in South-Western Nigeria. In Adahl K. and Sahlstrom B. (eds), *Islamic Art and Culture in Sub-Saharan Africa,* 71-98. University of Uppsala.

PICTON, J. 1996. The Masque of Words. In Arnaut K. and Dell E. (eds), *Bedu is my Lover,* 5-8. Brighton: Brighton Museum.

PICTON, J. 1997. Tracing the Lines of Art. In Picton (ed), *Image and Form.* London: SOAS.

POLE, L. 1999 *Iwa l'ewa: Yoruba and Benin Collections in the Royal Albert Memorial Museum, Exeter.* Exeter: Exeter City Museums.

WALKER, R. 1998. *Olowe of Ise: a Yoruba Sculptor to Kings.* Washington D.C.: Smithsonian Inst.

WALKER, R. 1962. The Symbolism and Ritual Context of the Yoruba *laba Shango. JRAI,* **92**, pp 23-37.

WESCOTT J. and MORTON, P., WILLIAMS 1962. The Symbolism and Ritual Context of the Yoruba Laba Shango. *JRAI,* **92**, 23-37.

Quest for the Cross River Skin-Covered Mask:

12

Methodology, Reality and Reflection

Keith Nicklin

A bold man has a big forehead.
Comment by Matthew Obi, an Elder of Odaljie-Mbube, Ogoja, Nigeria, concerning the prominent forehead of an Oyumne mask, in 1984.

This paper is an account of thirty years of research into a single genre of African art – that of Cross River skin-covered masks. Given the uniqueness of the genre and the variety of methods which were developed and applied in different field situations, I describe the reality of this experience, with its resulting achievements, qualified successes and downright failures. With regard to technology and cultural context I provide only an outline here, though the reader is given references to some of the relevant literature. I see this paper as a prolegomena, discursive rather than analytical, to the monograph on this subject which I intend to complete in due course; only then will my Quest truly have ended! For the time being, however, I hope that I have succeeded in my aim to present a project which demonstrates a case of appropriate ethnographic collecting rather than of cultural appropriation.

My firsthand experience of this genre dates from 1970, when, as an ethnographer newly appointed by Nigeria's Federal Department of Antiquities (now National Commission for Museums & Monuments), I was posted to South-eastern State (now consisting of Cross River and Akwa Ibom States). This part of Nigeria shares an international border with the Federal Republic of Cameroon, and apart from Calabar, old port and

Keith Nicklin

present-day capital of Cross River State, comprises mostly relatively little-known and sparsely populated rain forest, mangrove swamp and littoral regions. Modern towns such as Uyo and Eket in the south and Ikom and Ogoja to the north, however, are expanding rapidly, and tarred roads connect major settlements, with the Cross River now bridged at two points, near Itu and Ikom respectively.

Skin-covered sculpture, comprising carved wooden masks and figures, is unique to the Cross River forest region of southeast Nigeria and southwest Cameroon, and some contiguous areas (see map). The major skin-covered mask forms are as follows: cap masks or head-dresses depicting human, animal or therianthropic heads and figures, often mounted on a basketry base, carried on top of the head, and worn with a long gown of fibre or cloth which extends from the top of the masquerader's head to the ground; alternatively, a string costume, with or without fibre skirt, may be worn (fig. 1). The helmet mask covers the entire head and face of the wearer and is generally worn with a cloth costume consisting of separate top and hooped skirt. Both cap and helmet masks most frequently depict the human face, a male face worn to the fore and female face to the rear, in Janus mode, or multiple faces. Tableaux of human and animal figures or heads occur, especially in Igboland, at the western limit of distribution. Towards the north-eastern edge of distribution, especially among the Widekum of Cameroon the human figure cap mask is common, and also a type which Murray classified as the 'domed face mask' – a face mask in which the top of the mask extends over the wearer's head to a point at the back approximately level with the eyes.[1]

It is possible that the skin-covered sculpture genre derives from the custom of carrying trophy heads, as both animal hunting and intergroup warfare, the latter involving the taking of heads in hand-to-hand fighting, were institutionalised in the Cross River region prior to the colonial period. Skin-covered human and animal skulls are known from several museum collections throughout the world, and may still be found in the field (fig. 2) (Nicklin & Salmons 1997: 163-67). The human variety is often presented as a cap mask with a grotesque rectal gape, with incisors of the wild boar inserted into the original tooth sockets of the jaws. Scientific examination has shown that in at least a few cases human skin has been used to cover such masks, although the use of the skin of an animal in this way, usually wild rather than domestic, is much more frequent. The use of sheep and goat skin is common towards the eastern limit of distribution, for example amongst the Bangwa.

Figure 2: Left: Janus-faced skin-covered mask for Nkang warriors' association. Right: skin-covered cap mask containing an antelope skull, for the Bikarum hunters' association.

(Photograph: Keith Nicklin, 1971).

Skin-covered masks are generally the property of village-based sodalities or associations of warriors or hunters, and sometimes of lineage groups and entertainment fraternities or sisterhoods (vide Roschenthaler 1998: 38-49). Although in West Africa it is almost always men who wear carved masks, even when female characters are played, in the Cross River region skin-covered masks are sometimes worn by women, as follows: the cap, tableau form carried by women with face exposed, as among the Annang and Igbo; the open-faced helmet form, as among the Bangwa; and the cap mask form with wearer's face concealed, as among the Bokyi. Often, such masks belong to an age-set or regulatory association, and are used at monthly convivial palmwine parties, and at the initiation and ceremonial funeral or second burial of members. On the Nigerian side of the border in particular it is common for an aggressive male character or 'Beast' to interact with a gentle female persona or 'Beauty'. In such situations, knock-about humour and lewdness are normal (fig. 3) (Nicklin 1983 pl. 11).

One of my official briefs from 1970 until 1978 was to document the production and use of skin-covered masks, and to collect as many authentic examples as possible for the museums of Nigeria. This genre was definitely perceived by Dr. Ekpo Eyo, then Director of Antiquities, as an important and vanishing artform. Although an excellent collection of skin-covered masks was held at the National Museum, Lagos, many of which had been collected in the field by Kenneth Murray, who was also responsible for a well-documented card index of masks which he had seen and photographed in the field in the 1940s (Murray n.d.) skin-covered masks had never been the subject of intensive ethnographic investigation.

The German colonial official Alfred Mansfeld, who worked mostly in the upper reaches of the Cross River area of then Kamerun prior to World War I, published a little on the subject (Mansfeld 1908; 1924) especially

Keith Nicklin

Figure 3: Enyatu funerary masquerade near Ezekwe. A male character in 'hairy' plant fibre costume next to a female character wearing a skin-covered Janus-faced helmet mask decorated atop with mirrors and porcupine quills. The mask was made by Thomas Ogwogwo.
(Photograph: Keith Nicklin, 1984).

concerning some specimens of mostly Keaka and Anyang (both peoples may be subsumed under the Ejagham group) origin , including drawings of a sizeable collection which went to the Institute of Ethnography, Leningrad (Olderogge & Forman 1969). Mansfeld's British counterpart on the Nigerian side of the border during the same period, P. Amaury Talbot, described some examples of skin-covered mask, including the publication of field photographs (Talbot 1912), and lodged some specimens with both the Pitt-Rivers Museum, Oxford, and the British Museum. With the exception of material collected by Mansfeld, Talbot and Murray, at the time that I began my study of the subject, in most museum and private collections throughout the world it was the practice to attribute them to the 'Ekoi', which is, incidentally, a pejorative term for the Ejagham used principally by the Efik people in and around Calabar. Salesroom catalogues and some general accounts of African art frequently perpetuate the custom of using the term 'Ekoi head' to this day.

During my first field trip to Ejagham and Bokyi country in early 1971 I was able to examine and photograph a few specimens, despite the fact that in many villages I was informed that most of the indigenous art had been looted or destroyed during the Nigerian Civil War of 1967-70. I quickly came to realise that the only way of documenting the production of such a by now rarely-made artform bearing in mind that, three decades earlier, Murray, had failed to locate a single satisfactory artist, was to commission a competent myself. Accordingly, I commissioned two skin-covered masks from the first carver that I found who had had direct experience of the art. He was a young self-taught maker of wooden slit-drums, masks and figures, Patrick Adeh Achong from the Mbube village of Odajie, near Ogoja, in the northern savannah, part of the then South-eastern State. At the time of our meeting Patrick had already begun experimenting with the art of skin-covering, in order to meet commissions from local groups for the replacement of old, damaged or lost masks. He had not previously witnessed the covering of sculpture with skin-covering but he had talked to elders who had, and he had examined some old masks. One of his neighbours, by name Abo Oduk, was an accomplished maker of membrane drums, the heads of which are of antelope skin (Nicklin 1977: 43).

Working from a photograph of a cap mask which I provided, on the one hand, and from an old Janus-faced helmet mask of the Mbube men's association, Ntsebe, on the other, Patrick was commissioned to make two mask replicas. Most master carvers in south-east Nigeria do not sketch facial and other details on the wood before carving, but Patrick did. He acquired duiker skin from local hunters, shaved it with a knife, and soaked it in water for two to three days prior to applying it to the mask. In order to make the skin adhere to the wood and take on its shape, he tacked on scraps of modern roofing metal and of skin which were removed when the skin had dried. Some nails were also used to keep the skin in place, finally. Although skin-covered masks which he had previously made were decorated with industrially produced paints, rather than formerly used plant pigments, I instructed Patrick not to apply modern paint to the pieces he had made for the museum.

In sum, Patrick Achong had produced two works of reasonable quality, but the technical standard was short of that of the masters of this genre, especially in the absence of really traditional methods and materials of skin preparation and mask decoration. In a report of two years research on skin-covered masks to date, I published a detailed account of Achong's work, which, in the light of the growing fashion in south-east Nigeria for masks decorated in gloss paint of often brilliant colours, I expressed doubt that 'this new art form will ever achieve any great level of technical or aesthetic competence' (Nicklin 1974: 68).[2]

In 1971 I had also attempted to commission a skin-covered mask from an Annang carver from the renowned wood carving centre of Ikot Ekpene. I already knew from talking to Kenneth Murray, and from museum research in Lagos that the skin-covered mask trait had diffused into Annang territory. The artist assured me that he knew how to make skin-covered cap masks, so I provided him with a photograph of a skin-covered cap mask which I had seen earlier in an Ejagham village near Calabar, to work from. The result was a metre-high monstrosity, three times the size of the original, despite my careful instructions to the artist, with boot-polished, roughly-shaved goatskin partially adhering to the wood substructure only by the aid of 'Evostick' carpet adhesive. Since I could not proffer this piece to the national collections I paid for it out of my own pocket and for some years accommodated it as a characterful candle-holder and thief-deterrent in my unelectrified flat-cum-museum-store in Uyo.

The unfortunate coda to this account is that upon an inspection of the Lagos Museum reserve collection several years later I saw some examples of the same artist's work, much smaller than his original production, but otherwise rendered in the same crude manner. An unsuspecting member of the curatorial staff had obviously been duped by a dealer, and I was now wry witness to an unanticipated outcome of my own ethnographic endeavour. To the best of my knowledge I do not believe that other examples of this regrettable artform ever entered into indigenous use, despite the fact that I did see some specimens on sale at a craftshop in Ikot Ekpene during the mid to late 1970s, and I know that some local masquerade groups did 'shop' there.

A greater degree of success was achieved with the commission for a 'set' of Enyatu masks which I placed with Thomas Bebua of the Ekajuk village of Mfom, between Ikom and Yahe, in 1973. He produced two face masks decorated with modern paint, two skin-covered cap masks, and a skin-covered helmet mask. He did soak the skin in water prior to covering, but the standard of carving was mediocre, and he used non-traditional materials: nails to attach the skin to the wood, and a carpentry adhesive. The masks were acquired for the Oron Museum, but at this time Mr. Bebua was rather too old for further work to be undertaken with me. In his younger days he had probably been a competent carver with a rudimentary knowledge of covering masks with skin.

Keith Nicklin

Experimental work of this kind (Nicklin 1976) in the Palm Belt zone took on a new lease of life with the arrival in 1973 of Jill Salmons, on research attachment to the University of Nigeria, Nsukka. Beginning with leads from Murray's unpublished field notes at the Lagos Museum, her own fieldwork established that the practice of covering wooden sculpture with animal skin had penetrated some Annang, Ibibio, Efik, Ika and Igbo communities by way of an entertainment masquerade called Ikem, which, typically, employed a carved head-dress with hornlike coiffure, the whole often skin-covered. It would appear that Ikem was founded in the Calabar area at the turn of the century and, being a secular play, met the approval of the missionaries and a growing number of converts to Christianity, and so spread quickly. It reached its height of popularity during the 1930s and continued to be performed among a number of communities until the Nigerian Civil War (Nicklin & Salmons 1988).

Figure 4: Male skin-covered cap mask with corniculate coiffure for the Ikem play. Commissioned from Annang artist John Onyok by Jill Salmons for the National Museum Oron. (Photograph: Keith Nicklin, 1977).

During the mid-1970s Salmons commissioned many local artists who said that they had made masks for Ikem dance groups in the past, to make examples of these for the National Museum, Oron, now on its way to rehabilitation. The results were variable, and although technical competence generally did not meet that of the masters whose work had been collected earlier by Murray in the vicinity of the core area of skin-covered mask manufacture around Ikom, much of it was of good quality. Often the head-dresses were covered with domestic catskin, unsurprising in the more densely populated Palm Belt where game such as antelope is scarce. Two of the more outstanding artists in this area proved to be Annang artist John Onyok, who excelled in the production of a cap mask with remarkably tall corniculate coiffure fig. 4), and Ika artist Nwa Nkwa, who made pairs of head-dresses, the male with boldly executed horn coiffure, the female complete with a skin-covered representation of a crown of British type. Among the Ika, Ikem has become the main means by which they project their cultural identity to others. For example, at Nwa Nkwa's hometown, Urua Inyang, Ikem performances, using masks which he has made, take place annually, at funerals, and also for the entertainment of visiting dignitaries.

It was not until late 1973 that I was able to conduct an official research trip to Cameroon although by this time I had already ventured over the border several times by forest path.[3] In the course of this visit I conducted fieldwork in the Widekum and the Bangwa areas, and collected several pieces for the National Museum, Lagos (brought out, of course, under Cameroon Government permit). In addition, I spent time with Widekum skin-covered mask makers Joseph Tewire (fig. 5) and Nascup Asanga at Nen village in Momo Division, and, from them first received direct verification of the practice of covering small-scale human head and figure carvings with animal bladder, a highly elastic substance suitable for treating small and intricate carvings called *Atukom* and *Utaturu*. Larger domed face masks for the men's regulatory society, *Nchibe*, were found to be covered with the fresh, dehaired skin of either antelope or goat.

At Oshum village I interviewed carvers Pa Tanyi and Stephen Kawoh, who, after covering cap and domed face masks with fresh goat or antelope skin, secure it in place by tying tightly with string. Whilst still damp, the skin is rubbed with a dark coloured liquid called *ikan*, made by heating a certain leaf in water, and the mask smoked near a cooking fire. After drying, masks made in this way appear intensely black at first, and, when the string is removed, permanent

Figure 5: Widekum carver Joseph Tewire with newly-made Utaturu and Atukom figure cap masks. Collected by Keith Nicklin for the National Museum, Lagos.
(Photograph: Keith Nicklin, 1974).

cordage marks are clearly imprinted. From the examination of museum specimens before travelling to Cameroon, I knew that the use of string in this way was common amongst the Igbo, though usually absent from the work of more technically accomplished artists among the Ejagham and Bokyi. Whilst trekking through Widekumland, I was also able to witness domed face masks in use by *Nchibe* members, as well as Mpoh masqueraders wearing cap masks of human head form, the former worn with an embroidered gown, the latter with a body-hugging string costume and hooped skirt of unwoven raffia.

At Fontem, capital of the kingdom of Bangwa, arriving with the excellent credentials of having sat at the feet of Robert Brain – anthropologist at London University, and 'Friend of Bangwa' (see Brain 1976; Brain & Pollack 1971) – I gratefully accepted Fon Defang's invitation to stay at the palace. I also went to Fontem in the knowledge that, according to Dr. Brain, the skin of the first whiteman to reach Fontem, the German plantation agent Gustav Conrau, had been worn by a princess at a funeral in a nearby chiefdom. The Fon graciously granted me access to his ceremonial property, especially, at my request, to the skin-covered helmet masks and regalia of the 'Royal Society', as reported by Dr. Brain. In his younger days Chief Defang had himself practiced carving, and so went out of his way to help my enquiries (fig. 6). I also enjoyed the privilege of visiting one of Robert's main informants, Chief Fobella, who lived in mountain fastnesses above Fontem, stayed overnight in his polygamous home, and gratefully accepted the gift of one of his own skin-covered Royal Society masks upon departing.

Here it should be pointed out that although the Bangwa are a Bamileke people, with all the implications of being an hierarchical, Cameroon Grassfields-type society which this implies, much of their art and associated beliefs and institutions owe a great deal to their Cross River, traditionally more egalitarian, neighbours, especially the Ejagham, with whom they have maintained overland trade contact for centuries.

Keith Nicklin

Figure 6: Fon Defang outside his palace at Fontem with two Royal Society masks of which he said he was the author. Bangwa people, Cameroon. (Photograph: Keith Nicklin, 1978).

Although my visit to Fontem was an extremely rewarding one in respect of access to Royal Society masks, some of which were of superb quality, and I was able to gather much incidental data as to mask preservation and use, I was not able to remain long enough actually to witness masks in use. Equally frustrating, the prominent Fontem artist, Michael Atem, whose work had been favourably commented upon by Robert Brain, was 'out of town', working on a slit-drum carving commission in a remote settlement. Nevertheless, Brain's statement that, in Bangwa, 'Any pliable skin is suitable; monkey, antelope, sheep, even pig's bladder' was corroborated by my own enquiries, with the proviso that the skin of a sheep from a chiefly flock is preferred for the decoration of a Royal Society mask. The account of my 1973 Cameroonian fieldwork (Nicklin 1979), written and submitted for publication shortly after my return from that country, remained unpublished until after my second official visit to that country.

The latter took place in the dry season of 1977-78, when I was able to return to Fontem and also make contact with a number of artists in the Keaka area of Cameroonian Ejaghamland, and to visit Banyang country, south of Mamfe. At the Keaka settlement of Kembong a number of cap masks representing the human head were seen, in a style recognisable from some of the more naturalistic examples collected by Mansfeld. A skin-covered face mask with fresh plant fibre costume was seen at a masquerade performed in honour of my visit to the Banyang town of Tali (see Ruel 1969), by a group traditionally concerned with post-mortem examination of the entrails of suspected witches. At Fontem I spent many hours with the fun-loving and bibulous Michael Atem, carver to Fon Defang, who, though proudly showing me some fine house-post which he had recently made, diverted any serious enquiry concerning skin-covered masks. His main mask-making concern at the time was with multiple-faced Royal Society helmet masks, some with an aperture at the front to reveal the masker's face, 'in brightly coloured European hues' (Brain & Pollack 1971: 43).

The overall impression gained during my two Nigerian Government-sponsored trips to Cameroon was that a much greater number of artists continued to produce skin-covered masks on this side of the international border. Especially in the Widekum area, commercial demand for the art had been stimulated by a network of handicraft shops in the south-west part of the country, notably Bamenda, assisted by the government and with some international aid. It was clear from the general standard of many of the craftshop goods, carved as well as woven raffia work, that a reasonable degree of quality control had been achieved; more so than in the case of craft centres in places such as Ikot Ekpene in southeast Nigeria.

My ethnographic fieldwork in the Rio del Rey area of south-west Cameroon in 1988 and 1989[4] established south-western limits, to date, for the skin-covered mask genre, by the existence of a nondescript Ejagham-style cap mask seen in the Ekwe (men's leopard spirit association) lodge at Mundemba, and a fine horned coiffure cap mask originating from one of the Efut masters of Calabar (see Nicklin & Salmons 1988, map, Nicklin 1991: 7) performed as for a female pre-nuptial fattening rite, at Akpassang, on the Akwayafe River, which for part of its length marks the Nigeria/Cameroon border.

Among communities of the Balondo peoples of the densely forested Ndian Valley which I visited in 1988, no specimens of the genre were seen, my enquiries being severely inhibited by the iconoclasm inspired by a 'modernising' politico-religious movement of the late 1940s and early 1950s. This engendered the wholesale bonfiring of traditional material culture and seems to have been practiced with virtually Melanesian cargo cult ferocity throughout constituent Batanga, Bima, Ngolo, Bakundu, Balue and Mbonge territories. From my own research point of view, the situation was particularly disastrous, given the high degree of artistic achievement suggested by known works of the masters of skin-covered mask art practising among the Balondo, who are named Efut on the Nigerian side of the border, and the long-term demise of Efut culture in the face of that of the Efik, a dominant Ibibio sub-group of coastal and riverine Palm Belt.

From 1971 to 1973 I was able to document a number of skin-covered masks, including fine examples of Janus-faced helmet masks of the warrior's association, *Nkang*, cap masks both single- and Janus-faced of the male prestige association, *Oshirikong*, and a form of cap mask with a representation of vertical, plaited coiffure on top of the head, worn by a women's association called *Egbege*, among the Bokyi of the Ikom area. I also collected several Bokyi masks which had fallen into desuetude, for the Lagos Museum. This fieldwork was facilitated by the attachment to me of a series of undergraduate students from the University of Lagos. In most cases they were well-known members of their own communities, often former school-teachers now advancing their education, employed during the long vacation by the Department of Antiquities. Fieldwork now progressed fast.

I met Thomas Achagwu Ogwogwo of Ezekwe in Ukelle territory, near Ogoja, in the northern part of Cross River State, Nigeria, in the dry season of 1974. I commissioned a skin-covered helmet mask of the type which he usually made for men's *Enyatu* masquerade

Figure 7: Ukelle master artist Thomas Ogwogwo, assisted by his son, Columbus, finishing a skin-covered Janus-faced helmet mask, Enyatu, for the National Museum, Oron.
(Photograph: Keith Nicklin, 1974).

groups of his locality (fig. 7). From the very beginning I realised that in Ogwogwo I had found what I was looking for: a maker of skin-covered masks whose work equalled that of the best masters as represented in museum collections throughout the world. At this time Ogwogwo was a much respected member of the community, and although he bore no formal title, he was known affectionately among his people as 'Chief'. He had learnt to make masks by imitating his father, the late Ogwogwo Egana (Nicklin & Salmons 1984: 35: 41-2).

After the mask has been carved it is left to dry for several weeks. The sap from the *ezakpal* tree is applied to a sun-dried hide of either Duiker or Harnessed Antelope. The skin is folded, wrapped in leaves, and kept overnight by a smouldering fire. Early the following morning the skin is washed and the overnight action of the sap causes the hairs to fall from the skin. The glabrous skin is draped over the entire face of the mask, and pegged at either side of the eye and mouth apertures, base of nose and middle point of the ears. The skin is smoothed repeatedly with the fingers and thumbs. Ogwogwo uses his tongue and lips to knead and press the skin into the contours of the mask. After repeating this process for a while the mask is put to one side to commence drying.

In the production of a Janus-faced mask, prior to covering with skin the female face may be rubbed with a red pigment, namely a paste made by roasting, pulverising and then mixing with water billets of wood from a forest tree, *Pterocarpus*. Typically, he begins skin-covering at dawn. Before noon the skin on the mask begins to dry and harden and change from white to translucent light brown in colour. The female face assumes a cinnamon hue, due to presence of the pigment on the wood below. By mid-afternoon the mask is ready for painting. On the previous day Ogwogwo will have collected sap from a forest tree called *okaduk*. This sap is applied all over the male face of the mask. In so doing the colour of the sap changes in colour through pink to dark brown, finally hardening to give a glossy effect. Then the features of the female face are delineated: eyebrows, lips, the rim of the ears, and scarification and tattoo marks. In the late afternoon, the teeth and sometimes the 'blind' female eyes of the new mask may be whitened with a pigment made from roasted forest snail shells, ground up and mixed with water. Finally the mask is polished with a cloth dipped in palmoil, so that the skin covering on the female face is raised to a gleaming chestnut colour, whilst that of the male face becomes a rich brown, almost black.

Frustratingly, during the mid-1970s, although I was able to visit Chief Ogwogwo from time to time, and he always produced excellent work for me, my duties with regard to the rehabilitation of the National Museum, Oron, curtailed fieldwork time. Through Ogwogwo, I established contact with another Ukelle carver, Thomas Lukpata, and commissioned work from him also. His usual output for local clients comprised carved wooden figures representing deceased lineage members, and skin-covered Janus-faced helmet masks for the *Enyatu* association, often incorporating carved representations of the cattle egret into the superstructure.

Throughout this period, whenever in the Ogoja area, I visited and stayed with Patrick Achong's delightful family in Odajie-Mbube. Partly through my own patronage, and also a growing reawakening of local demand which my interest stimulated, the quality of Patrick's work improved. He was able to achieve a better adherence of the skin to his sculptures, and with the aid of an imported hair dye normally used by greying villagers, obtained from local markets, his mode of decorating masks improved. From certain Bokyi communities, especially through the good offices of Councillor Daniya at Iso-Bendighe, near Ikom, I was able to commission replicas of skin-covered masks still in use. These were exchanged for original pieces, and owners compensated in cash and in kind for the transferral of spiritual power from the old to the new masks. In this way the interests of the mask owning institutions were protected, no negative impact made by the collecting process upon indigenous belief systems, and the Nigerian museum authorities made a significant contribution to the revival of a generally declining traditional artform.

An unforeseen down-side came in the train of my commissioning of mask replicas. During the late 1970s I was informed by Patrick Achong that a Nigerian man, purporting to be my colleague or friend, had passed through some of the Bokyi and Mbube locations where I had done fieldwork. He had collected some masks, of which he said copies were to be made and later presented in place of the originals, in the manner which I had established. No replicas were made and the originals not returned to the owners. I was told about this person's activities also on my return to the Ogoja area in 1984, before which he had returned, too. I had never met the man and his identity remains a mystery to the present day. I have little doubt, however, that he was an art dealer, 'running' old masks overseas, probably to the USA, and that he was well-briefed, having read at least my 1974 publication in the journal African Arts. I have discussed the impact of the illicit traffic in cultural property from this part of the world, due to the demands of Western collectors, elsewhere (Nicklin 1975: 86-8; 1981: 259-60). Another negative by-product of my own research and publication was the attention of overseas collectors which this work seemed to be drawing to my subject matter, although I followed the usual convention of not revealing place names concerning important pieces still *in situ*. Increasingly, also, from private collectors as well as curators, I received requests to identify skin-covered masks held in the West, from photographs of the pieces.

Over the years I established a firm friendship with Patrick, and in effect became a member of the Odajie *Enyata* association of which he was a leader, attending *ad hoc* palmwine drinking parties and funerary masquerades as much participant as observer (fig. 8). Patrick's artwork now having reached a highly competent stage, I took him to meet Chief Ogwogwo at Ezekwe. The encounter went well, Ogwogwo freely sharing his trade 'secrets' with the younger artist. As a result Patrick learned of the traditional skin dehairing and softening process of the old skin-covered mask artists, and materials and methods of decoration.

Nevertheless, in his subsequent work, Patrick did not always adopt Ogwogwo's technology. In essence he remained an artist whose ways of working remained somewhere between that of the traditional artist represented by Ogwogwo, and those who freely employed industrially produced tools and materials. The continuing contrast in the work of both Ogoja artists presented me with an ideal, laboratory-like situation with direct access to the best of the traditional artist's output, as well as that of an innovative individual whose work responded to new challenges as it matured.

Keith Nicklin

200

From my early fieldwork in Nigeria and Cameroon I was impressed by the relative care taken by many of the guardians of skin-covered masks on behalf of the associations owning them (Nicklin 1983: 123-27). This included rubbing with palmoil and palm kernel oil, and wrapping in banana leaves, a sleeping mat of woven screwpine or of bark cloth. Among the Bokyi bark cloth was believed to offer resistance to termite attack (Nicklin & Salmons 1979). Such a package, in the best cases, would be suspended by a single piece of cord or cane and kept in the smoky atmosphere near a cooking fire – a situation providing maximum protection of insect and rodent attack, and relatively warm and dry and so mould-free. I had become aware of the shortcomings of museum preservation and storage methods, not only in ill-equipped African museums, but also in the West where storerooms and showcases had predominantly over-dry atmospheres causing the skin to shrink and crack.[5] At the Oron Museum, where most of the pieces which I collected after the early 1970s were kept, the coastal situation was extremely humid for most of the year, and the electrical supply very unreliable.

I had resisted Patrick Achong's requests for employment at the Oron Museum for some time, partly on account of my own research in his home area, but in the end recommended his appointment there in the hope that his skills could be utilised in the development and application of technologically appropriate methods for the preservation at Oron of skin-covered masks and other artefacts in the national collections. For bureaucratic and other reasons beyond my control this programme was never implemented, but Patrick did continue mask-making there in order to demonstrate his skills at a small 'Craft Village' in the grounds, and accepted a few commissions from mostly expatriate visitors. Always enterprising, Patrick also took the initiative to sell some of his wares at Calabar international airport, on the other side of the Cross River estuary from Oron. After several years at Oron he returned home to Odajie.

Patrick's presence at Oron greatly aided the success of a masquerade group which I founded among museum staff there, called 'Urban Gorilla', which was modelled on his *Enyatu* group in Odajie, as Patrick had for long been a skilful drummer, masquerader and dancer. Although 'Urban Gorilla' was a convivial palmwine-drinking club, it also had the serious purpose of encouraging somewhat urbanised personnel to re-discover social activities and traditional utensils whose use had been discouraged during the colonial period and frowned upon by the missionaries. It also provided me with my valuable first experience of African masquerade actually from *inside* a suffocating, hairy fibre costume. Patrick Achong was one of the group of artists and craftspersons which I selected to travel to the Lagos Museum in 1977, proudly to demonstrate their work to Nigerian and overseas visitors to FESTAC, the Black and African Festival of Arts & Culture.

In April 1977, approximately one year before I left Nigerian Federal Government employment and returned to England, the new exhibition at the National Museum, Oron, was opened to the public. This included a prominent display of skin-covered masks, using specimens collected earlier, from the Lagos Museum, as well as older specimens collected since 1970, and newly commissioned pieces made by Ogwogwo, Lukpata, Nwa Nkwa and Achong. Among the works of the latter artist was a production sequence made in order to show the stages of skin-covered cap mask manufacture, and an Ejagham cap mask collected by Murray, in its original leaf storage wrapping. Wherever possible, specimens were labelled as to name of carver, village of origin, ethno-linguistic group and administrative locality. The display was illustrated with enlarged photographs showing mask production and use. To the best of my knowledge the Oron display was the first detailed and fully contextualised exhibition of skin-covered masks (Nicklin 1977: 21-7; 1978: 10-12).

During the mid- to late-1970s I extended my search for skin-covered masks into the forested Middle Cross River around Obubra, among the Bahumuno and Agoi peoples, and Ejagham peoples including the Northern and Southern Etung. In the latter group I lived for some months at Nsofang on the southern bank of the Cross River and from here visited riverside communities on the Nigerian side of the border by dugout canoe, as well as those which could only be reached by walking many miles along forest paths – following routes which constituted an overland network once part of the slave-trading hinterland of Old Calabar. I became a member of several age-set groups in Nsofang which frequently met at night to party and for grave-digging. From time to time skin-covered masks were employed in funerary ceremonies, and a particularly fine skin-covered human skull was produced for my close inspection at one settlement near Nsofang, now that I was trusted not to betray the owners of such a grisly article to the authorities. In the course of enquiries into metal-working communities including Abiriba and Item in the Ngwa Igbo area west of the Middle Cross River, enquiries were made about skin-covered masks, and a competent Cross River Igbo artist Obunyan Okpori of Amaoke Item.

Before and after my marriage to Jill Salmons in 1975, she occasionally accompanied me on extended research, especially in Bokyi and Southern Etung country, and improved the standard of data which was able to attain in respect of women's affairs. It is true to say that interaction with most informants was intensified when working as a couple and became altogether more fruitful, when my wife's pregnancy became general knowledge throughout the area of our fieldwork operations. Our first son was born in 1977 and from the moment of our very first appearance with him, naturally hairless in early infancy, especially in the villages of south-west Cameroon, our enquiries moved with the greatest ease. Previously a 'loner' I had not anticipated that a wife and baby could be such a valuable research asset.

After departing Nigeria in 1978 it was not possible for me to resume fieldwork until the dry season of 1983/84.[6] As Keeper of Ethnography, I had persuaded the then Director of the Horniman Museum, David Boston, that the scientific value of the skin-covered masks held there would be much enhanced by the addition of some newly commissioned material from Nigeria, and that this would provide an excellent opportunity for updating part of the existing ethnographic displays at the Horniman in an exciting manner. Accordingly, I prepared for a three-month trip, the aim being, among other things, to acquire work from the four principal Nigerian masters: Ogwogwo, Lukpata, Achong and Nwa Nkwa, representing areas whose work was absent from the existing Horniman holdings. I also purposely focussed on these individuals as I knew that with them, especially Chief Ogwogwo and Patrick Achong, I might be able to achieve my objectives in the short time available.

Given Nigerian legislation forbidding the exportation of 'antiquities', as well as my own ethical position and Horniman Museum collecting practice, I knew that I would not be able to collect any material which had been used in an authentic African ceremony; a few such pieces, given to me by friends in Ogoja and elsewhere, were in fact duly donated to the National Museum, Oron. However, in practice, I enjoyed the same advantages of attachment to a respected Nigerian institution (the National Commission for Museums & Monuments) that I had enjoyed in the 1970s. When a senior police officer arraigned me in the course of an *Enyatu* masquerade, held in the main street of Odajie shortly after my arrival, fellow members of my old sodality made him quietly withdraw. 'If the police arrest Nicklin, *Enyatu* will arrest the police' they announced!

Upon arrival at Patrick's compound I found that he had started carving a four-faced helmet mask, commissioned by the local headteacher, Matthew Obi, on behalf of the people of Odajie, whom he had persuaded to found a new masquerade group, called *Oyumene*. After consultation with the elders it was agreed that I should pay for two such masks and that they would choose which one they preferred, after which I would be free to take the other mask to London. They had feared that if this arrangement was not put in place, I would effectively commandeer Patrick's efforts so that they would have to wait indefinitely for their own mask, a reasonable assumption in the circumstances.

Figure 9: Janus-faced skin-covered *Enyatu* helmet mask (female face to fore). Commissioned from Thomas Ogwogwo for the Horniman Museum in 1984. (Photograph: Bernard Brandham, 1984).

Arrangements with Chief Ogwogwo were straightforward, and he immediately embarked upon the Horniman commission for helmet and cap masks (fig. 9). Apart from acquiring the masks, of equal importance was to video-record the entire process of manufacture with both Ogwogwo and Achong. Given the fact that the two artists lived around fifty miles apart and the fact that I was then inexperienced in video-recording, in addition to which my equipment was heavy, sensitive to heat, shock and dust, and required the battery packs to be recharged at somewhat distant power sources, I had a tough task indeed. Moreover, I met the hottest dry season in living memory. Nevertheless it was completed successfully, and some video-recording done even of Nwa Nkwa's work far to the south of the two Ogoja locations.

In the vicinity of Ogwogwo's village, with him I attended a number of funerary masquerades employing skin-covered masks. How do you dance, drink palmwine, take notes, photograph and video-record simultaneously?

Upon such occasions both artist and ethnographer need to appear both 'cool' and multi-talented and, to a certain extent, in this 'liminal' state, they are, at least for the time being, interdependent. It is my conviction that the Africanist ethnographer at his (her) peril, ignores recognition of the importance of his (her) own public performance and entertainment value. It was, after all, distinguished anthropologist Marcel Mauss who insisted upon the central importance of mutual giving and receiving in social situations. I had not participated in quite this way with Thomas Ogwogwo before, and it was, for me, a recognition of the laurels that I had won by making it possible for him to see himself on TV. A local missionary had arranged for me to play back some of my video recordings on his TV set, in colour, and this had left Thomas and myself spellbound. We were both new to video in those days.

Back at Odajie it so happened that near the agreed collection date of the four-faced helmet mask, the mother of the head of a local College had died, and the Principal, being a man of means, wished to initiate a performance of the mask previously commissioned by Matthew Obi. I was invited to the occasion, and Matthew kindly arranged for my admission even to the secret aspects of introducing a new skin-covered mask to the community. I thus witnessed the 'birth' of the new mask and its emergence into public view. Patrick Achong was there, dancing before the slit-drum played by the blind musician who had taught him. If ever there was a case of arm-of-museum embracing local artist, who in turn communally celebrated his new creation among his own people with the aid of local *and* international sponsorship, this was *it*.

Having spent the morning videoing a magnificent performance of the Obassi-Njom witch-finding masquerade in a Bokyi settlement many miles away, I had spent the greater, hotter part of the day videoing the Mbube funerary masquerade. At Odajie I positioned myself from the most advantageous positions, mostly on top of a high, shadeless pile of jagged cement blocks, with my cameras. Afterwards, in an almost delirious state, at the generator-powered house of the Clan Head, the whole performance of the afternoon's masquerade was re-played on his own TV set. By this time I was too exhausted and short of the light, videotape, battery power, inspiration and sobriety needed to film the participants in an exuberant 're-play'. Such is the power of television.

At the end of the project I had succeeded in videoing, in the case of Ogwogwo and Achong, the entire process of skin-covered mask manufacture. At Ezekwe this included sacrificial offerings to the tree deity, Logwa, the actual felling of the tree to be used for carving, and the gathering of tree saps for dehairing and pigmenting. I had videoed masquerades using skin-covered masks in the vicinity of Ogwogwo's home. With Achong I had managed to video-record a mask made by him, almost identical to the one made for the Horniman Museum, in action at the compound of the artist's neighbour.[7]

Upon my return to the Horniman a display of skin-covered masks was mounted which included older specimens side-by-side with the new pieces. All the masks were provenanced in detail, in the case of the new masks beginning with the name and locality of the artist. The masks were arranged in a manner which could be 'read' from left to right, reflecting the west to east distribution of the actual origin of the pieces. This was important as the genre shows a distinctive regional variation in style. Place-names and ethno-linguistic groupings were provided on showcase maps, and three text panels covered the topics, in turn, of techniques of production, stylistic variation and use and meaning. On open display adjacent to the vitrine were two masquerade figures, one wearing a string gown topped with a skin-covered triple-faced Bokyi cap mask of the type worn by the Osirikong association, the other a Janus-faced Enyatu helmet mask made by Ogwogwo, and wearing a cloth gown decorated with strands of coloured wool, produced for the display by an Ukelle tailor (Nicklin 1987: 90-2).

As part of the re-display of the African collections, the skin-covered mask exhibition remained in place in the South Hall for a number years during the 1990s, before being re-located to the North Hall, where it remained until being dismantled in preparation for the *African Worlds* gallery which opened in Spring 1999. A skin-covered mask component is part of this exhibition, elucidating the artistic patronage in which the Horniman had itself participated through my 1984 fieldwork. Photographs of skin-covered mask artists appear in the accompanying display booklet, and, by directly quoting the words of Thomas Ogwogwo, one of them was allowed to 'speak' on their behalf, thus demonstrating the important principal of the indigenous 'voice' inherent in *African Worlds*.

Accordingly, the final words of this paper are those of Nigerian skin-covered mask-master Thomas Achagwu Ogwogwo, spoken in response to my question to him concerning the light-coloured female face and dark-coloured male face of a Janus-faced *Enyatu* helmet mask made for the Horniman Museum in 1984: 'The beauty of a woman can attract a man. Darkness on a man's face means that he is strong. A hunter wears a black face – he is dirty from the bush'.

Notes

1. K.C. Murray (1903-72) Nigeria's first Surveyor, and, later, Director of Antiquities; he founded the museum movement in Nigeria (see Nicklin 1999: 95 ff). The document referred to is his 'List of Classes' (unpublished typescript, National Museum, Lagos).

2. On leave in England, 1972-73, I gave a lecture to the Art Panel of the Royal Anthropological Institute in London, somewhat facetiously entitled 'Skinheads in Old Calabar'. This covered the ground of my first write-up, published in 1974. Bernard Fagg arranged for a selection of my fieldwork colour transparencies to be copied for the Pitt-Rivers Museum, University of Oxford.

3. I travelled by road from near Ikom, under the auspices of my employers. Although I received a good reception from staff at the Bamenda Museum, one of whom acted as my guide in the Widekum area, I spent only one month in the country as I failed to obtain a visa extension.

4. I spent the first three months of 1988 as a Scientific Advisor to an Adventure Training Expedition staged by Sphinx Battery, Royal Artillery, British Army on the Rhine. Our base was at Mundemba, administrative headquarters of the newly established Korup National Park, and a good starting point for survey work in the rain forest. We received much practical support from

the local government administration in Mundemba, as well as from staff of the Worldwide Fund for Nature involved in the management of Korup. Approximately one year later I returned to the same area for three weeks as Ethnographic Advisor to a group making a documentary film for the Central Office of Information in London, entitled 'The Molecule Mine'.

5. In 1973 I established contact with the British Leather Manufacturers' Research Association, and in due course some photomicrographs of skin specimens which I had collected in the field were kindly provided by Ms. Betty Haines. However, my efforts to initiate a research project to examine the technical properties of skin-covered masks, with a view to the improvement of their care in museums, remained in abeyance until 1998, when the Keeper of Conservation at the Horniman Museum, Louise Bacon, succeeded in obtaining funding from the Gabo Trust for this purpose. I collaborated with this project with Ms. Sophie Julien, whose report was recently issued (Julien 1999).

6. This work was financially sponsored by the Horniman Fund (administered by the Royal Anthropological Institute) and an equipment grant from the Central Research Fund, University of London. Material assistance was generously provided by the Nigerian National Commission for Museums & Monuments, including the use of a vehicle and staff driver.

7. Although I have shown selections of this video material at many university and museum locations in Britain and the USA since 1984, whilst in employment at the Horniman Museum I was too pre-occupied with other duties and lacking in necessary funds and equipment to arrange for the editing of this material into a suitable documentary programme or programme series. I now very strongly believe that such work would be fully justified in terms of the high technical quality of the original tapes, the uniqueness of the subject matter and its historic importance in relation to long-term display in the Horniman's ground-breaking *African Worlds* gallery.

Bibliography

BRAIN, R. 1972. *Bangwa Kinship and Marriage.* Cambridge: Cambridge University Press.

BRAIN, R. 1976. *Friends and Lovers.* London.

BRAIN, R. and POLLACK, A. 1971. *Bangwa Funerary Sculpture.* London: Duckworth.

JULIEN, S. 1999. *An Investigation into Skin-Covered Masks in the Horniman Museum* [Project report, Collections conservation and care section]. London: Horniman Museum.

MANSFIELD, A.1908. *Urwald-Dokumente.* Berlin: Reimer.

MANSFIELD, A. 1924. *Westafrika aus Urwald und Steppe.* Munchen: Muller.

MURRAY, K. n.d. *List of Classes.* Unpublished typescript. Lagos: National Museum.

MURRAY, K. n.d. *Notes on Ikom.* Unpublished typescript. Lagos: National Museum.

NICKLIN, K. 1974. Nigerian Skin-Covered Masks. *African Arts,* 7, 3.

NICKLIN, K. 1975. The Rape of Nigerian's Antiquities. *African Arts,* **8**, 3.

NICKLIN, K. 1976. *Experiments in the Renewal of a Traditional Art Form in Southeastern Nigeria.* Paper given at the Symposium on Contemporary Nigerian Art, University of Nigeria, Nsukka.

NICKLIN, K. 1977. *Guide to the National Museum Oron.* Lagos: National Museum.

NICKLIN, K. 1978. The Utilization of Local Skill and Materials in a Nigerian Museum. *Museums Journal,* **78.**

NICKLIN, K. 1979. Skin-Covered Masks of Cameroon. *African Arts,* **12,** 1.

NICKLIN, K. 1981. Rape and Restitution: the Cross River Region Considered. *Museum* (UNESCO), **33,** 4.

NICKLIN, K. 1983a. No Condition is Permanent: Cultural Dialogue in the Cross River Region. *Nigerian Field,* **48.**

NICKLIN, K. 1983b. Traditional Preservation Methods: Some African Practices Observed. *Museum* (UNESCO), **35,** 2.

NICKLIN, K. 1987. The New African Display at the Horniman Museum. *Museum Ethnographers Group Newsletter,* 21.

NICKLIN, K. 1991. Ekpe in the Rio del Rey. *Tribal Art.* Genève: Musée Barbier-Mueller.

NICKLIN, K. 2000. Ekpu: the Oron Ancestor figures of South Eastern Nigeria. London & Coimbra: Horniman Museum & Gardens & Museu Antropologico da Universidade de Coimbra.

NICKLIN, K. and SALMONS, J. 1976. Bokyi Brakcloth: an Ethnograpic Retrieval Study in S.E. Nigeria. *Baessler-Archiv,* **20.**

NICKLIN, K. and SALMONS, J. 1984. Cross River Art Styles. *African Arts,* **18,** 1.

NICKLIN, K. and SALMONS, J. 1988. Ikem: The History of a Masquerade in South East Nigeria. In Kasfir, S. (ed), *West African Masks and Cultural Systems.* Tervuren: Royal Museum for Central Africa.

NICKLIN, K. and SALMONS, J. 1997. Les Arts du Nigéria du Sud-Est. Les Ogoni et les Peuples de la Cross River. In Martin, J. (ed), *Arts in Nigeria.* Paris: Réunion des Musées Nationaux.

OLDEROGGE, D. and FORMAN, W. 1969. *Negro Art from the Institute of Ethnography, Leningrad.* London: Hamlyn.

ROSCHENTHALER, U. 1993. *Die Kunst der Frauern: Zur Komplementaritat von Nacktheit und Maskierung bei den Ejghm im Sudwesten Kameruns.* GAM-media: Berlin.

ROSCHENTHALER, U. 1998. Honoring Ejagham Women. *African Arts* **31:2**

RUEL, M. 1969. *Leopards and Leaders: Constitutional Politics Among the Cross River people.* London: Tavistock.

TALBOT, P. 1912. *In the Shadow of the Bush.* London: Heinemann.

Tradition as Object of Derision and Desire:

The Bedu Masquerade

of North-Eastern Côte d'Ivoire

13

Karel Arnaut

I collected the four Bedu masks which are now on display in the *African Worlds* gallery of the Horniman Museum during a two-month trip (June-July 1998) to the Bondoukou region (Côte d'Ivoire) (fig.1).[1] This was the last in a series of similar projects which involved ordering masks either for display in museums (The British Museum, London, and The Royal Pavilion, Brighton) or for local use (Bondoukou city and Boroponko) over a period of several years. All these projects were set up as part of a programme to enhance the interaction between myself as researcher and the Bedu mask users/makers by assuming different positions in the domain of Bedu masquerade.

The first step, of course, was for me to become an active participant in Bedu masquerading: the simple feat (that seemed so sensational at the time) of joining the crowd dancing in circles around the masks. As I got acquainted with Bedu chiefs and was initiated into the masquerade in several villages, I could also take part in the painting of the masks and the making of the costumes. Up till now I was allowed once to perform with the mask myself albeit in a rather passive way. During the annual initiation session of children and youngsters into the Bedu mask at Nandibin, I sat behind the mask and made the habitual 'ou, ou' sounds (imitating an undefined ferocious animal) in order to scare the initiands.[2] Finally, by ordering masks for external consumption or by sponsoring the production of Bedu masks for local use, I gained access to the sculpting

Figure 1: Bedu
masks in the
African Worlds
Gallery.
(Photograph: Horniman
Museum).

process which until then was kept away from me. Having gone through these processes once, I simply had to repeat the same procedure for obtaining the four Horniman Bedu masks; the only new thing was negotiating the videoing of the entire production process. Near the end of the latter project my research assistant, Ali Ouattara, stated that we had now gone all the way – we had disclosed, witnessed and recorded, all there was to be known about the Bedu masquerade.

Although it certainly carried also a very positive message, I prefer to look back at Ali's statement as an attempt at closure. It was not the first time Ali came to that kind of *conclusion* and many others at different stages – even very early on in my research – tried to establish that what I had been told or shown so far was somehow penultimate, that going beyond that point was difficult, dangerous, impossible, or just pointless. At the same time, most of the 'closure statements' I received left open the possibility of continuing the ongoing dialogue. Except in a few cases, the dialogue indeed continued. In sum, the many moments of relative closure marked situations when the normal course of action/discourse was temporarily interrupted, a moment when at least the tempo of interaction was slowed down.

Closure

This article explores three cases of closure in the context of the Bedu masquerade. The first is a case of discursive closure in the course – in fact at the very beginning – of an interview with the keeper of the Bedu masks at the village of Nandibin in 1994. The second and third are cases of closure-in-performance, one could be called 'traditional', the other 'modern'. The second case explores how in traditional Bedu masquerade, Bedu is confronted with its double, a parody of Bedu and tradition in the Zòrògò performance. The mockery of Zòrògò is found to have an effect of 'closure' on the Bedu masquerade-as-tradition. In the third case, we observe the staging of 'tradition' and of Bedu masks during a political meeting of the Parti Démocratique de Côte d'Ivoire (PDCI) at the village of Tambi in 1995. In each case 'closure' is rather different, but in the literature the concept is found applied to both kinds of contexts.

To start with the latter case, the staging of 'tradition', has been documented and variously described as folklorisation, reification, canonisation, etc. To my taste, the most apt definition has been provided by Raymond Williams (1977: 122) when he described 'archaic culture' as 'that which is wholly recognised as an element of the past, to be observed, to be examined, or even on occasion to be consciously "revived", in a deliberately specialising way'. The phenomenon of 'closing culture' in Africa was brought to our attention by Terence Ranger (1983: 261-2) who documented 'the whole body of reified "tradition" invented by administrators, missionaries, "progressive traditionalists", elders, and anthropologists'. This is most clearly observable in the domain of African traditional art where canonisation by tribal art experts is 'powerful, one sided, and usually final' (Kasfir 1992: 45). In the domain of performance Anne Doquet (1999) documents processes of 'reduction' in Dogon masquerading in response to cultural tourists who want to witness in real life the kind of authentic Dogon culture they have seen displayed in ethnographic museums – the masquerade tradition in turn obtaining *in situ* the 'fixité' of a museum object (Doquet 1999: 632). These few examples seem to suggest that traditionalisation in its many guises occurs in a confrontation between fluid traditions and appropriating, commodifying, and classifying agents. However in order to avoid the trap of ethnocentrism, we need to take into account Peter Pels' observation that 'the notion of invented tradition privileged European agency and regarded the tradition too much as an ideology imposed on, rather than co-authored with or resisted by, sections of colonised groups' (Pels 1997: 177, and see Berman 1998: 332). In a recent reassessment of his own seminal article of 1983, Terence Ranger (1993: 63) equally deplores the essentialising 'cleavage that "the invention of tradition" assert[ed] between custom and invented tradition'. After all, he says, 'the history of modern tradition has been much more complex than we have supposed' (ibid.: 82). However, acknowledging co-authorship with 'elders' (Ranger), local artists (Kasfir) or mask dancers (Doquet) must not efface the power inequality that opposes traditionalist workers to traditionalising patrons but should, above all, frame both agents within a shared performance of re-imagining tradition. A splendid example of this can be found in Achille Mbembe's description of post-colonial political 'spectacles' in Africa. Mbembe clearly distinguishes 'ordinary people' from the moguls of national politics ('le commandment') but describes a relation of 'intimacy' (1992a) or 'conviviality' (1992b) between them. In the case of the PDCI-meeting at Tambi we will see how the staged tradition is conspicuously subject to 'closure': manipulation, reification, and homogenisation in the presence of national political power. At the same time, it is 'tradition' that helps create the intimate space shared by national politicians and local peasants.

The opening statement in the interview with Kouakou can be productively identified as an instance of discursive closure. In its broadest sense, the latter phenomenon has been described at the micro-level of closings in conversation (e.g. Kendon 1992), at the macro-level of 'fixing' ethnic or national identity in large discursive formations (e.g. Geschiere and Meyer 1998; Blommaert and Verschueren 1998), as well as at the meta-level of social theory, for instance in the work of Chantal Mouffe and Ernesto Laclau (Torfing 1999).

I open this article with a rather detailed analysis of the Kouakou statement because it contains elements of these different uses of closure in discourse and performance by attempting to foreclose on the asked-for historiography of Bedu and 'the ancestors', but at the same time delineating the limits of possible research into the matter, and above all, by relocating agency from the researcher to the elders, including Kouakou himself.

Significantly also, the Kouakou statement is situated at the beginning of an hour-long interview in which *I* was asking the questions and Kouakou told a great deal about such critical matters as the Bedu masquerade. It is an obvious case of relative closure, as I said before, a moment of resistance and reflection. This applies albeit in a different way, I think, to the Tambi performance as well. One may describe the staging of 'tradition', including Bedu masks, as an instance of reification, but only by considering its double aspect of (1) opening-up tradition to (relative) strangers and the (national) public, as well as (2) posing 'tradition' as an index of local identity, 'everlasting' political will, and relative autonomy – something we could call, after Appadurai (1995), the closure of locality.

I have thought it productive to cast this analysis of closure and aperture of 'tradition' in discourse and performance, in an argument about desire and derision. The main reason for doing so is that these two terms cover and cut across the intentions of the many 'traditionalising agents' involved: the elders, the local artists, the mask dancers, as well as the researchers, including myself, and the national politicians. Looking back at my research experience it now seems clear to me that among the elders, artists, dancers, Ali, and myself grew a consensus about our shared desire to witness/build/perform a Bedu masquerade in all its traditional, authentic splendour. This seriousness and zeal was interrupted by moments of derision either staged and public like in the case of the Zòrògò performance or impromptu and individual. At these moments, to use Mbembe's words, tradition revealed 'its own arbitrariness, its own potential for opacity, simulacrum and distortion' (1997: 151).

Kouakou is about to speak...

A particularly complex instance of a 'moment of closure' occurred during a formal interview I had with the Bedu chief of Nandibin, Kouakou, on 4 March 1994 (fig. 2). The interview took place near the very

Figure 2: Kouakou, keeper of the Bedu masks of Nandibin, in front of his house. (Photograph: Karel Arnaut, Nandibin, March, 1995).

beginning of my first stay in the village, at the occasion of an annual feast which includes Bedu mask performances.[3] The days before, I had spoken to other elders some of which were directly concerned with the Bedu masquerade. One of them, Kouadjo, was chief of Dèbabin, the Dèba village quarter that owns the Bedu masks of Nandibin. In the presence of Kouakou, Kouadjo had spoken of the village of Sanwi, the place of origin of the Kulango 'somewhere in the north'. In the interview with Kouakou from which the opening statement below is taken, I was trying to go one step further in linking the migration history of the Kulango with the history of the Bedu masquerade. By asking how Bedu was there (in Sanwi), how it was transferred and how it was 'here' (Nandibin), when it arrived, I was trying to elicit a Bedu (art) history. Considering the fact that I had been quite unsuccessful in reconstructing a Bedu art history in other villages, the fact that I had just arrived in the village, and that I was interviewing Kouakou for the first time, I was definitely moving quickly, also as it appears, to his taste. Kouakou was first and foremost signalling to me to 'hold my horses'. He opened his answer to the first question with the following statement:

1. You come with something (weighty/grave).
2. [6s] Well, when they [ancestors] left there and came here,
    they came and found it here hé ,
    he [Bedu] does not go anywhere.
3. But as they have come,
    you must know that this place is his.
4. But this dates back long ago.
5. Once we got older and found this around here;
    it is not as if it is ours.
6. It is the thing of the ancestors
7. But when it is said that it is man who built it,
    you must know that we lie.
8. Someone makes a joke, but it is not a joke.
9. It happens that at a given moment along your way you see someone who
    resembles the white man who sits here;
9a. and he calls you;
9b. he says 'Come here';
9c. he says 'My name?', 'Do you know me?';
9d. and you say 'I don't know you';
9e. and he says 'and your ancestors?';
9f. 'that is where they come from'
10. That we have seen.
11. When we see this,
    and we say that we can unveil the world's secret,
    you must know that we lie.
12. When grandfather was born, he has found it, truly.
    He has found it with his grandfather, before it came to me in my turn.
13. So, that is generally how it happened.

Kouakou's response expands elegantly on the symmetry which I was trying to set up between the history of Bedu and the history of the ancestors (i.e. the Kulango, the ethnic group to which most of the people of

Nandibin belong) by indicating the difficulties in knowing them both – the 'lying' of line 7 (about Bedu) and 11 (about the ancestors' history). I take these lines to delimit the two scenes in which the text can be divided.[4] In the first scene, lines 1 to 6 recall the confrontation between Bedu and the ancestors while the second scene (8-11)[5] tells about a confrontation between a white man and 'we' or 'you' – respectively myself, and Kouakou, Kouadjo and a small group of bystanders. In the coda (12-13) Kouakou repeats his earlier point about Bedu being found while constructing a 'we' that comprises his grandfather (the ancestors) and himself linked through a continuous line of descent.[6]

The elegance – the poetics if you like – of Kouakou's answer largely resides in the parallels between scene 1 and 2. At the beginning of each scene one finds a situation of coming and going (2 and 9). This is followed by a confrontation, respectively between the ancestors and Bedu (2 to 5) and between locals and a white man (9 to 9f). The two scenes likewise oppose 'something that is there' to 'something that moves'. In the first scene Bedu is in place and the ancestors are migrating ('coming'); in the second scene it is the white man who is in place ('seated') and 'they' moving ('come here', 9b). Through these parallels Bedu and the white man, on the one hand, and the ancestors and the locals on the other hand are associated. The situation is as follows:

BEDU : WHITE PERSON : ANCESTORS : LOCALS

Nonetheless, this state of affairs, depicted in two scenes which talk about the past, respectively about the distant and the near past, is somehow destabilised by two verses which describe a present state of affairs: the 'you come' of the opening line, and the 'it came to me in my turn' of the coda. In line 1 Kouakou could refer to my recent arrival in the village or the first-time visit to his house. In line 12 Kouakou reconfirms the fact that he indeed is keeper of the Bedu mask. A further opposition is constructed between the two scenes in terms of silence/speaking.[7] In the first scene the ancestors who came and found did *not* ask any questions, while the white man of scene 2 plainly came, sat down, and started asking questions right away. These elements I take as implicit means to expose the association of Bedu and white man as an anomaly and evoke a new or desired state of affairs in which the white man found the locals in place in the same way as the ancestors found Bedu.

Kouakou's opening statement could be read as a poignant description or even critique of the actions of the impetuous white researcher, and, of course, of the loquacious Kouadjo who may have been particularly embarrassed by line 11, knowing that the day before he unveiled an albeit public secret about the origin of the Kulango ancestors. Together with this, Kouakou formulates a general warning: speaking about Bedu (7) and unveiling the ancestral past (11) is no small matter: the active participation in the dialogue the researcher is trying to trick elders and locals into, could lead to lies and fantasies (7 and 11), turning these serious matters into a joke (7).

Reading the opening statement as a protocol for action, more can be learned. It may seem that the statement tries to relocate agency in the speaker (and the present elders and locals), while subtracting agency from the researcher, the white man, who is going too far by assuming the position of somebody who is there ('seated', 9) and whose 'calling' (9a) and asking questions (9c, 9e) is definitely out of order.[8] The scheme of action that emerges from the opening statement is that the participation of the elders/locals in the dialogue will henceforth be based on *their* initiative. In other words, the elders/locals are reinstated as active participants, instigators and decision makers, rather than people who are bound to act in response to the researcher's inquiries and inquisitive behaviour.

A final, rather more technical point bears out how some of these moments of closure are, quite literally, to be understood as temporal obstructions, as obstruction in time. In the course of the first scene Kouakou speaks slowly even stately, while from line 9 onwards he starts speeding up. Particularly the dialogue in direct speech (9a-9f) as well as the final lines (12-13) are articulated energetically, very much akin to his normal way of speaking during the remainder of the interview and in most of the later conversations. The extent to which Kouakou was temporising during the first scene becomes clear by counting the number of characters spoken per second: 7.8 characters per second in the first scene and 13.5 characters per second in the second scene (including the coda). This observation confirms how scene 1 and 2 are constructed analogically: the creative work, the construction of the argument, is done in the first scene while the problematic is merely transposed from the distant past to the near past and from Bedu to 'ancestral history' in the second scene. Again, read as a protocol for action, the change in tempo in the opening statement illustrates 'temporal resistance' as opposed to normal, rather animated dialogue and interaction. In retrospect, from that point onwards indeed things moved quite swiftly: during the same interview I learned a lot about Bedu at Nandibin, the day after I was initiated into the Bedu mask, and over the two following days I was shown a great deal of what happened behind the scenes of the annual feast.

But still, Bedu remained 'a thing of the ancestors'. This statement was reiterated as a set-sentence many times in different contexts. Most significantly, even after I had found out about (and participated in) the manufacturing of Bedu masks and costumes by men, and the painting of the masks by women, this image persisted both in the words of locals and in my conception of things. To use Kouakou's phrasing, after I had seen that Bedu was made by men, it remained located beyond historical time and disconnected from a specific place or area. In its timeless and placeless omnipresence, I took it to be an exemplary instance of a religious entity (such as God, spirit, or 'genius'). This image was further corroborated by the observation that speaking about Bedu was assuming a great deal of authority over 'things ancestral'. In the same sense, I felt that the religious enormity of Bedu explained the presence of an, albeit contested, hierarchy of authorised exegetes.

However, looking back at how, when, and by whom this image was used – like I did in the analysis of Kouakou's opening statement – I am less than ever convinced that from it *the* characteristics of Bedu can be inferred. The statement is quite meaningless in itself and must be placed within its discursive context and in a particular course of action. The Kouakou case leads us to believe that Bedu as 'a thing of the ancestors' must be seen within larger strategies of speaking about and dealing with 'tradition'.

In the next section I will give an account of how the Bedu masquerade, in its traditional guise, is talked about and performed. Here I hope to make clear how the 'timeless and placeless omnipresence' of Bedu is constructed in the organisation of the cult. Nonetheless this analysis also reveals the political and basically counter-traditional aspects of the Bedu masquerade.

The traditional Bedu masquerade

The Bedu masquerade is a relatively widespread phenomenon among the Kulango, Nafana, Degha, Hwela, and Abron of the 'northern Bondoukou region'.[9] The northern Bondoukou region is that part of the Bondoukou province ('département') that lies to the north of the city of Bondoukou, between the road to Bouna and the border with Ghana (see map). The choice of this region has historical and political relevance: its population shares an eventful 18th century of migrations resulting in their coming together in and around the then booming city of Bondoukou, attractive as it was as trade-centre and gold-producing area. Soon after the villages and small chiefdoms were colonised by a group of Akan immigrants, known as the Abron, who created the Gyaman kingdom through negotiation and the use of armed force (Terray 1995). The economic and political importance of Bondoukou city, the migrations it brought about and the interaction between villages in the northern hinterland of the city, accounts for the complex ethnic make-up of the region even at

Map: 1 Bondoukou region.

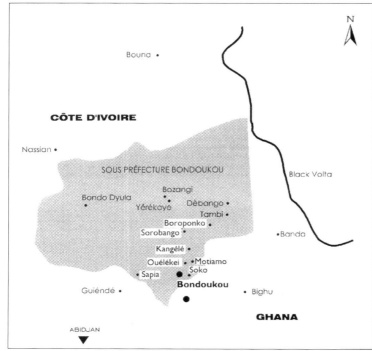

the village level. This populational complexity articulates itself also in the Bedu masquerade, in the way it is differentially organised and positioned into the ritual calendars of different villages and groups of villages.

Bedu performances take place during new year festivals which can last one or several weeks, and, depending on the ritual calendar in use, are organised near the beginning or near the end of the dry season (October to April). Bedu is a night masquerade involving one or more Bedu masks (large plank mask + costume that covers the entire body of the dancer), songs and dances, and comic side-acts. Bedu is a communal event, open to villagers (men, women, and children), visitors, and strangers.

The preparation and organisation of the masquerade is in the hands of a limited group of people who, through kin or interest, have become involved in the production and the management of the performance; this special interest group is led by one or more keepers of the Bedu mask. As a new year festival, Bedu is sometimes compared to other communal purification or renewal festivals which also occur in the region and are more widely known: the Odwira or Yams feast of the Akan peoples of Ghana and Côte d'Ivoire, the Christmas of the Christians, and the end-of-Ramadan celebration of the Muslims.

Very much like the Odwira, Bedu has a political component. Bedu is located in a political space – the village – whose internal division and organisation is displayed and renegotiated in the course of the performances. The main difference with Odwira is that the latter focuses on the authority of the king and the political centre, while Bedu is (also) posited as an alternative authority. While, following McCaskie (1995), Odwira may be considered as an annual key-event in the 'recherche hégémonique' of the Asante political centre, Bedu to a certain extent, can be seen as a counter-hegemonic agent. Bedu has the potential to confront and interrogate the political power of the village chief, in particular, and the socio-economic power of men, in general.

The overall image of the Bedu masquerade that is established throughout narratives and performances, can be presented under three themes: time, space, and authority.

Time. The historical narratives on Bedu are what one could call 'foundational' rather than historical: they tell about the origin of the masquerade in an unspecified past time, that is, they recount (1) the discovery of the wild Bedu by a hunter, (2) its transfer from the bush to the village and (3) the transformations which the Bedu of the bush underwent before becoming the Bedu of the village. This foundational narrative is further dehistoricised by the fact that the transfer (the capturing and domestication by men) of the 'animal' is annually re-enacted in the coming and going of the mask to and from the village.

Only during the time of the Bedu dances is Bedu said to reside in the village. During the rest of the year Bedu stays in the bush – it is kept in the village but is not 'active'. The yearly arrival of Bedu in the village is marked by it being re-painted by women and making a tour of the village – the only day-time Bedu performance – saluting the newly born, children, elders and the houses of the recently deceased.

The foundational narratives, the annual re-enactment of Bedu's coming into existence, the gendered moments in the cycle of its production by men – hunters, sculptors – and its reproduction by women, and the focus on members situated at the extremes of the life-cycle (babies and elders), all these features deeply embed Bedu in the cyclical time-frame of societal continuity. Moreover, Bedu's 'cyclicality' is in some cases modernised through its association with other annual feasts such as Christmas/New Year.[10]

Space. Bedu is not only ancestral in a 'societal' way, but also in a political way. While the foundational narratives stress the importance of the bush as place of origin, the Bedu performances rather point to its place of destination in the village, as unit of political organisation. In a number of Kulango villages, the Bedu performances form part of an annual celebration of a 'creative' moment in the history of the village. These moments are marked by the death of an important forefather and/or foremother. The commemoration of these ancestors, a combination of processions and sacrifices, involves movements between the bush and the village, and particularly the activation of the frontier zone between these two. These movements somehow match Bedu's who arrives from the bush at the beginning of the celebrations and leaves at the end. In between these two moments, Bedu, does not participate in the to-and-fro between village and bush, but stays within the confines of the village, and more importantly, Bedu never enters the 'royal quarters'. These are the quarters inhabited by the people eligible to high office, they are the matrilineal descendants of the ancestors commemorated during the annual feast. In all, these examples give an idea of how the movements of Bedu mark spatial boundaries and segmentations. It is beyond the scope of this paper to go into more detail about this, but let it suffice to say that the operations directly connected to Bedu (initiation, painting, touring the village, dancing, sacrifices, etc.) are located in particular places; these locations and the groups of people associated with them, demonstrate the internal divisions within the village, mark certain hierarchies, in other words, reveal the discontinuities within the relevant political unit, the village. The procession which most clearly marks the divisions and hierarchies within the village, consists of a large group of unmarried girls who visit the different village quarters. After having visited the place in the bush where the creator of the village is buried, the girls, dressed only in a 'traditional' loincloth – consisting of (red) beads and (red) cloth – come back to the village. Here they visit the different quarters and, more importantly, they perform dances and songs around painted clay mounds (*dingo*) which are associated to the Bedu masks and to particular ancestor groups. This procession is the most public of performances that marks the political and ritual hierarchies and divisions in the village.

Authority. In songs and movements, Bedu dances address issues of adult morality and social reproduction (the problem of adultery, the care for children) which are explicitly linked to the relationship between people and the earth (immoral behaviour is said to 'spoil the earth', affect fertility, or, in general, to jeopardise the cycle of natural and human reproduction). Bedu's special power to heal and protect (especially babies and elders) is derived from its origin in the bush. However, to the extent that Bedu is domesticated (captured and tamed) and communal (kept and managed by particular people from particular village quarters) it becomes politicised and its power partly subsumed under village authority. Guardianship of Bedu is inherited and remains within the same matrilineage/quarter (*bin*). Depending on the alliances of the quarter that keeps the Bedu, with other village quarters, certain tasks concerning Bedu (dancing, music making, painting) can be put out to tender. The Bedu that arises from this, is a political animal that is 'of the ancestors', more specifically, of

Figure 3: Man demonstrating Bedu dancing by using a miniature Bedu mask, sculpted by Yao Gbegbetou.
(Photograph: Karel Arnaut, Tambi, August, 1993).

Figure 4: Comedians (kawakòsè) confronted with small Bedu mask (Jadjié) during Bedu performance.
(Photograph: Karel Arnaut, Nandibin, March, 1995).

particular ancestors and not, or less, of others. This is most clearly observed in the fact that Bedu is '*persona*' non *grata* in the royal quarters. The incompatibility between royal and Bedu authority construes a Bedu that is an alternative power and makes for the tensions that exist between Bedu and the village authorities.

Bedu dances, tradition parades and their double in Zòrògò

The above is a description of the Bedu masquerade, in the strict sense of the word. Looking at the ceremonial context, one must take into account the backside of Bedu, that is, the Zòrògò performances. Zòrògò can be seen as the 'unserious', the playful, the hilarious or to say it with Mbembe, the 'obscene and grotesque' side of Bedu. Prior to the period of Bedu dances or to a particular Bedu performance, Zòrògò

Figure 5: The large Bedu mask (bèdu sosoonro) dances in a stately manner during the Bedu performance. Remark how unlike in the case of Jadijé (fig. 3) the whole body is enveloped by the costume.
(Photograph: Karel Arnaut, Nandibin, March, 1994).

performances take place. Zòrògò dances consist mainly of male and female groups of adults and children singing and behaving in a playfully offensive way. Both gendered groups insult each other using obscene language and using grotesque objects to represent each others sexual organs – a pestle for the penis and a mortar for the vagina being the common attributes. The role of Bedu masks in Zòrògò performances is peripheral but not insignificant. The Bedu mask operating during Zòrògò at Nandibin is the smaller of the two, and it is at no point the focus of attention of the dancers. In many respects, the 'Zòrògò' Bedu is a 'lesser' masquerade: its size reminds of the miniature Bedu masks which adults and children produce for fun or decoration (figs. 3 & 4); the costume is less thick and does not completely envelop the dancer's body; and finally it does not 'walk' stately as the large Bedu does (fig. 5), but it 'runs' and 'plays around' not only in the central dancing square, like the Bedu proper, but in the village at large. The main task of the Zòrògò Bedu consists in roaming the village and the dance floor to check whether the unmarried girls – the ones who, a few hours earlier, have been involved in the procession described above – are in 'traditional' loincloth and do not cover themselves with a piece of fabric. It is common practice for the girls to keep themselves covered unless the small Bedu mask shows up. This tension between the chastity of the girls and their forced semi-nakedness is formally explained as that between the contemporary apprehensiveness of girls for showing their breasts and the strict demands of tradition. However, from casual conversations mainly with elder men, it transpires that the girls in traditional outfit are also seen as sexually attractive. This somehow articulates with the sexually explicit language and movements of the Zòrògò dances to shape a general context conductive to extra-marital sexual relationships which are said to be allowed during the Zòrògò period.

The phenomenon of showing unmarried or marriageable girls in various 'traditional outfits' is found in other performances in Bondoukou and the villages immediately to the north. The most well-known is the

Figure 6: On the platform of the Donzoso and Limamso quarter, the unmarried girls dance all night during Kouroubi. The djomo head-dress is usually hidden beneath a headscarf kept in place by a string with 3 pompons. (Photograph: Filip Erkens, Bondoukou, February, 1997).

Figure 7: Abena Hélène (right) who has been excised 3 weeks ago, just before the parade through the village with about 40 other newly excised girls. (Photograph: Karel Arnaut, Tambi, December, 1994).

annual Kouroubi ('night of destiny') event held two days before the end of Ramadan at the mainly Muslim town of Bondoukou. Here unmarried girls are dressed in modern colourful dresses but wear two 'traditional' items: the special headpiece and head-dress (*djomo*) and the whisks (fig. 6). Another rather more local event, takes place in Tambi when the newly excised girls leave the special camps where they have been staying for three weeks, for a parade through the village (fig. 7). Here the traditional outfit consists of the loincloth which the unmarried girls of Nandibin also wear, and the typical Kouroubi head-dress. Again, in all three cases the beauty of the girls is celebrated in view of a future marriage. Only the Nandibin Zòrògò, however, makes the sexual connotations of this pageant explicit through association with bawdy songs and movements.

As said, Zòrògò is a clearly delimited 'moment of freedom' which stops as soon as the drummers switch to Bedu dance rhythms.[11] Almost instantaneously, the atmosphere of the performance changes, it becomes more serene. The battle of the sexes is abandoned and the participants focus on the movements of the large Bedu that dances in the centre. Nonetheless, at least two elements of Zòrògò spill over into the Bedu performance. Firstly, due to the interventions of the small Bedu, the unmarried girls are kept in traditional outfit. Secondly, the Zòrògò technique of 'grotesque' mimicry is found during short side-performances in which the ways of the 'traditional' farmer (fig. 8) are parodied. The latter performance requires some explanation. Impersonating 'the traditional farmer' albeit in a serious way, appears to be a relatively widespread phenomenon in the northern Bondoukou region. It usually forms part of a parade of groups representing the people of the village, comprising various occupations – farmers, hunters, potters, – associations – youth or women's organisations – and status groups – the traditional chiefs, the (former) slaves, etc. Parades of this kind, I have encountered, for instance, during the village anniversary feast of Motiamo and at the inauguration of the new market building

Figure 8: Comedians impersonating 'the traditional farmer' do their classic act: ushering little chickens into the chicken basket.
(Photograph: Karel Arnaut, Nandibin, March, 1995).

Figure 9: Farmers' delegation during village parade at the occasion of the opening of the new market building at Nandibin.
(Photograph: Karel Arnaut, Nandibin, April, 1994).

in Nandibin in 1994 (fig. 9). In these parades, the 'traditional farmer' is a set item. The 'farmer' *tableau vivant* consists of a small group of people (men and women) who present themselves clad in recognisably poor cloths – the kind of clothes people wear when going to work on the field – and carrying two standard attributes: a hoe, and a basket which can contain a water reservoir, food, but which is said to have been used originally to transport chicks which are too small to be left alone at the house and are therefore taken to the field.

In the periphery of Bedu performances 'the farmer' is staged, employing the parodic technique of amplification seen at work in representing genital organs: actors dressed in rags carry an oversized 'chicken basket' supplemented by an equally gigantic 'fan' (fig. 4). The performance mainly consists in making a caricature of the clumsiness of the farmer who ushers his little chickens into the basket (fig. 8).

It is beyond my present purpose to give a fine analysis of these ceremonial practices, as diverse as excision ceremonies, village feasts, masquerading, and instances of vernacular Islam. Similarly, rather than concentrating on the Zòrògò parodic techniques, I primarily want to look at the material Zòrògò uses to deride, and describe what happens to this material (tradition, Bedu, etc.) in the process. In that respect, we cannot miss the point that the choice of 'the farmer', 'the unmarried girls', and the Bedu masquerade, as the focus of parody and hilarity cuts deep into the heart of tradition. All three items are explicitly recognised as 'things of the past' and are annually or occasionally staged in 'serious' processions or parades: the newly painted Bedu masks during their day-time presentation to the village, the unmarried girls after their annual visit to the grave of the village founders, and the farmers during the special occasions of village parades. Although this would need further arguing, it seems as if Zòrògò capitalises on their partial objectification as things and parade - items to decontextualise and parodically recontextualise these three exemplary instances of tradition. In other words, Zòrògò further reifies tradition by turning it into an object of derision. In that sense

I consider it as an instance of 'closure-in-performance'. In his study of the full performance (from rehearsals to première) of a nativity play in a Mexican town, Richard Bauman (1996), detected a similar double operation of mockery and apprehension. Commenting on Bauman's study, Silverstein & Urban (1996: 13-14) observed: 'we see here not only how the text [of the play] as authoritative (and representative of tradition and shared culture) is faithfully re-enacted, but also how the performers mock and fight against the text, creating in part a Bakhtinian carnivalesque spirit or irreverence, even as they celebrate textual fixity, authority, and the continuity of culture'. This can be found back in the *full* Bedu performance – Bedu as 'authoritative cultural' text *and* Zòrògò as parody – whereby Zòrògò traditionalises Bedu precisely by 'fixing' it in its cultural grandeur and ridiculing it as such.

In the following case – Bedu display as part of a political meeting – we can see this reification of tradition being taken one step further. Again we will remark the three items – Bedu, the marriageable girls, and the farmers – , among others, being displayed, now in a context which is quite straightforwardly meant to evoke and celebrate 'tradition'.

Bedu and Bédié at Tambi, 1995

Figure 10: The large Bedu accompanied by a delegation of the 'excised girls' enters the village square at Tambi during the political meeting 'PDCI notre tradition'. (Photograph: Karel Arnaut, Tambi, April, 1995).

Tambi is a relatively large Nafana village in the eastern part of the northern Bondoukou region, very near the border with Ghana. On the 16 April 1995 the village organised a meeting for the PDCI (Parti Démocratique de Côte d'Ivoire) under the slogan 'PDCI, notre tradition'. The local variant of this slogan read 'La tradition continue a Tambi: Moh Yao François' and was printed on caps, T-shirts, and cloth especially designed for the occasion. The first slogan went with the image of president Bédié, the latter with the image of the named village chief wearing his Akan-style royal crown and attire. The slogans were indeed a nice piece of copy-writing but their inventiveness matched the ingenuity with which the entire event was set up. In order to grasp some of the topics of the event, I need to explain very briefly the political situation in Côte d'Ivoire and the Bondoukou region at that time and the historical-ethnic overtones.

In December 1993, Henri Konan Bédié replaced the deceased President Félix Houphouët-Boigny, thereby removing the Prime Minister, Alassane Ouattara, from office. Bédié decided to stay in office until the next presidential elections of October 1995. In the run-up to the multi-party elections of 1995 – after 30 years of single-party rule, democratic elections were reinstated in 1990 – a new political party, the RDR (Rassemblement des Républicains) was created in 1994 and Alassane Ouattara became one of its leading figures. In the spring of 1995, rumour had it in the Bondoukou region, which used to be a PDCI-stronghold, that the RDR was rapidly gaining ground in the predominantly Muslim 'Grand Nord' of Côte d'Ivoire and that the Muslims of Bondoukou were about to switch their support to the RDR.[12] The meeting at Tambi took place at a moment when the PDCI was trying to re-establish links with the North. So, the most obvious meaning of 'PDCI, notre tradition' was the call not to change one's 'traditional' loyalty for the reigning party.

The meeting was set up around the visit of a PDCI-minister, Gbon Coulibaly, a Senufo from the Korhogo region. In the official speeches the minister stressed the ancient links between the Nafana of Tambi and the Nafana and Senufo of the North. The prehistory of this renewal of alliances is that in the course of the early 18th century groups of Senufo-Nafana migrated to the Bondoukou region and set up major settlements in the

Figure 11: Awaiting the arrival of the PDCI minister, the image of president Henri Konan Bédié is shown in between the two important Bedu masks of Tambi, the one of Tapang (left) and of Trasco (right).
(Photograph: Karel Arnaut, Tambi, April, 1995).

northern hinterland of the town of Bondoukou, in Tambi, Banda, and Soko (Terray 1995: 310-15). Having been separated from each other for about 200 years the Nafana dialects of the Senufo-Nafana and the Bondoukou-Nafana are now mutually unintelligible. Nonetheless, the 'tradition' in the slogan was traced through the Nafana/Senufo from Tambi to their ancestral land in Korhogo. In conversations and in speeches, people were reminded of the historical alliance between another Gbon Coulibaly, the famous Senufo leader, and Houphouët-Boigny in the early years of the PDCI-RDA before and just after independence. Through this historical bond, a link was forged between Bédié, the successor of Houphouët, and the peoples of the North, the offspring, so to speak, of the old Gbon Coulibaly. In other words, traditionalising the PDCI, was effected by discursively tying the past to the present, through various lines of descent.

These pre- and post-colonial 'traditions' of allying with and voting for the PDCI were made abundantly tangible in the overwhelming presence of 'tradition' on display. The minister was received by about 10 delegations of local groupings. On one side of the village square stood 'the farmers', 'the hunters', 'the slaves', and the Nafana chiefs from Tambi and its satellite village, Boroponko. At the two other sides of the square stood the audience accompanied by music bands from Tambi, and from Boroponko a person wearing the Senufo-style Do mask, a masquerade which this village took over from the Muslim village of Sorobango. The climax of this parade was the display of the two main Bedu masks of Tambi (belonging to the Tapang and Trasko village quarters) accompanied by a small delegation of girls who had been excised in December of the previous year (fig. 10). Near the time the minister was expected to arrive, this group appeared, walked across the square, and took position near the place where the minister was about to leave his car and enter the village (fig. 11).

Because of another event at that time – tellingly the, in my view, far more significant ('traditional') annual feast at Nandibin where I resided– I did not spent enough time after the PDCI-meeting in Tambi to be able to sufficiently research the reception of this unusual display. However, from later comments I gathered that it was thought particularly well done and not at all an aberrant use of 'tradition'. More importantly for our present purposes, it must be clear how this instance of Bedu display seemingly escapes the discursive grip of cyclicality, village-bush dynamics, and intra-village factionalism.

Time. The above Bedu performance is a particularly non-recurrent event – it breaks through the closed circle of the ceremonial calendar. As a day-time performance, it somehow connects with the annual 'greeting' of the village. As such, it is an out-of-season presentation of Bedu after its return from the bush. The cyclicality of the traditional Bedu masquerade is further deeply transformed by stressing both the linearity of tradition while retaining its unchanging character – the slogan 'la tradition continue' bears this out clearly.

Space. In terms of the use of space, the Tambi Bedu performance is atypical in at least two respects. Instead of being peripheral to the chiefdom it shared its space, and instead of walking around and marking the internal divisions within the village, Bedu circulated in the centre as if it was 'traditionally' dancing. Seen like this, the 'PDCI' Bedu performance is an 'out-of-place' greeting parade; Bedu behaves like it is greeting but this is effected in a space that is organised like a standard dance formation. Except, Bedu is not surrounded by a counter-clockwise moving circle of dancers but by a wide circle of static groups, representatives of the village and its traditions, frozen in space. Further to the use of space, we must notice that the event is structured as a confrontation between 'the village' (including its neighbours amongst whom it enjoys a certain stature) and the national space of politics (whose coming to the village could be a proof of respect). The joint use of the slogans, one referring to the PDCI, the other to its local leader/representative attest to this.

Authority. The extraordinary amalgamation of religious and political authority in the organisation of the PDCI meeting, can to a large extent be found back in the person of Koffi Dadié who, at the time, combined three functions: (1) he was chief of the Trasko quarter of Tambi, (2) keeper of the Bedu mask of Trasko, and (3) sécrétaire PDCI (representative of the PDCI) for the village. It is quite obvious that Bedu was directly confronted with supreme political power, posing next to the effigy of the president, greeting its representative, and being accompanied by people wearing images of the village chief. In the construed opposition between national and local politics, between Bédié and Moh Yao François, Bedu retains its oppositional stance towards the village chief, by taking sides with the PDCI through the Bedu chief and PDCI-representative, Koffi Dadié.

The PDCI Bedu performance can be productively considered, I think, as an instance of closure-in-performance, in different respects. As for the use of time, Bedu is indexing tradition, a 'thing' that exemplary connects the past with the present. Its association with the excised girls bear this out. During an earlier stay at Tambi in 1992, I did some work on the excision which revealed how the people responsible for it as well as the subjects of this practice were well aware of the fact that it was against the law and very much against the grain of modern (metropolitan/European/French) public opinion. This was turned into a point of honour, and used to illustrate how Tambi was able to resist national and international condemnation and built a modernity of its own without losing respect for its traditions. Bringing out, together, Bedu and the excised girls, was a very clear statement in the face of a national politician from the Muslim north: Tambi was determined to keep excising girls and dance pagan masks. The same village-outside world opposition is constructed through homogenising the communal space, patronised by Yao François and unified by its resolve to continue the tradition. I would like to think of Yao François and the other traditional chiefs from Tambi and its neighbouring villages as representatives of the 'political society' and of the many groupings – (male and female) farmers, hunters, slaves, etc. – as representatives of the rural 'civil society'. In between these two, Bedu seems to mediate, capitalising as it can on its double image as a counter-force to political authority but immediately concerned with the well-being of the entire village as political and social community.

The serious and stereotyped representation of the different groups could be described as a form of 'canonisation', the forging of explicit links between past and present as instances of traditionalisation, and the use of 'tradition' in slogans, speeches, and display, indications of reification. I argue that all these are elements in a process of relative closure. This closure, however, operates not within tradition, like in the case of Zòrògò, but on the level of village-based tradition as opposed to the outside world. Although this may, in turn, reify the complex event that we have seen at Tambi – and I will somewhat 'liquidify' it in the conclusion to this paper – I believe it useful to consider it as an instance of 'closure of locality' by the use of tradition.

Two final notes on the uses of tradition

In the introduction of this article I raised, what I recognised as a central problematic, the issue of agency in the closure of tradition. The cases of Kouakou's statement and of Tambi's Bedu performance seem to confirm that traditionalisation occurs in a confrontation between fluid traditions and appropriating, commodifying, and classifying agents. I have however inserted the case of Zòrògò in between the two, in order to destabilise this opposition between authentic and reified tradition. The case of Zòrògò indicates that in traditional performance, tradition is – certainly only partially, but still – objectified, isolated as an object of derision. This conclusion is meant to discourage any reflex to identify 'fluid tradition' with authentic Africa and 'appropriating agents' with external traditionalising forces such as national politicians, international public opinion, or European tourists and researchers. In my description of the Zòrògò performance I have deliberately used the terms 'grotesque' and 'obscene' because these are used by Mbembe (1992a) to expose the key-characteristics of post-colonial political spectacles, very much like the one we have witnessed at Tambi. From his description it becomes clear that agency is almost entirely located with the political-economic centre of the post-colonial state who decides 'on the timing and location of those occasions which state power organises for dramatising its own magnificence', who chooses 'the actual materials used in the ceremonial displays through which it makes manifest its majesty', and who assumes the function of stage-director of these 'spectacles, for its "subjects" to watch' (Mbembe 1992a: 4). However, in the case of Tambi, although it can be assumed that the timing and the location of the event were set by the PDCI, it is obvious enough how the local community provided the 'actual materials' and to a large extent stage-directed the happening. Therefore, it may not make too much sense to try to disentangle who is appropriating who – or in Jewsiewicki's words – 'who is cannibalising who' (in Barber 1997: 6). The co-authorship, argued for by Pels (1997), must be taken seriously, not only in the case of colonial ethnography, but also in political performance in post-colonial Africa. In other words, reading the Zòrògò of Nandibin and the PDCI-meeting at Tambi together – in actual fact they took place within the same fortnight in 1995 – invites us to abandon the idea of the state-driven folklorisation of custom or tradition and examine the complicity with which locals mobilise traditional 'reifying' techniques to please the tradition-seeker. Finally, looking at what happened in Tambi through the eyes of Mbembe, we realise the utter absence of laughter, of the grotesque and the obscene, in the same sense that Bedu without Zòrògò would be considered incomplete. Only a detailed ethnographic account of the Tambi happening could clarify whether the mockery of Zòrògò is 'present' by it being conspicuously absent, consciously repressed, or actively banned. Nonetheless, a trace of the Zòrògò-esque distancing from the serious tradition-on-display is found back in the 'closure of locality'.

Reading the case of discursive closure by Kouakou together with the events at Tambi, we find similar techniques at work in both:
1. traditionalising through connecting with the past ('grandfather' in line 12; the old Gbon Coulibaly) with the present (Kouakou/the elders; the present Gbon Coulibaly).
2. relocating agency by opposing the local interests (respecting unknown history; tradition) to the external ones of the white person (research) or the PDCI (winning the elections).

These few observations indicate that I may need to look at the above instances of reification not so much as processes of 'closure of tradition' rather than 'closure by tradition'. I take this idea from Ranger who suggested we take into account the multi-authored processes of re-imagining tradition by replacing the 'invention of tradition' by 'the invention by tradition' (1993: 76). In the Kouakou statement and the Tambi happening a confrontation is imagined between local interests and an agent who is perceived as a 'traditionalising patron' –

a researcher who is taken to be interested in authentic tradition; a politician who is supposed to like the idea of voting-PDCI-as-tradition. In both cases also, one is trying to salvage local integrity – Kouakou by relocating agency and in Tambi by massive mobilisation of local tradition as counter-force. In this resides, I believe the dynamics and the relative autonomy of the rural societies under consideration: their capability to use the overt and widespread desire for tradition against the desirous.[13] Expressing locality, signalling autonomy and cultural willpower through tradition and *at the same time* exposing tradition in all its splendour, clearly requires a double use of tradition: the serious and the mocking, the Bedu and the Zòrògò use. From both uses arises a different 'tradition', one as object of desire and the other as object of derision.

Notes

1. The field collecting project (1997-98) was financed by the Horniman Museum & Gardens (Sahel Project 2). Research was also conducted while I was a D.Phil student at the University of Oxford (1991-1995). For this I was financialy supported by the *Philip Bagby Studentship in Social Anthropology* (Oxford) and by the *NFWO* (Belgium).

2. The name of the village 'Nandibin' is fictitious. As most of my ethnographic work focusses on that village I prefer to respect its privacy and that of its people with whom I shared so much.

3. Up to then I had been staying in the village of Sorobango, was tipped about an extraordinary Bedu dance at Nandibin and decided to have a look – after that event, I spent 6 more months in the village.

4. Here I follow to a limited extent the terminology introduced by Dell Hymes (1996) for ethnopoetic analysis, distinguishing 'scenes', 'verses' and 'lines'. Due to lack of linguistic competence I have made several simplifications in the above transcription: (1) with the exception of verse 9 where I distinguish several lines, most lines are grouped to verses, and in these cases the two terms are used interchangeably, and (2) I do not distinguish stanzas as Hymes does.

5. The numbers between brackets refer to the line numbers of the interview excerpt.

6. For an analysis of traditionalisation (as discursively tying the present to the past), see Bauman (1992). Most interestingly, in his description Bauman uses the 'art world' metaphor of provenance – traditionalising is 'an act of authentication, akin to the art or antique dealer's authentication of an object by tracing its provenence'– and kinship terminology – the narrator in question contextualises his story 'by situating it in a lineage of other tellings or commentaries (ibid.: 140).

7. For a perceptive appraisal of the difference between speaking and silence as duplicated in the human versus mask, and village versus bush oppositions, see Walter Van Beek's study of Dogon masquerade (1991: 68).

8. Allocating agency/authority to entities who are apparently more passive ('being there', 'seated') than the ones who are moving, coming, arriving, must be understood within the logic of 'firstcomers' who retain important powers over 'latecomers' (see Kopytoff 1987; Arnaut 1997).

9. The *locus classicus* for a general introduction into the Bedu masquerade is Bravmann (1974), but see also Bravmann (1979). For an account of the 'discovery' of the Bedu mask in its traditional habitat – the mask was showing up in collections since the late 1950s but had never been seen performing *in situ* – see Williams (1968). For a critical reconstruction of the invention of the Bedu mask tradition, see Arnaut (forthcoming).

10. In some parts of the northern Bondoukou region, Christmas is one of the variables taken into account when determining

the dates of the ritual period (*dafiago*) in which the Bedu performances take place.

11. I explicitly refer to Fabian's use of the term in his 1998 book. Although I do not directly use terms and quotes from this book, his questions on mimesis (26-27) and the co-presence of tradition and modernity (73-4) greatly inspired this paper.

12. For more details on the 1993-1995 period of political unrest and particularly the north-south division in Côte d'Ivoire, see Paul N'Da (1999: 101-114)

13. Here, again, I take my lead from Ranger (1993: 102) who observed 'the continued dynamics of a rural society, dynamic under the guise of traditionalism, and autonomous from the overarching state'.

Bibliography

APPADURAI, A. 1995. The Production of Locality. In Fardon, R. (ed), *Counterworks: Managing the Diversity of Knowledge*, 204-225.

ARNAUT, K. 1997. *Performing the Past: the Political History of Nandibin and the Yearly Feast of Fanlo.* Paper presented at the Institute of Social and Cultural Anthropology, Oxford University, May 1997.

ARNAUT, K. *forthcoming*, 2000. The Natural History of Museum labels: Fragments of the 'Bedu' and 'Sakrobundi' Art History (Côte d'Ivoire). *Annales of the Royal Museum for Central Africa.*

BARBER, K. 1997. Introduction. In Barber, K. (ed), *Readings in African Popular Culture,* 1-11.

BAUMAN, R. 1992. Contextualisation, Tradition, and the Dialogue of Genres: Icelandic Legends of the Kraftaskáld. In Duranti, A. and Goodwin, C. (eds), *Rethinking Context: Language as an Interactive Phenomenon,* 125- 146.

BAUMAN, R. 1996. Transformations of the World in the Production of Mexican Festival Drama. In Silverstein, M. and Urban, G. (eds.), *Natural Histories of Discourse,* 301-328.

BERMAN, B. 1998. Ethnicity, Patronage and the African State: the Politics of Uncivil Nationalism. *African Affairs,* **97**, 305-341.

BLOMMAERT, J. and VERSCHUEREN, J. 1998. *Debating Diversity: Analysing the Discourse of Tolerance.* London: Routledge.

BRAVMANN, R. 1974. *Islam and Tribal Art in West Africa.* Cambridge: Cambridge University Press.

BRAVMANN, R. 1979. Gur and Manding Masquerades in Ghana. *African Arts,* **13**, 1, 44-51, 98.

DOQUET, A. 1999. Les Masques Dogon: de l'Objet au Musée de l'Homme à l'Homme Objet de Musée. *Cahiers d'Etudes Africaines,* **39**, 3-4, 917-635.

FABIAN, J. 1998. *Moments of Freedom: Anthropology and Popular Culture.* Charlottesville: University Press of Virginia.

GESCHIERE, P. and MEYER, B. 1998. Globalization and Identity: Dialectics of Flow and Closure: Introduction. *Development and Change,* **29**, 601-615.

HYMES, D. 1996. *Ethnography, Linguistics, Narrative Inequality: Towards an Understanding of Voice.* London: Taylor & Francis.

KASFIR, S. Littlefield 1992. African Art and Authenticity: a Text with a Shadow. *African Arts,* **25**, 2, 41-53.

KENDON, A. 1992 The Negociation of Context in Face-to-Face Interaction. In Duranti, A. and Goodwin, C. (eds), *Rethinking Context: Language as an Interactive Phenomeno.* 323-334.

KOPYTOFF, I. 1987. *The African Frontier: The Reproduction of Traditional African Societies.* Bloomington: Indiana University Press.

MCCASKIE, T. 1995. *State and Society in Pre-Colonial Asante.* [African Studies Series 79]. Cambridge:

Cambridge University Press.

MBEMBE, A. 1992a. Provisional Notes on the Postcolony. *Africa,* **62**, 1, 3-37.

MBEMBE, A 1992b. The Banality of Power and the Aesthetics of Vulgarity in the Postcolony. *Public Culture,* **4**, 2, 1-30.

MBEMBE, A. 1997. The 'Thing' and its Double in Cameroonian Cartoons. In Barber, K. (ed), *Readings in African Popular Culture,* 151-163.

N'DA, P. 1999. *Le Drame Démocratique Africain sur Scène en Côte d'Ivoire.* Paris: L'Harmattan.

PELS, P. 1997. The Anthropology of Colonialism: Culture, History, and the Emergence of Western Governmentality. *Annual Review of Anthropology,* **26**, 163-183.

RANGER, T. 1993. The Invention of Tradition Revisited: the Case of Colonial Africa. In Ranger, T. and Vaughan, O. (eds.) *Legitimacy and the State in Twentieth Century Africa. Essays in Honour of A. H. M. Kirk-Greene,* 62-111.

TERRAY, E. 1995 *Une Histoire du Royaume Abron du Gyaman: des Origines à la Conquête Coloniale.* Paris: Karthalla.

TORFING, J. 1999. *New Theories of Discourse: Laclau, Mouffe and ?i?ek.* Oxford: Blackwell.

VAN BEEK, WOUTER, E. 1991. Enter the Bush: a Dogon Mask Festival. In Vogel, S. (ed), *Africa Explores 20th Century African Art,* 56-73.

WILLIAMS, D. 1968. The Dance of the Bedu Moon. *African Arts,* **2**, 1, 18-21, 72.

WILLIAMS, R. 1977. *Marxism and Literature.* Oxford: Oxford University Press.

Notes on Contributors

Emmanuel Nnakenyi Arinze worked in the Nigerian Museum Service for over twenty years, before he went into private consultancy (Heritage Consultancy Bureau). He is the chairman of the West African Museums Programme and president of the Commonwealth Association of Museums. In 1999 he was made an honourary curator of the Horniman Museum. He has published *The Use of Cultural Heritage in Nigerian Education* (1983), *Museums and their Communities* (1995) and *Museums and History* (1999).

Karel Arnaut is currently teaching at the Department of African Languages and Cultures, Ghent University (Belgium). He holds a degree in Art History and did extensive field research in the Bondoukou region (Côte d'Ivoire) for his D.Phil. at the Institute of Social and Cultural Anthropology (Oxford University).

Phil Cope is an arts and heritage consultant, and chairperson of the educational charity, The Haiti Fund. He coordinated Valley and Vale, a Welsh community arts team, and set up a community theatre company in Athens, Greece. He was the principal of an Algonkin Native Indian Community College, Quebec, and taught at the Imperial Court in Tehran, Iran. His research in Latin America resulted in the publication *Creating Meaning, a Book About Culture and Democracy*, the exhibition and video *La Lucha*, and three exhibitions of objects and his own photographs on aspects of Haitian art and culture.

Michèle Coquet holds a doctorate in anthropology. She is an africanist working at the CNRS research center 'Systèmes de pensée en Afrique Noire' (ESA 8048). Apart from numerous articles, she has published two books *Textiles Africains* (1993) and *Arts en Cour* (1996), both published by Adam Biro, Paris.

Joseph Eboreime is curator of the National Museum of Benin, Nigeria and an honourary curator of the Horniman Museum, London.

Keith Nicklin is Visiting Curator of the Horniman Museum and Fellow of the Royal Society of Arts. From 1970 to 1978 he served as an ethnographer in charge of Cross Rover State for the Nigerian Commission for Museums and Monuments and was largely responsible for the rehabilitation of the National Museum, Oron, after the civil war of 1967-70. From 1982 to 1994 he was Keeper of Ethnography at the Horniman Museum.

Michael Pennie is a sculptor and Professor of Sculpture at Bath Spa University College. He has written about travel, art and life in West Africa – his most recent book is *Adventures with Lobi, an abc*. He has curated several touring exhibitions: *West African Journeys* was shown throughout Britain, and *LOBI* is now part of the Ghana Museum and Monuments Board collection and is to be the nucleus of a new museum in Wa, Upper West Region of Ghana.

John Picton is Reader in African Art in the University of London, Department of Art & Archaeology, School of Oriental and African Studies. From 1961 to 1970 he worked in Nigeria for the Nigerian government Department of Antiquities; and from 1970 to 1979 at the British Museum. He moved to SOAS in 1979. His research and publication interests include Yoruba and Edo (Benin) sculpture, masquerade, textile history in West Africa, and 20th-century developments in the visual arts of Africa.

William Rea teaches in the Department of Anthropology at Goldsmiths College, University of London. He gained his PhD in 1994 from the Sainsbury Research Unit. He carried out research into the masquerade traditions of Ikole-Ekiti and the wider Ekiti region between 1990-91 and in 1996. He is currently working on a book *No event, no history*, which explores the politics and aesthetics of Ikole Ekiti masquerades.

Polly Richards is a freelance designer and part-time PhD student at S.O.A.S. (University of London). She gained practical experience making mas' (masks) for Notting Hill (where she was born) and Trinidad. For the past two years Polly has been engaged as a designer, in setting up Hackney Building Exploratory, the UK's first interactive centre about the built environment. She has made 5 visits to the Dogon (totalling 10 months) since 1994.

Jill Salmons read History and West African Studies at the Universities of Warwick and Birmingham respectively. During the 1970s she conducted fieldwork in southeastern Nigeria as Commonwealth Scholar at the University of Nigeria, Nsukka. Author of numerous papers, she is Senior Lecturer in Art History at the School of Art & Design, Worcester College of Technology.

Anthony Shelton taught Critical Museology at the University of Sussex (1991 - 1998). He is currently Head of Collections (Research and Development), at the Horniman Museum, and Honorary Research Fellow in Anthropology, University College, London.

Tania Costa Tribe was born and educated in Brazil, and obtained her PhD at the University of Essex. She now lectures at the School of Oriental and African Studies, University of London, where her research and teaching interests include the arts of the African Diaspora and the theory of art. She has written several articles on these subjects (including candomble) and is now preparing a book on the arts of Latin America.

Hein Vanhee holds an MA in Anthropology from the Sainsbury Research Unit at the University of East Anglia and is presently working at the Department of Contemporary History of the University of Ghent. His current doctoral research looks at the impact of Catholic missionaries in the beginning of the twentieth century on regional politics and trade in Mayombe, Congo-Kinshasa. Under difficult circumstances, he made research visits to Mayombe in 1998 and 1999.

Jan Vansina is Professor Emeritus at the University of Wisconsin-Madison where he taught from 1973 to 1994. Among art historians he is best known for his seminal book *Art History in Africa: An Introduction to Method* (1984). His work on oral history in Central Africa brought him world-wide renown and culminated in the publication of *Paths in the Rainforest* (1990). Amongst his most recent work is the autobiography *Living with Africa* (1994).